214

Feb. 1973

J2

OTTO KAISER

ISAIAH 1–12

THE OLD TESTAMENT LIBRARY

OTTO KAISER

ISAIAH 1-12

A Commentary

SCM PRESS LTD
BLOOMSBURY STREET LONDON

Translated by R. A. Wilson from the German
Der Prophet Jesaja/Kap. 1–12
(Das Alte Testament Deutsch 17)
second edition 1963
published by Vandenhoeck and Ruprecht,
Göttingen

334 00726 7
FIRST PUBLISHED IN ENGLISH 1972
© SCM PRESS LTD 1972
PRINTED IN GREAT BRITAIN BY
W & J MACKAY LIMITED
CHATHAM

In memory of my brother
KARL KAISER
who was killed on 26 November 1941
and my friend and fellow theological student
KLAUS MORTZFELDT
who died on 7 October 1949

Isaiah 35.10

CONTENTS

vii

EDITOR'S NOTE

PROGRESS ON the commentary on the book of Isaiah in *Das Alte Testament Deutsch*, from which the Old Testament Library translation is being made, has been dogged with misfortune and delayed long beyond the original plan. Bishop Volkmar Herntrich, originally selected as the commentator on Isaiah 1–39, died after the completion of his commentary on Isaiah 1–12, but without being able to finish the balance of the work. To avoid an unsatisfactory compromise, the German publishers thereupon allowed the first part to go out of print and reassigned the project to Dr Otto Kaiser of Marburg. His commentary on Isaiah 1–12 appeared in 1960, and was followed by a revised version in 1963; the commentary on Isaiah 13–39 has yet to appear in Germany.

Meanwhile, a commentary on Isaiah 40–66 by Dr Claus Westermann appeared in Germany in 1966 and was translated into English in 1969.

Given these circumstances it seemed best for the Old Testament Library to follow the German pattern and issue the commentary on Isaiah 1–12 separately. It follows the pattern of other volumes in the series apart from the fact that the material normally to be found in an introduction is included in the comments on 1.1. A commentary on Isaiah 13–39, also by Dr Kaiser, should by available in English in the mid 1970s.

ABBREVIATIONS

AcOr(L)	*Acta Orientalia (Leiden)*
AfO	*Archiv für Orientforschung*
AJSL	*American Journal of Semitic Languages and Literatures*
ANET	*Ancient Near Eastern Texts relating to the Old Testament*, ed. J. B. Pritchard, 1950; 2nd ed. 1955
ANVAO	Avhandlinger utgitt av Det Norske Videnskaps-Akademi i Oslo
AOB	*Altorientalische Bilder*, ed. H. Gressmann, 2nd ed. 1927
AOT	*Altorientalische Texte*, ed. H. Gressmann, 2nd ed. 1926
ArOr	*Archiv Orientální*
ATD	Das Alte Testament Deutsch, ed. A. Weiser
AThANT	Abhandlungen zur Theologie des Alten und Neuen Testaments
BAL	Berichte über die Verhandlungen der Sächsischen Akademie der Wissenschaften zu Leipzig
BASOR	*The Bulletin of the American Schools of Oriental Research*
BAT	Die Botschaft des Alten Testaments (Stuttgart)
BBB	*Bonner Biblische Beiträge*
BEvTh	Beiträge zur Evangelischen Theologie
BFChTh	Beiträge zur Förderung christlicher Theologie
BH	*Biblia Hebraica*, ed. R. Kittel, 7th ed. 1951
BHTh	Beiträge zur historischen Theologie
BJRL	*The Bulletin of the John Rylands Library*
BK	Biblischer Kommentar. Altes Testament, ed. M. Noth, 1955ff.
BKD	Beiheft zu *Kerygma und Dogma*
BRL	K. Galling, *Biblisches Reallexikon* (HAT I. 1, 1937)
BSt	Biblische Studien
BWANT	Beiträge zur Wissenschaft vom Alten und Neuen Testament
BZAW	Beihefte zur *Zeitschrift für die alttestamentliche Wissenschaft*
CBQ	*The Catholic Biblical Quarterly*
CR	Corpus Reformatorum
CRE	*Christus und die Religionen der Erde. Handbuch der Rel. Gesch.*, ed. F. König
CT	Cahiers Théologiques
Cult. Bib.	*Cultura Biblica*

DUZ	*Deutsche Universitäts-Zeitung*
EvTh	*Evangelische Theologie*
ExpT	*The Expository Times*
FRLANT	Forschungen zur Religion und Literatur des Alten und Neuen Testaments
GK	Gesenius-Kautzsch, *Hebrew Grammar*, ET by A. E. Cowley, Oxford, 2nd ed. 1910
HAT	Handbuch zum Alten Testament, ed. O. Eissfeldt
HNT	Handbuch zum Neuen Testament, ed. G. Bornkamm
HSAT	Die Heilige Schrift des Alten Testaments, ed. E. Kautzsch and A. Bertholet, 4th ed. 1922ff.
HUCA	*Hebrew Union College Annual*
IB	Interpreter's Bible
ICC	International Critical Commentary on the Holy Scriptures of the Old and New Testaments
JAOS	*The Journal of the American Oriental Society*
JBL	*Journal of Biblical Literature and Exegesis*
JBR	*The Journal of Bible and Religion*
JNES	*Journal of Near Eastern Studies*
JPOS	*Journal of the Palestine Oriental Society*
JQR	*The Jewish Quarterly Review*
JSS	*Journal of Semitic Studies*
JTS	*The Journal of Theological Studies*
KHAT	Kurzer Hand-Commentar zum Alten Testament, ed. K. Marti
LuQ	*The Lutheran Quarterly*
LXX	Septuagint (Greek translation of the Old Testament)
M	Massoretic Text
OBL	*Orientalia et Biblica Lovaniensia*
PJB	*Palästinajahrbuch*
RAAO	*Revue d'Assyriologie et d'Archéologie Orientale*
RB	*Revue Biblique*
RGG	*Die Religion in Geschichte und Gegenwart*, 3rd ed. 1957ff.
RHPhR	*Revue d'Histoire et de Philosophie Religieuses*
RHR	*Revue de l'Histoire des Religions*
RSO	*Revista degli Studi Orientali*
RSR	*Recherches de science religieuse*
RV	Religionsgeschichtliche Volksbücher
SAT	Die Schriften des Alten Testaments in Auswahl
SBA	Sitzungsberichte der Berliner Akademie der Wissenschaften, philosophisch-historische Klasse
SN	*Supplements to Numen*
SNVAO	Skrifter utgitt av Det Norske Videnskaps Akademie i Oslo

StKHVL	Studier utgiv. av. Kungl. Humanistiska Vetenskapssam-fundet i Lund
StTh	*Studia Theologica*
SVT	*Supplements to Vetus Testamentum*
Targ.	Targum
TDNT	*Theological Dictionary of the New Testament*, ET of *TWNT*, tr. and ed. G. W. Bromiley
ThB	Theologische Bücherei
ThLZ	*Theologische Literaturzeitung*
ThR	*Theologische Rundschau*
ThSt(B)	Theologische Studien, ed. K. Barth
ThStKr	*Theologische Studien und Kritiken*
ThZ	*Theologische Zeitschrift*
TICP	Travaux de l'Institut Catholique de Paris
TThSt	Trierer Theologische Studien
TWNT	*Theologisches Wörterbuch zum Neuen Testament*, ed. G. Kittel and G. Friedrich, ET: *TDNT*
Ug.Man.	C. H. Gordon, *Ugaritic Manual*, 1955
UUÅ	Uppsala Universitets Årsskrift
Vg	Vulgate (Latin translation of the Bible by Jerome)
VT	*Vetus Testamentum*
WA	M. Luther, *Werke*, Kritische Gesamtausgabe, Weimar ed., 1883ff.
WMANT	Wissenschaftliche Monographien zum Alten und Neuen Testament
WZ-Halle	*Wissenschaftliche Zeitschrift der Martin-Luther-Universität Halle-Wittenberg*
WZ-Greifswald	*Wissenschaftliche Zeitschrift der Ernst-Moritz-Arndt-Universität, Greifswald*
ZÄSA	*Zeitschrift für Ägyptische Sprache und Altertumskunde*
ZAW	*Zeitschrift für die alttestamentliche Wissenschaft*
ZDMG	*Zeitschrift der deutschen Morgenländischen Gesellschaft*
ZDPV	*Zeitschrift des Deutschen Palästinavereins*
ZEE	*Zeitschrift für evangelische Ethik*
ZKTh	*Zeitschrift für katholische Theologie*
ZThK	*Zeitschrift für Theologie und Kirche*

BIBLIOGRAPHY

COMMENTARIES

A. Bentzen, 1943; J. A. Bewer, 1950; C. J. Bredenkamp, 1887;
A. Condamin, 1905; F. Delitzsch, 1st ed., 1886, 4th ed., 1889;
C. F. A. Dillmann, 1890; C. F. A. Dillmann and R. Kittel, 6th ed.,
1898; B. Duhm, HAT III.1, 1st ed., 1892, 4th ed. 1922; W. Eichrodt,
1960; O. Eissfeldt, 1922; F. Feldmann, 1925/26; J. Fischer, 1937;
G. Fohrer, 1960; G. B. Gray, ICC, 1912; V. Herntrich, 1950;
H. W. Hertzberg, 1st ed. 1936, 2nd ed., 1952; E. J. Kissane, 1941;
E. König, 1926; K. Marti, KHAT 10, 1900; C. von Orelli, 1st ed.,
1887, 3rd ed., 1904; O. Procksch, 1930; H. Schmidt, SAT II.2, 2nd
ed., 1923; R. B. Y. Scott and G. D. Kilpatrick, IB 5, 1951, 149–773;
J. Steinmann, 1950; J. Ziegler, 1948.

OTHER WORKS: A SELECTION

ABRAMSKI, S., ' "Slag" and "Tin" in the First Chapter of Isaiah',
    Eretz Israel 5 (*Mazar Festschrift*), 1958, pp. 105–7 (Hebrew;
    English summary p. 89*)
ALBRIGHT, W. F., 'The Son of Tabeel (Isaiah 7.6)', *BASOR* 140,
    1955, pp. 34f.
ALT, A., 'Tiglathpilesars III. erster Feldzug nach Palästina', *Kleine
    Schriften* II, 1959, pp. 150–62
'Jesaja 8.23–9.6. Befreiungsnacht und Krönungstag', *Kleine
    Schriften* II, pp. 206–25
'Menschen ohne Namen', *Kleine Schriften* III, 1959, pp. 198–213
ANDERSON, R. T., 'Was Isaiah a Scribe?', *JBL* 79, 1960, pp. 57f.
BENTZEN, A., 'Zur Erläuterung von Jes. 5.1–7', *AfO* 4, 1927, pp. 209f.
BIRD, T. E., 'Who is "the Boy" in Isaias 6.16?', *CBQ* 6, 1944,
    pp. 435–43
BLANK, S. H., 'The Current Misinterpretation of Isaiah's *She'ar
    Yashub*', *JBL* 67, 1948, pp. 211–5
'Immanuel and which Isaiah?', *JNES* 13, 1954, pp. 83–98
'Traces of Prophetic Agony in Isaiah', *HUCA* 27, 1956, pp. 81–92
Prophetic Faith in Isaiah, 1958

BOEHMER, J., '"Dieses Volk"', *JBL* 45, 1926, pp. 134–48
  'Der Glaube und Jesaja. Zu Jes. 7.9 and 28.16', *ZAW* 41, 1923,
    pp. 84–93
BROWNLEE, W. H., 'The Text of Isaiah VI.13 in the Light of DSIª',
    VT 1, 1951, pp. 296–8
BRUNO, A., *Jesaja, eine rhythmische und textkritische Untersuchung*, Stock-
    holm, 1953
BUCHANAN, G. W., 'The Old Testament Meaning of the Knowledge
    of Good and Evil', *JBL* 75, 1956, pp. 114–20
BUDDE, K., 'Über die Schranken, die Jesajas prophetischer Botschaft
    zu setzen sind', *ZAW* 41, 1923, pp. 154–203
  'Jesaja 8.6b', *ZAW* 44, 1926, pp. 65–7
  'Verfasser und Stelle von Mi. 4.1–6 (Jes. 2.2–4)', *ZDMG* 81, 1927,
    pp. 152–8
  *Jesajas Erleben. Eine gemeinverständliche Auslegung der Denkschrift des
    Propheten (Kap. 6.1–9.6)*, 1928
  'Zu Jesaja 8, Vers 9 und 10', *JBL* 49, 1930, pp. 423–8
  'Zu Jesaja 1–5', *ZAW* 49, 1931, pp. 16–40, 182–211; *ZAW* 50,
    1932, pp. 38–72
  'Das Immanuelzeichen und die Ahaz-Begegnung, Jes. 7', *JBL* 52,
    1933, pp. 22–54
BULMERINCQ, A. v., 'Die Immanuelweissagung (Jes. 7) im Lichte der
    neueren Forschung', *Acta et Comm. Univers. Dorpat* 37.1, 1936,
    pp. 1–17
CROOK, M. B., 'A Suggested Occasion for Isaiah 9.2–7 and 11.1–9',
    JBL 68, 1949, pp. 213–24
DEQUEKER, L., 'Isaïe VII.14: *wqr't šmw 'mnw'l*', *VT* 12, 1962,
    pp. 331–5
DRIVER, G. R., 'Linguistic and Textual Problems: Isaiah I–XXXIX',
    JTS 38, 1937, pp. 36–50
  'Two Misunderstood Passages of the Old Testament', *JTS*, NS 6,
    1955, pp. 82–87
  'Abbreviations in the Massoretic Text', *Textus* 1, 1960, pp. 112–31
EATON, J. H., 'The Origin of the Book of Isaiah', *VT* 9, 1959,
    pp. 138–57
EISSFELDT, O., '*nūaḥ* "sich vertragen"', *Schweiz. Theol. Umschau* 20.3/4,
    1950, pp. 23–26
ELLIGER, K., 'Prophet und Politik', *ZAW* 53, 1935, pp. 3–22
ENGNELL, I., *The Call of Isaiah: an Exegetical and Comparative Study*,
    UUÅ, 1949, 4

FAHLGREN, K. H., 'hā'almā. En undersökning till Jes. 7', SEÅ 4, 1939, pp. 13–24

FEUILLET, A., 'Le signe proposé à Achaz et l'Emmanuel (Isaïe VII. 10–25)', RSR 30, 1940, pp. 129–51

FICHTNER, J., 'Zu Jes. 7.5–9', ZAW 56, 1938, pp. 176
'Jesaja unter den Weisen', ThLZ 74, 1949, cols. 75–80
'Jahwes Plan in der Botschaft des Jesaja', ZAW 63, 1951, pp. 16–33

FOHRER, G., 'Zu Jesaja 7.14 im Zusammenhang von Jesaja 7.10–22', ZAW 68, 1956, pp. 54–6
'Jesaja I als Zusammenfassung der Verkündigung Jesajas', ZAW 75, 1962, pp. 251–68

FULLERTON, K., 'The Interpretation of Isaiah 8.5–10', JBL 43, 1924, pp. 253–89

GALLING, K., 'Ein Stück jüdaischen Bodenrechts in Jes. 8', ZDPV 56, 1933, pp. 209–18

GEHMANN, H. S., 'The Ruler of the Universe. The Theology of the First Isaiah', Interpretation 11, 1957, pp. 269–81

GINSBERG, H. L., 'Some Emendations in Isaiah', JBL 69, 1950, pp. 51–60

GORDON, C. H., "Almah in Isaiah 7.14', JBR 21, 1953, p. 106

GRAHAM, W. C., 'Isaiah's Part in the Syro-Ephraimite Crisis', AJSL 50, 1933/34, pp. 201–16

GRAY, J., 'The Kingship of God in the Prophets and Psalms', VT 11, 1961, pp. 1–29

GUTHE, H., Jesaia, RV II.10, 1907

HAMMERSHAIMB, E., 'Immanuelstegnet (Jes. 7.10ff.)', Dansk Teologisk Tidsskrift 8, 1945, pp. 223–44
'The Immanuel Sign', StTh 3, 1949, pp. 124–42
'On the Ethics of the Old Testament Prophets', SVT 7, 1960, pp. 75–101

HENTSCHKE, R., 'Gesetz und Eschatologie in der Verkündigung der Propheten', ZEE 4, 1960, pp. 46–56

HESSE, F., 'Wurzelt die prophetische Gerichtsrede im israelitischen Kult?', ZAW 65, 1953, pp. 45–53

HOOKE, S. H., The Sign of Immanuel, 1955

HUMMEL, H. D., 'Enclitic Mem in Early Northwest Semitic, especially Hebrew', JBL 76, 1957, pp. 85–107

HVIDBERG, F., 'The Masseba and the Holy Seed', Mowinckel Festschrift, 1955, pp. 97–9

IWRY, S., 'Massebah and Bamah in IQISᵃ 6.13', JBL 79, 1957, p. 232

JENNI, E., 'Jesajas Berufung in der neueren Forschung', *ThZ* 15, 1959, pp. 321–39

JEPSEN, A., 'Die Nebiah in Jes. 8.3', *ZAW* 72, 1960, pp. 267f.

JIRKU, A., 'Zu Eilebeute in Jes. 8.1, 3', *ThLZ* 75, 1950, col. 118

JONES, D., 'The Tradition of the Oracles of Isaiah of Jerusalem', *ZAW* 67, 1955, pp. 226–46

JUNKER, H., 'Ursprung und Grundzüge des Messiasbildes bei Isaias', *SVT* 4, 1957, pp. 181–96
'Die literarische Art von Jes. 5.1–7', *Biblica* 40, 1959, pp. 259–66
'Sancta Civitas Jerusalem Nova. Eine formkritische und über-lieferungsgeschichtliche Studie zu Jes. 2', *TThSt* 15 (*Wehr-Festschrift*), 1962, pp. 17–33

KELLER, C. A., 'Das quietistische Element in der Botschaft des Jesaja', *ThZ* 11, 1955, pp. 81–97

KISSANE, E. J., '"Butter and Honey shall he Eat" (Is. 7.15)', *OBL* 1, 1957, pp. 169–73

KÖHLER, L., 'Zum Verständnis von Jes. 7.14', *ZAW* 67, 1955, pp. 48–50

KRAELING, E. G. H., 'The Immanuel Prophecy', *JBL* 50, 1931, pp. 277–97

LACHEMAN, E. R., 'A propos of Isaiah 7.14', *JBR* 22, 1954, p. 43

LATTEY, C., 'The Emmanuel Prophecy: Is. 7.14', *CBQ* 8, 1946, pp. 369–76
'The Term '*Almah* in Is. 7.14', *CBQ* 9, 1947, pp. 89–95
'Various Interpretations of Is. 7.14', *CBQ* 9, 1947, pp. 147–54

LIEBREICH, L. J., 'The Position of Chapter Six in the Book of Isaiah', *HUCA* 25, 1954, pp. 37–40
'The Compilation of the Book of Isaiah', *JQR* 46, 1956, pp. 259–77; *JQR* 47, 1957, pp. 114–38

LINDBLOM, J., 'Gibt es eine Eschatologie bei den alttestamentlichen Propheten?', *StTh* 6 (1952), 1953, pp. 79–114
A Study on the Immanuel Section in Isaiah. Isa. 7.1–9.6, StKHVL, 1957–58, 4

MORAN, W. L., 'The Putative Root '*tm* in Is. 9.18', *CBQ* 12, 1950, pp. 153f.

MORENZ, S., '"Eilebeute"', *ThLZ* 74, 1949, cols. 697–9

MORIARTY, F. L., 'The Immanuel Prophecies', *CBQ* 19, 1957, pp. 226–33

MOWINCKEL, S., 'Die Komposition des Jesajabuches Kap. 1–39', *AcOr(L)* 11, 1933, pp. 267–92

'Immanuelprofetien Jes. 7. Streiflys fra Ugarit. I', *Norsk Teologisk Tidsskrift* 42, 1941, pp. 129–57

MÜLLER, H.–P., 'Uns ist ein Kind geboren, Jesaja 9.1–6 in traditionsgesichtlicher Sicht', *EvTh* 21, 1961, pp. 408–19

PFEIFFER, R. H., 'Assyria and Israel', *RSO* 32, 1957, pp. 145–54

PORÚBSAN, S., 'The Word *'ot* in Isaiah 7.14', *CBQ* 22, 1960, pp. 144–59

REYNOLDS, C. B., 'Isaiah's Wife', *JTS* 36, 1935, pp. 182–5

RIGNELL, L. G., 'A Study of Isaiah 9.2–7', *LuQ* 7, 1955, pp. 31–5
'Das Orakel *Mahersalal Has-bas*, Jes. 8', *StTh* 10, 1957, pp. 40–52
'Isaiah Chapter One', *StTh* 11, 1958, pp. 140–58
'Das Immanuelszeichen. Einige Gesichtspunkte zu Jes. 7', *StTh* 11, 1958, pp. 99–119

ROBERTSON, E., 'Isaiah Chapter I', *ZAW* 52, 1934, pp. 231–6

SCOTT, R. B. Y., 'The Literary Structure of Isaiah's Oracles', *Studies in Old Testament Prophecy presented to T. H. Robinson*, 1950, pp. 175–86

SEELIGMANN, I. L., *The Septuagint Version of Isaiah*, 1948

SEIERSTAD, J. P., *Die Offenbarungserlebnisse der Propheten Amos, Jesaja und Jeremia*, SNVAO 1946, II. 2.

SNAITH, N. H., 'The Interpretation of El Gibbor in Isaiah IX 5', *ExpT* 52, 1940/41, pp. 36f.

STAMM, J. J., 'La Prophétie d'Immanuel', *RHPR* 23, 1943, pp. 1–26
'Die Immanuel-Weissagung, ein Gespräch mit E. Hammershaimb', *VT* 4, 1954, pp. 20–33
'Neuere Arbeiten zum Immanuel-Problem', *ZAW* 68, 1956, pp. 44–53
'Die Immanuel-Weissagung und die Eschatologie des Jesaja', *ThZ* 16, 1960, pp. 439–55

STEINMÜLLER, J. F., 'Etymology and Biblical Usage of *'Almah*', *CBQ* 2, 1940, pp. 28–43

STENNING, J. F., *The Targum of Isaiah*, 1949

THOMAS, D. W., 'A Note on the Meaning of *jāda'* in Hosea 9.9. and Isaiah 9.8', *JTS* 41, 1940, pp. 43f.

TORCZYNER, H., 'Ein vierter Sohn des Propheten Jesaja. Zu Jes. 9.5', *Monatss. Wiss. Jud.* 74, NS 38, 1930, pp. 257–9

VISCHER, W., *Die Immanuel-Botschaft im Rahmen des königlichen Zionsfestes*, ThSt (B) 45, 1955

VOGT, E., 'Filius Tāb'ēl (Is. 7.6)', *Biblica* 37, 1956, pp. 263f.

VRIEZEN, T. C., 'Essentials of the Theology of Isaiah', *Israel's*

Prophetic Heritage (Muilenburg Festschrift), 1962, pp. 128–46

WEIL, H. M., 'Exégèse d'Isaie 3.1–15', *RB* 49, 1940, pp. 76–85

WHITLEY, C. F., 'The Call and Mission of Isaiah', *JNES* 18, 1959, pp. 38–48

WILDBERGER, H., 'Die Völkerwallfahrt zum Zion, Jes. 11.1–5', *VT* 7, 1957, pp. 62–81

'Die Thronnamen des Messias, Jes. 9.5b', *ThZ* 16.4 (*Eichrodt-Festschrift*), 1960, pp. 314–32

WOLFF, H. W., *Immanuel. Das Zeichen, dem widersprochen wird*, BSt 23, 1959

Frieden ohne Ende. Eine Auslegung von Jes. 7.1–7 und 9.1–6, BSt 35, 1962

WÜRTHWEIN, E., 'Der Ursprung der prophetischen Gerichtsrede', *ZThK* 49, 1952, pp. 1–16

'Jesaja 7.1–9. Ein Beitrag zu dem Thema "Prophetie und Politik"', *Karl Heim-Festschrift*, 1954, pp. 47–63

ZIEGLER, J., *Untersuchungen zur Septuaginta des Buches Jesaias*, 1934

Isaias, 1939

COMMENTARY

CHAPTER 1.1

The Heading

1 The vision of Isaiah the son of Amoz, which he saw concerning Judah and Jerusalem in the days of Uzziah, Jotham, Ahaz and Hezekiah, kings of Judah.

[1] In its present setting, this heading is meant to refer to all the sixty-six chapters of the Book of Isaiah. In the form in which it occurs, it may be due to the most recent editor, to whom we owe the final compilation and redaction of all the prophecies contained in this book. It cannot come from Isaiah himself, for he would scarcely have given information of this sort concerning his own lifetime and career. Moreover, a new heading is given in 2.1. It is no longer possible to tell whether ch. 1 once formed a small collection on its own, or whether the prophecies it contains originally had a place within the collection of the sayings of Isaiah which begins with 2.1 and possibly extends to ch. 32 (cf. the comment on 2.1 below). In any case, the present heading must go back to the redactor who gave the chapter its present position, because he found it possible to use this chapter as a programmatic summary of the whole preaching of the prophet. In spite of the oracles against foreign nations in chs 13–23 (27) it is not impossible that he chose it for the whole book as it stands, with the intention of specifying Jerusalem and Judah as those to whom the prophecies of Isaiah (and those attributed to him) are principally addressed.

There are also internal reasons for recognizing the heading as the work of a later writer. Whereas Isaiah himself explicitly mentions a vision only in one passage, 6.1ff., here his whole preaching is described as 'the vision'. Hebrew possessed neither a specific expression for the reception of prophecy solely in the form of words, nor an inclusive expression corresponding to our word 'prophecy'.[a] In the course of time, the terms 'to see' and 'vision' came to fulfil the latter function, and this implies that visions were originally predominant and were later understood as the characteristic means of revelation[b] (cf. 2.1; 13.1; 29.10). Moreover, for reasons so far unknown, those to whom the prophet's preaching was addressed are named in the order Judah and Jerusalem, whereas Isaiah himself prefers the older reverse order (cf. 3.1, 8; 5.3; 22.21).

The name of the prophet can be translated as 'Yahweh is salvation'. Looking back upon it, it is as though it were a summary of everything which Isaiah said to his people (cf. the comment on 12.3–6). We have no knowledge of his origins. All we have is the name of his father Amoz,[c] who must not be confused with the prophet Amos. If his untrammelled dealings with his king (cf. 7.3ff.) and with the high priest of the Jerusalem temple (cf. 8.2) cannot be explained by his status as a prophet, it might be supposed that he was born into a noble family of Jerusalem.[d] Since in 20.2b it is assumed that he wore sackcloth and sandals, the everyday clothing of an ordinary man, it is perhaps more accurate to speak of him as a free citizen with a farm, possessing full rights.[e] The lack of biographical detail in the heading bears witness to the fact that the importance of the prophet lies not in his human situation and standing, but in his task. What is important is not what Isaiah was as a man, but the fact that God desired and still desires to speak through his words.

The historical situation. God placed his prophet in a particular period, the last third of the eighth century BC, the years of which were decisive for the whole of Israel. The weakening of the Aramaean state of Damascus by the Assyrian king Adadnirari III in the year 800, and

---

[a] Cf. Michaelis, *TDNT* V, p. 330.

[b] Cf. *ZAW* 70, 1958, p. 110.

[c] R. T. Anderson, *JBL* 79, 1960, pp. 57f., tries to identify him with the owner of the seal of the same name published by D. Diringer, *Le inscrizioni Antico-Ebraiche Palestinesi*, 1934, p. 235 plate XXI. 11, so that by profession he would have been a *sōpēr*, a scribe. But the age of the seal does not seem to be in accordance with this. On the Jewish tradition cf. *b. Megilla* 15a and *b. Sota* 10b, with the critical comment of Delitzsch, *ad loc.*

[d] It is not possible to agree entirely with Delitzsch that the mention of the puzzling 'valley of vision' (22.1) shows that he dwelt in the lower city. Cf. also Ziegler on 22.1.

[e] Cf. J. P. Seierstad, *Die Offenbarungserlebnisse der Propheten Amos, Jesaja und Jeremia*, SNVAO 1946, II. 2, pp. 118 and 166.

the temporary decline of the internal power of the Assyrian kingdom which followed, permitted the northern kingdom of Israel, under its king Jeroboam II (787/6–747/6), and the southern kingdom of Jerusalem and Judah, under its king Uzziah, to flourish once again; the latter came to the throne in 786, while his father Amaziah was still alive. When Uzziah contracted leprosy in 758/57, his son Jotham exercised the regency on his behalf, continuing to do so until 743/42.[a] He, too, was able to make use of this period of freedom from disturbance from outside enemies, during which the economy of the whole country expanded, to continue his father's policy undisturbed, to increase and complete the fortifications of the capital and the country, and probably in addition to carry out a successful campaign against the Ammonites (cf. II Chron. 27). But Assyria was approaching the period of its greatest power. Tiglath-pileser III (745–727) conquered the whole Near Eastern world up to the Egyptian border in a few years. Ahaz, who acted as regent from 743/42 to the death of Uzziah in 735, and was sole ruler until 726/5,[b] saw in the early years of his regency the conquest of King Menahem of Israel by the Great King, who also made Damascus and the Phoenician cities of Tyre and Byblos pay tribute. An alliance was formed against Assyria under the leadership of Hanno of Gaza, Pekah, the usurper of the throne of Israel, and Rezin, king of Damascus, who set their hopes on Egyptian help, whereupon Tiglath-pileser conducted a surprise campaign in 734 which penetrated as far as the Brook of Egypt, the *nahal musur*, and probably founded the province *Du'ru* at that time in the region of the Israelite coastal plain.[c] With immense new effort, the former allies once again attempted to regain their freedom. In order to increase their forces, they sought in 733 to incite the Davidic kingdom to join their alliance. There was a plan to dethrone King Ahaz, who was opposed to the scheme, and to replace him by a more pliant person, apparently a foreigner (cf. 7.6). Against the emphatic warning

[a] Since according to 6.1 Isaiah was called in the year that king Uzziah died, that is, in 735, the mention of Jotham in the heading of the book (1.1) derives from a misunderstanding of his status as regent, as though he had been sole ruler. Thus it demonstrates the secondary character of 1.1.

[b] For the chronology of Uzziah and Jotham cf. A. Jepsen, *Die Quellen des Königsbuches*, Halle, 1953, pp. 41ff., which should be preferred to that put forward by J. Begrich, *Die Chronologie der Könige von Israel und Juda*, BHTh 3, Tübingen, 1929. Cf. also E. Kutsch, *RGG*³ III, cols. 942ff.

[c] Cf. A. Alt, *Kleine Schriften zur Geschichte des Volkes Israel*, II, Munich, 1953, pp. 150ff.

of Isaiah, Ahaz turned to the Assyrians for help. The result of the war fought by Syria and Ephraim was the annexation of the northern and eastern provinces of the northern kingdom, which took place in 733 (cf. 8.23), the conquest and sack of Damascus in 732, and the voluntary subjugation of the southern kingdom, which had dangerous cultic consequences (cf. 7.2). The hegemony of Assyria remained uncontested until the death of Tiglath-pileser.

Hoshea then allowed himself to be drawn into a new revolt against Assyria, as a consequence of which he himself lost both his throne and his freedom in 724, while in 722/21 his kingdom ceased to exist as an independent state. Hezekiah, the successor of King Ahaz (725/4–697/6), at first took part neither in the revolt of his neighbour Hoshea, nor in the Syrian and Philistine revolt of the year 720. Not until 713–11 did he allow himself to be led into a cautious participation in the disturbances which emanated from Ashdod, and were stirred up by the Ethiopian Pharaoh Sabako (cf. 18.1–6); from these, however, he was able to withdraw in good time. On the death of Sargon II in the year 705, all the states of the Near East joined together in a single alliance, which included the Babylonian king Merodach-baladan, as well as the majority of the states of southern Palestine. Once again, Sabako promised his help. At this time Hezekiah removed the Assyrian cultic objects, as well as the altar of burnt offering set up by Ahaz (cf. II Kings 16.10f.; 18.4), and entered into negotiations with the Babylonians (cf. ch. 39) and the Egyptians (cf. 30.1–5, 6–7, 8–14, 15–17; 31.1–3, 4–5, 8f.). Isaiah's warnings went unheeded (cf. 28.7–13; 29.13–14; 28.14–22). Sennacherib, the successor of Sargon II, was at first held back by having to crush other revolts in his kingdom before he could set out for Palestine. In 703 Merodach-baladan fled before him. In 701 he appeared in the West, and conquered one after the other those cities of Syria and Phoenicia which had not chosen to submit to him voluntarily. Only Sidon, Ashkelon, Ekron, and Judah offered any resistance. The Egyptian army sent to relieve them was defeated at Eltekeh, thirty miles west of Jerusalem. The fate of the Davidic kingdom, and of the capital city in its enclave, seemed to be sealed. The country towns and fortifications were conquered one after the other. Once Lachish had fallen, Hezekiah was left with no political course other than complete submission. He bought the freedom of Jerusalem by paying a heavy tribute. The Shephelah was divided between the kings of Ashdod, Ekron and Gaza.[a] Later, though we do

---

[a] Cf. *AOT*, 2nd ed., pp. 352ff.

not know when, but possibly while Hezekiah was still alive, the separated districts were restored to Jerusalem.

The judgment of the great historian Eduard Meyer on the fate of the principalities of Syria and Palestine was that they were brought to ruin by a blind trust in the power of their native gods.[a] The judgment of Isaiah on the fate of his own people was different. This was: 'If you will not believe, surely you shall not be established' (7.9). But the answer to the question whether his whole preaching consisted of provincial prejudice expressed in the concepts of traditional belief, and of blindness towards the realities of the political situation, or whether it was ultimate truth, cannot be decided by a detached consideration, but only by the personal decision of whoever reads his words. Anyone who is touched by the saving will of the God who loves righteousness, as interpreted in prophecy, can find in his statements, meant for an earlier age and an earlier kingdom, authoritative counsel and the word of God for himself.[b]

CHAPTER 1.2–9

A Word to the Survivors

2 Hear, O heavens, and give ear, O earth,
for Yahweh is speaking:
'Sons have I reared and brought up,
but they have rebelled against me.
3 The ox knows its owner
and the ass its master's crib.[c]
But Israel does not know,
my people does not understand.'
4 Ah, sinful nation,
a people laden with iniquity,
brood of criminals,
band of evildoers!
They have forsaken Yahweh,

[a] *Geschichte des Altertums*, II. 2, Darmstadt, [3]1953, p.436.
[b] For the historical events, see M. Noth, *The History of Israel*, rev. tr. by P. R. Ackroyd, [2]1960, pp. 162ff.; A. Scharff and A. Moortgat, *Ägypten und Vorderasien im Altertum*, Munich 1950.
[c] *beʿālāw* is a *pluralis majestatis*.

despised the Holy One of Israel,
drawn themselves back.

5 Why will you still be smitten,
that you continue to rebel?
The whole head is sick,
and the whole heart faint.

6 From the sole of the foot even to the head
there is no point ⟨in him⟩ whole,ᵃ
but bruising and boils
and raw wounds.
They are not pressed out, or bound up,
or softened with oil.

7 Your country – a desolation!
Your cities – burnt with fire!
Your land – in your very presence
aliens devour it. ⟨   ⟩ᵇ

8 And the daughter of Zion is left
like a booth in a vineyard,
like a lodge in a cucumber field,
like a watch-tower.

9 If Yahweh Sebaoth
had not left us a few survivors,
we should have been like Sodom,
and become like Gomorrah.

[2–9] This passage first attained its present position at a late stage
in the formation of the Book of Isaiah, if not in fact at the final redaction. It is easy to see why the compiler or redactor, working with a
conscious purpose, gave it its present place at the head of the whole
book, for it seems to contain in a concise form the whole legacy of the
prophet to posterity: it is only thanks to the grace of God that Israel
has not wholly succumbed to the judgment which has threatened it
time and again since the days of Isaiah. By giving the passage this
emphatic position, the scribe working at a later period accepted a
prophetic oracle belonging to a previous age as a valid interpretation
of the situation of his own community, living in the expectation of the
final judgment. The passage consists of two parts: vv.2 and 3 contain an accusation by Yahweh, and vv.4–9, a taunt against Israel

ᵃ Following D. D. Hummel, *JBL* 76, 1957, p.105, M must be regarded as a
scribal error for an original *'ēn bᵉmō tōm*.

ᵇ 'And the desert is like the overthrowing ⟨of Sodom⟩' (cf. *BH*) can be
excluded as a gloss based on v.9.

by the prophet. The solemn appeal to heaven and earth as God's witnesses, as required by ancient cultic usage, suggests that the temple of Jerusalem was the place where Isaiah delivered this prophecy. Verses 7–9 show that the invasion of Sennacherib and the reduction of the southern kingdom to the city state of Jerusalem had already taken place (cf. II Kings 18.13–16; Taylor Cylinder, col. III. 23–26),[a] so that the whole passage dates from the year 701 or shortly after. Perhaps the accusation on the part of Yahweh permits a conclusion to be drawn about the occasion of this prophecy. It would be understandable for Isaiah to have contrasted God's accusation with the lament of the people over their unfortunate fate. Thus the *Sitz im Leben* of the prophecy would be the solemn celebration of this lamentation. But whereas the assembly would have looked for an oracle of salvation from the prophet, he answered them with this call to remember their own guilt.[b]

[2–3] *God's accusation against his people*. Isaiah appears like a herald of judgment in the solemn assembly, and appeals to heaven and earth to listen to Yahweh's accusations against Israel, as his witnesses (cf. Deut. 4.26; 30.19; 31.28; 32.1; Ps. 50.4).[c] They can testify that God, the partner and guarantor of the covenant concluded with his people, has been faithful to the obligation into which he has entered of his own free will. He has brought up his people as a father brings up his children, and is therefore entitled to expect from them the thankfulness of children, expressed in complete obedience. In Israel, as in virtually all nations of the ancient world, a father possessed the power of life and death over his children. The duty of a child was to honour him (Ex. 20.12); to rebel against him, either by word or by deed, brought death (cf. Ex. 21.15, 17).[d] Parallels to the transference of the concept of fatherhood to God exist in other Semitic religions. The Mesopotamian storm-god Enlil was regarded as the father of the gods, while the god of the primeval ocean and of wisdom, Ea, was thought of as the father of the first man. In Ugarit, El

[a] Cf. Alt, *PJB* 25, 1930, pp. 8off. = *Kleine Schriften* II, pp. 242ff.; *AOT*, 2nd ed., pp. 352ff.

[b] As a result of a failure to recognize the cultic situation, vv. 2–3 and 4–9 are often dealt with as independent units. It is more difficult to decide whether 1.2–9 and 1.10–20 are directly associated in time, as well as with regard to their setting. Cf. also the comment on 1.10–20 below.

[c] Cf. K. Baltzer, *ThLZ*, 1958, col. 585; E. Würthwein, *ZThK* 49, 1952, p. 15 n. 2.

[d] Cf. Nötscher, *Biblische Altertumskunde*, Bonn, 1940, pp. 74f.

was worshipped as the father of the gods and of men.[a] Moreover, the Old Testament regarded the heavenly servants as the sons of Yahweh (Pss. 29.1; 82.6). But because of the close association with the nature myths of neighbouring peoples, Israel very rarely referred to its God as father, and did so principally in order to emphasize the incontestable authority which God possessed over his people (cf. Ex. 4.22f.; Deut. 14.1; Ps. 89.26; Isa. 63.16; 64.8; Jer. 3.4; 31.9; Mal. 1.6). Whereas those who worshipped heathen gods considered themselves their natural children, Israel knew that it was the son of God only as the result of God's free act of election (cf. Hos. 11.1).[b] Yahweh has brought his people through all the ills of childhood, and given them a respected position among other nations. Israel's response to this care has been ingratitude and rebellion. Israel has broken God's covenant, by turning repeatedly to other gods and infringing God's moral demands. If the kingdom of David is now shattered, it is not Yahweh, but the people, who are under accusation. The monstrous and unnatural attitude of Israel is emphasized by a comparison with the faithfulness of animals towards their owners. Israel compares very badly with the animals: its behaviour is less reasonable than that of mere cattle (v. 3). The ox and the ass *know* their masters, that is, they associate with them on terms of trust and obedience. For the Israelites, knowledge is never a purely intellectual process, but always includes a practical relationship, a fact to which the usage of the verb *yd'* 'to know' in a sexual sense bears witness (cf. Gen. 4.1). Thus in the Old Testament the knowledge of God is to know 'what Yahweh wills, and to act accordingly.'[c] But Israel has refused to give to its God the childlike obedience that is due to him. If there is a God, then godlessness either in practice or in theory is in an ultimate sense irrational, and a disguised suicide. The community of the old and the new covenant held the belief that the deity of God has been clearly perceived ever since the creation of the world in the works of creation (cf. Ps. 19.1f.; Ecclus. 17.5ff.; Rom. 1.18ff.). Just as Paul regards all the confusion and error of mankind as a consequence of denying the deity of God, the consequence of which is ultimately death (Rom. 6.23), so those who listen to the prophet, the people through whose

[a] Cf. Gordon, *Ugaritic Manual*, Rome, 1955, Text 2:25; *Krt* 37, 151, 278. For related Egyptian concepts cf. Kaiser, BZAW 78, 1959, pp. 7f.

[b] Cf. Quell, *TDNT* V, pp. 959ff.

[c] S. Mowinckel, *Die Erkenntnis Gottes bei den Alttestamentlichen Profeten*, Oslo, 1941, pp. 6f.

history God desires to be glorified before the whole world, and to overcome the blindness of all nations (cf. Gen. 12.3), are meant to recognize their own position as a consequence of the anger of God. They, who have really deserved death, are still alive. But at the moment the prophet cannot yet proclaim the grace of God, because the people will pay no heed to the whole seriousness of judgment at the present hour.

[4–9] *Only the grace of God has preserved Israel from total disaster.* Like a whirlwind, the prophet's rebuke falls upon the assembled people, in order to break their defiance. They, who are members of the chosen people of God (Ex. 19.f.; Lev. 19.2), are behaving like a band of criminals, who selfishly set themselves above the laws of society (v. 4). They have broken the covenant of Yahweh, and nevertheless dare to contend with God. The monstrousness of this attitude is emphasized by the title given to God, 'the holy one of Israel', which is characteristic of Isaiah.[a] He, whose power and mighty judgment fills the whole earth (cf. 6.3), is rejected by men, his own creatures. Because the holiness of God consumes everything impure and ungodly in the world like a burning fire (cf. 30.27; Jer. 23.29), Israel calls down God's punishment by its own behaviour (v. 5). But what blows must fall upon it, before it recognizes its sin and does sincere penance? Its position is deadly serious: Israel is already like one who is sick and has been plagued, on whose body no whole place can be found, and whose central organs, the head and the heart, have not been spared. His wounds are still fresh and have not been dressed (v. 6, cf. Luke 10.34). Verse 7 passes from the image to reality. The whole country has been laid waste by Sennacherib's forces. Its cities have been reduced to rubble and ashes. The prophet is not exaggerating. According to Sennacherib's own claims, forty-six fortified places and numerous small towns were besieged and taken by storm. He claimed to have carried off 200,150 people, as well as numerous cattle.[b] A harsh tribute was laid upon Hezekiah (cf. II Kings 18.15f.). As far as the borders of the city state of Jerusalem, the fields were given over to the ancient hereditary enemy, the Philistines. Only Jerusalem remained

---

[a] It seems to occur in Isaiah as an echo of his experience at his call. Whether, however, it was first formulated by him is doubtful, though this is argued by Procksch, *TDNT* I, pp. 93f., for it is found is Pss. 71.22; 78.41; 89.18. The divine title as such may be drawn from the language of the cult. Cf. H. Ringgren, *The Prophetical Conception of Holiness*, UUÅ 12, 1948, pp. 27f.

[b] Cf. *AOT*, 2nd ed., pp. 352ff.

as a pitiful remnant of the former flourishing empire of David (v. 8).
But this Jerusalem was no longer the proud and self-conscious royal
city which had been able to consider itself unassailable (cf. Ps. 46).
The prophet presents the extraordinarily dangerous situation of the
city to his hearers in two comparisons: the city is like a booth of
branches, an overnight lodge, which the guards in harvest time set up
for a few days and nights.[a] The prophet was enjoined in the moment
of his call to make Israel obdurate by his words, until the cities lay
waste without inhabitant, and the houses were without men and the
land was utterly desolate (6.11), and this has now been fulfilled,
just as has his warning against the plans for a revolt, that they should
flee before the Assyrians until they were no more than a remnant,
like a banner on a hill (30.17). But is what is gathered here in the
temple the holy seed? The closing words of the prophet sound like an
incantation: 'If Yahweh Sebaoth had not left us a few survivors, we
should have been like Sodom, and become like Gomorrah' (v. 9). It
would have been right and fair for God to have brought his people
to the end that they deserve, by destroying Jerusalem for ever, as he
once destroyed the accursed cities of Sodom and Gomorrah (cf.
Gen. 19; Rom. 9.29; Amos. 4.11; Isa. 1.10; Jer. 23.14; Lam. 4.6;
Zeph. 2.9). To survive the judgments of God is due to an act of his
grace. Will Israel understand that it has only been given a brief
period of probation? We are able to see further than the prophets,
and to recognize that the people did not hear the word of God and
the voice of his prophet. Consequently the woe (cf. v. 4)[b] pronounced over them was fulfilled again and again. This was not
recognized until later: 'The steadfast love of the Lord never ceases,
his mercies never come to an end; they are new every morning; great
is thy faithfulness' (Lam. 3.22). He who said that, sat amongst the
ruins of Jerusalem.[c] In the light of this prophecy, the Christian church
may join Calvin in asking a similar question to that of Rom. 11.17ff.,
whether it is not in the same position as the Israelites were at that
time: 'Adoption as the child of God laid upon them the obligation to
worship him in purity. But we have a double obligation. And this is

    [a] Such huts were set up even before the time of harvest, to protect unripe grapes
or cucumbers that were not yet fully grown from theft. Cf. H. Guthe, *Monographien
zur Erdkunde* 21, Bielefeld and Leipzig, ³1927; G. Dalman, *Arbeit und Sitte in
Palästine* I, Gütersloh, 1928, p. 161. On the construction cf. *ibid*, II, Gütersloh,
1932, p. 61.
    [b] Rendered above by 'Ah!'
    [c] Cf. also Matt. 23.37ff.; Rom. 9–11.

not only because we are redeemed by the blood of Christ, but because he has made us worthy of his gospel, he who redeemed us once for all; and thereby he has preferred us to all those whom he still permits to remain in the blindness of their ignorance. If we do not recognize this, how much graver will the punishment be of which we are worthy? For the more fully and richly the grace of God has been poured upon us, the greater the ingratitude of which we will be convicted.'[a] The tiny number of those who are faithful must in fact be thought of in a tension between Luke 12.32; I Cor. 1.26ff. and Rev. 3.14ff. The outward and inner weakness of the church of Jesus Christ is not simply identical.[b]

CHAPTER 1.10–20

The True Worship of God

10   Hear the word of Yahweh,
      you rulers of Sodom!
      Give ear to the teaching of our God,
      you people of Gomorrah!
11   'What to me is the multitude of your sacrifices?'
      says Yahweh,
      'I have had enough of burnt offerings of rams
      and the fat of fed beasts;
      I do not delight in the blood of bulls,
      or of lambs, or of he-goats.

[a] J. Calvin, CR 64, p. 29 (Commentary on Isaiah): *Adoptatio Dei obstrictos tenebat, ut eum pure colerent; duplex nostra obligatio est. Nempe quia non solum redempti sumus Christi sanguine, sed quia nos suo evangelio dignatur, qui nos semel redemit; atque hoc modo profert omnibus, quos adhuc ignorantia obcaecatos manere sinit. Haec si non agnoscimus, quanto graviore poena digni erimus? Quo enim plenius et uberius effusa est in nos gratia Dei, eo maioris ingratitudinis nos convincet.* Cf. also M. Luther, WA 31, 2, p. 4.14ff.: *Hic habes divinae paternitatis titulum erga nos, sed quales gerimus nos erga tantum et talem patrem?. . . . Sumus ingrati, contemnimus, blasphemamus eum, scilicet beneficiis Dei alimur, ut simus per haec hostes eius.* 'Here you have the title of the fatherhood of God towards us, but how do we conduct ourselves towards a father so great and so inclined as he?. . . . We are ungrateful, and despise and blaspheme him; that is, we are nourished by the good things God does for us, but in such a way that we become his enemies.'
[b] Cf. Calvin, CR 64, p. 28.

12 When you come ⟨to see⟩ᵃ my face,
    who requires this of you, the trampling of my courts?
13 Do not continue to bring me vain offerings;
    incense is an abomination to me.
    New moon and sabbath and the calling of assemblies
    I cannot endure –
    ⟨fasting⟩ ᵇ and rests from work.
14 Your new moons and your appointed feasts
    my soul hates.
    They have become a burden to me,
    I am weary of bearing them.
15 When you spread forth your hands,
    I will hide my eyes from you;
    even though you make many prayers,
    I do not listen;
    your hands are full of blood.
16 Wash yourselves; make yourselves clean;
    remove the evil of your doings
    from before my eyes.
    Cease to do evil,
17 Learn to do good.
    Seek justice,
    help ⟨the oppressed⟩,ᶜ
    defend the fatherless,
    plead for the widow.'
18 'Come now, let us plead together',
    says Yahweh.
    'Though your sins are like scarlet,
    they shall be as white as snow;
    though they are red like crimson,
    they shall become like wool.
19 If you are willing and hear,
    you shall eat the good of the land;
20 But if you refuse and rebel,
    you shall be devoured ⟨by⟩ ᵈ the sword.'
    For the mouth of Yahweh has spoken.

[10–20] The content and situation of the two following passages, vv. 10–17 and 18–20, is closely similar to that of the previous passage,

ᵃ Cf. *BH*.
ᵇ Cf. *BH*.
ᶜ Cf. *BH*.
ᵈ Read *beḥereb* with 1QIsa. Another possibility is to follow Driver in reading: *ḥereb tō'kelū*, 'You shall devour the sword' (BZAW 77, p.42).

vv. 2–9. Under God's command, the prophet has begun by an accusation in the name of God, the point of which was made clear by his own taunt which followed; and it is the same scene that he assumes here. Israel is being judged before a court. Since God's judgment upon his people formed a fixed theme in the great Israelite harvest festival (cf. Ps. 50),[a] we have no need of the references to sacrifice and the courts of the temple in vv. 11ff. to recognize the occasion on which Isaiah pronounced his prophecy.[b] Clearly the assembled people, with the nobles at their head (v. 10), had given evident expression to their displeasure at the preceding utterance of the prophet. In view of the oriental temperament, it is scarcely possible to exaggerate the liveliness of the scene. It would have been argued that the sacrifices were a sufficiently clear sign of the people's faithfulness to Yahweh in the covenant.[c] What did the prophet really want from them? Isaiah's answer is not given on his own authority. He does not think of defending himself. Once again, he lets God speak. As in a dispute in civil law, he lets Yahweh approach his opponents for a discussion, and suggests an agreement. 'If you are willing and hear, you shall eat the good of the land.' In a different way from the sayings which we possess from his early period, he is struggling here to open the eyes of his people to their true position in the sight of God, and to spare them further punishment.

[10–17] *The false and the true worship of God.* This is a speech forming part of the discussion before the court. While the prophet began by solemnly calling heaven and earth as witnesses to the God of the covenant who was rising up to give judgment, he now turns imperiously and sternly to the assembled people (v. 10). The comparison between the desperate situation of Jerusalem and the two cities which disappeared from the face of the earth through the judgment of God is still in his mind (v. 9). But it is given a new twist by the reaction of the assembly to the prophecy that has just been concluded. Just as

[a] For further details cf. Weiser, *The Psalms*, OTL, 11. II. Hartwell, 1962, pp. 35ff., 64ff.; Würthwein, *ZThK* 49, 1952, pp. 1ff.; a different view is taken by F. Hesse, *ZAW* 65, 1953, pp. 45ff.

[b] Guthe and Procksch already recognized the cultic setting. Fohrer considers that this was merely adopted by Isaiah as imagery.

[c] The considerable extent of the sacrifices assumed is no objection to the late dating of the passage. Budde says: 'In time of trouble men learn not only to pray, but also to sacrifice' (*ZAW* 48, 1931, pp. 25f.). The inner link between 1.1ff. and 1.10ff. has also been defended by Rignell, *StTh* 11, 1958, p. 146. But cf. Eichrodt, *Der Heilige in Israel*, BAT 17.1, Stuttgart, 1960, *ad loc.*

the inhabitants of Sodom violated God's commandments, the assembly now opposes Isaiah. In order to emphasize that the words he has just spoken were utterly serious, and furiously provoked, he calls the city officials responsible for the public administration of Jerusalem and the administration of justice,[a] 'rulers of Sodom', and the men of the chosen people, 'people of Gomorrah'. They must listen to the teaching of God.[b] The people feel that through their own sacrifices, they are sufficiently proved to be truly pious and obedient, and are secure in their own works. Slain offerings, of which God received the fat, the priests the right breast, and the sacrificing congregation the rest as a meal; burnt offerings, which were wholly consecrated to God, and burnt upon the altar; and food offerings of cereals and fruits, have been offered in abundance, as has also the sweet-smelling incense offering.[c] All the prescribed feasts days have been faithfully observed. The Sabbath, the new moon,[d] penitential fasts,[e] rests from work[f] and solemn assemblies have been conscientiously carried out by them, with all their prescribed rites. Isaiah presents his God as speaking of these 'pious' and 'holy' works in terms of unsurpassed contempt. God stands as it were helpless before the profusion of sacrifices that are offered. He is fundamentally weary of this whole activity. Neither the sacrifices with their offerings and manipulations of blood (cf. Lev. 17.10–14; 3.2; 4.6) nor the whole system of feasts can obtain his favour. When people hasten to the temple in order to see the face of God there (cf. Pss. 42.2; 63.2; 27.4; 84.2), God regards it as a disfiguring of the sanctuary. He even turns a deaf ear to prayer uttered

---

[a] For this meaning of qāṣīn cf. R. Hentschke, *Die Stellung der vorexilischen Schriftpropheten zum Kultus*, BZAW 75, 1957, p.94 n.3; Isa.3.6f.; 22.3; Micah 3.1, 9.

[b] For the linguistic usage of tōrāh cf. below on 2.3. Hentschke, *loc. cit.*, points out that Isaiah is here exercising a function that properly belonged to the priests.

[c] On the archaeology of Israelite sacrifice cf. Nötscher, *Biblische Altertumskunde*, pp.320ff.; on its theological significance, von Rad, *Old Testament Theology* I, tr. D. M. G. Stalker, 1962, pp.250ff.; Vriezen, *An Outline of Old Testament Theology*, tr. S. Neuijen, 1958, pp.288ff.; Eichrodt, *Theology of the Old Testament* I, tr. J. A. Baker, 1961, pp.141ff.; H. J. Kraus, *Worship in Israel*, tr. G. Buswell, 1966, pp.122ff.

[d] In the Old Testament the new moon is the first day on which the moon can be seen again; cf. Num. 10.10; 28.11–15; I Sam.20.5.

[e] Cf. I Sam.7.6; Jer.14.12; Joel 1.14; 2.15; Jonah 3.5, 7; Nötscher, *Biblische Altertumskunde*, pp.363f.

[f] For the meaning of 'aṣārā cf. Neh.8.18; II Chron.7.9 and Kutsch, *VT* 2, 1952, p.65.

with outspread hands,[a] the most ancient attitude of prayer, and an expression of the fellowship between God and man.[b] Two completely opposed views on this passage are found among exegetes. Some see in it a fundamental rejection of the sacrificial cult, comparable to Amos 5.22ff. and Jer. 7.21ff., regarding it as a work of man not commanded by God.[c] Others, however, understand it only in its polemic context, as limited to the situation in which it was uttered: here Isaiah is not passing judgment on the legitimacy of sacrifice as such, but on its uselessness and even harmfulness as a result of the breach of the covenant relationship, which was itself the primary basis of the sacrificial ordinances.[d] The history of religion can provide justification for both views. In favour of a fundamental rejection of the sacrificial cult by Isaiah, one can point to the example of Amos, and to the historical study of religion, which shows that the greater part of Israelite sacrificial practice was of Canaanite origin.[e] In favour of the limited, polemic understanding of the passage, it can be shown that the documents of Israelite law, from the Book of the Covenant to the Priestly Document, all bear witness to an automatic belief in the divine origin of the sacrificial cult. A choice between one view and another cannot therefore be made on the basis of general considerations, but only by evaluating the statements of the text itself. Verse 12 in fact clearly attacks not merely the driving of cattle into the forecourt of the temple for the celebrating of sacrifices, but also the intention of seeing the face of Yahweh. But this polemic can hardly be taken as a fundamental attack on the whole procedure, but must be understood in the light of vv. 16f. No one may appear on the holy hill who does not fulfil Yahweh's moral commands (cf. Ps. 15). From this it follows that the statements in vv. 13b and 14 likewise do not contain a fundamental rejection of the feasts, for they provided the occasion for looking on the face of Yahweh (cf. Ex. 23.17; Deut. 16.16). In the case of v. 15 it is quite obvious that only in this particular case

[a] For the attitude of prayer cf. I Kings 8.54; II Chron. 6.13; Dan. 6.10; Luke 22.41; Acts 7.59. Outstretched hands were an expression of the desire for union, the bended knee of humility and reverence.

[b] Cf. Mowinckel, *Religion und Kultus*, Göttingen, 1953, p. 116.

[c] Cf. Procksch; defended in detail recently by R. Hentschke, BZAW 75, pp. 94ff.

[d] Cf. Marti, Fischer, Kissane, Hertzberg, Steinmann, Herntrich, Ziegler, *ad loc.*; Rignell, *StTh* 11, pp. 147ff., who believes that there was heathen influence on the cult; Eichrodt, *Theology of the Old Testament* I, p. 169 n. 1.

[e] Cf. Hentschke, BZAW 75, p. 96; Rudolph, HAT 12, 2nd ed., on Jer. 7.12ff.; Weiser, ATD 24 on Amos 5.25; ATD 20 on Jer. 7.21ff.

is prayer not heard; for it is quite simply impossible that Isaiah should have rejected prayer as such. In view of these observations the statements concerning sacrifices can be understood in the same sense.

Sacrifice was 'an action which took place in a realm beyond man and his own subjective being[a] and which only became a true act of salvation through the declaration of the priest (cf. II Sam. 24.23; Amos 5.22; Hosea 8.13; Jer. 14.12; Ezek. 20.40f.; 43.27; Mal. 1.10).[b] While the extravagant sacrifices are still burning on the altar, the prophet begins to speak, instead of the priest, and in the power of the Spirit gives an authoritative declaration of the rejection of the sacrifices.[c] Just as Samuel once insisted to Saul that Yahweh loved obedience in concrete terms more than sacrifice (cf. I Sam. 15.22; Micah 6.6–8; Pss. 50.5ff.; 51.6–19), Isaiah here declares the sacrifices, festal assemblies and prayers to be worthless, and even an insult and annoyance to God, because their only purpose is to shield men against God's claim upon their whole life. God cannot and will not accept any sacrifice which is offered to him as a mere substitute, on which he is obliged to compromise. The freely given obligation which he took on in giving the law of sacrifice becomes void, if the people do not at the same time show by their whole attitude that they in their turn feel themselves bound by the whole ordinance. Here Isaiah is attacking a perversion of meaning which has threatened all human worship through the centuries: sacrifice, worship and prayer only keep their true sense as long as in them men are really concerned to encounter the holy God. If man tries to make use of them to give himself security in the sight of God, then they become a blasphemy; sacrifice becomes a means of self-justification, the celebration of feasts the occasion of mere emotional exaltation, and prayer a meaningless, craven or hypocritical wailing. The people have received a hard blow from God. Yet they do not offer themselves to God, but seek to placate the living God with their dead works. They are stained with blood from the sacrifices, and that is how they stand in the sight of God: they are guilty.

Verse 16 apparently uses cultic expressions: the people are to wash themselves clean. But guilt cannot be washed away with water, and cannot even be set aside by better deeds in the future. It must be forgiven. Thus in the demands that follow Isaiah is not describing the

---

[a] von Rad, *Old Testament Theology* I, p. 253.
[b] *Ibid.*, pp. 261f.
[c] Cf. E. Würthwein, *ThLZ* 72, 1947, cols. 148f.

means, but only the precondition for God's forgiveness. If God is to withhold, by a free decision, based upon his saving will, the word of judgment which hangs over the people of the covenant (cf. 6.9ff; 9.8ff.), if God is to let himself be bound once again by the covenant ordinance, from which both sacrifice and prayer derive their validity, then the people itself must first return to this ordinance, by ceasing to sin.[a] As an example of the doing of good that is required of them, Isaiah mentions the judicial honesty of the people, which is manifested in the protection of its weakest members, the widows and orphans (cf. 10.2; and also James 1.27; Rom. 12.1ff.).

[18–20] *The conditional offer of pardon.* This is a speech of reconciliation. The long statement of the prophet comes to an end. God challenges the assembled people to a legal dispute. The sentences that follow are not ironical, but serious in intention. It is not Yahweh's intention to mock his partners in the covenant, who for a long time have been so self-righteous, by saying to them: 'You know perfectly well the way to wash yourselves clean!' – if your sins are like scarlet, is it going to be possible to wash them as white as snow?[b] Rather, he draws their attention to his own power of forgiveness, which is not limited by the deepest human guilt. Even though your guilt is blood-red, like scarlet and purple,[c] and even if by human and divine law it has made your lives forfeit, he still has the power to obliterate this guilt (v. 18, cf. II Cor. 5.17). The assembly of God, which has lost its kingdom and its country through its own guilt, can receive both again as a gift from its creator and Lord, if it now at last becomes wholly serious in doing his will, and practises righteousness (v. 19). The comparison of v. 18 emphasizes once again the greatness of the guilt, in order to make the grace of God seem even greater and more desirable. For the grace of God can only be properly understood by

[a] On the link between promise and warning in the prophetic preaching cf. R. Hentschke, *ZEE* 4.1, 1960, pp. 51ff

[b] Against Duhm, Marti and Balla, *Die Botschaft der Propheten*, Tübingen, 1948. Fohrer, *ad loc.*, understands v. 18b as the acceptance of an objection which the hearers could make against the 'instruction' in vv. 10–17: if the cult is not a means of salvation, one can nevertheless take refuge in the grace and mercy of God.

[c] Scarlet was produced from the eggs and bodies of the kermes worm, which lives in oak trees, and crimson (purple) from the slime of certain molluscs; cf. Nötscher, *Biblische Altertumskunde*, p. 216. On snowfalls in Palestine cf. Dalman, *Arbeit und Sitte* I, pp. 231ff. On the average there are up to three days of snow a year in the mountains, and the snow has been observed to lie for up to twelve days. Usually it melts immediately.

someone who knows that he has deserved death, and that this death will indubitably overtake him if he rejects the outstretched hand of his God. If the people will not repent even now, then even the city of Jerusalem and the remnant are condemned to destruction, and abandoned to the sword of the enemy (v. 20). Just as according to tradition Moses presented his people with a choice of life and death (cf. Deut. 30.19), so also does Isaiah, so that they may choose life. Pointing to the fact that Yahweh himself has spoken, and that he is entirely serious in his twofold offer, the prophet concludes this eloquent poem.

CHAPTER I.21–28

The Purification of Jerusalem

21 Ah, how the faithful city
    has become a harlot.
    ⟨Zion⟩ᵃ was full of justice
    and righteousness lodged in her. ⟨   ⟩ᵇ
22 Your silver has become dross,
    your beer is adulterated. ⟨   ⟩ᶜ
23 Your princes are rebels
    and companions of thieves.
    Everyone loves a bribe
    and runs after gifts.
    They do not defend the fatherless,
    and the widow's cause does not come to them.
24 Therefore the Lord says,
    Yahweh Sebaoth,
    the Mighty one of Israel:
    'Ah, I will get me comfort from my oppressors,
    and avenge myself on my enemies.
25 *I will turn my hand against you*ᵈ

ᵃ Cf. *BH.*
ᵇ Cf. *BH.*
ᶜ Cf. *BH.*
ᵈ Verse 25a is a gloss.

and will purify your dross ⟨in the furnace⟩[a]
and remove all your lead.

26 And I will restore your judges as at first,
and your counsellors as at the beginning.
Afterward you shall be called: "City of
righteousness,
faithful city".'

27 Zion shall be redeemed by justice
and those in her who turn, by righteousness.

28 But evildoers and sinners shall be destroyed together,
and those who forsake Yahweh shall be consumed.

[21–28]. This speech cannot be dated with certainty. The similarity between the thought of v. 23 and 3.12–15; 5.22–24 and 10.1–4 suggests that it belongs to the beginning of the prophet's ministry, as does the proclamation of judgment in vv. 24f., which appears to assume a political situation which is still undisturbed. Isaiah begins with a lament in the style and rhythm of a funeral elegy (3 + 2), which passes into a reproach, vv. 21–23. This is followed by the threat of judgment on the part of Yahweh, vv. 24–26. The reference to v. 21 in v. 26 provides an organic conclusion to the prophetic proclamation of judgment, and shows that the following verses, 27 and 28, were not originally joined to them, but are the work of a later hand.[b]

[21–23] *Jerusalem the harlot*. With the prevailing religious and moral situation in the city in mind, the prophet breaks out into a funeral lamentation over the city, although it is still flourishing (cf. Lam. 1.1; 2.1; 4.1). At the beginning of the history of God's dealings with his people, Jerusalem was a fortress of justice, in which the ordinance of the covenant was genuinely in force. The city has lost this noble title under the rule of unfaithful judges. Consequently, it is like a girl of good repute, who has fallen into wrong ways and become a harlot. The prophet is not deceived by outward appearances; for him, what is decisive in passing judgment on the future of the city of God is not its prosperity and apparent security, but the attitude of its inhabitants, and especially of its ruling class, towards God's demand for righteousness. Isaiah compares the city to silver, which has once again turned to an ore mixed with lead,[c] and with wheat beer which has been

---

[a] Cf. *BH*.

[b] Duhm, Marti, Procksch, Fohrer and Eichrodt, *ad loc.*; cf. also Fohrer, *ThLZ* 77, 1962, col. 747.

[c] Cf. S. Abramski, *Eretz Israel* 5, 1958, p. 89*.

adulterated with water (v. 22). Both images emphasize how the city has fallen in esteem in the sight of God. The men who ought to be concerned with keeping law and order – in their capacity as royal officials, the judges are here called princes[a] – are only concerned with seeking their own advantage (v. 23). Whoever has the most to offer them obtains their support. Judges have become companions of thieves, and those who should maintain order are destroying it. Those classes who are without influence and property, especially the widows and orphans, who rely on strangers to plead their cause, cannot find a righteous advocate (cf. 1.17; 10.2).

[24–26] *The purifying judgment of Yahweh.* Through this state of affairs, Jerusalem calls into action the giver and guardian of the covenant ordinance, who tolerates no other God besides himself (Ex. 20.1–5), and who is in particular the advocate of the defence-less.[b] The prophet stresses the all-inclusive power of God, by calling him Yahweh Sebaoth,[c] the Mighty One (or 'the Bull') of Israel (v. 24, cf. Gen. 49.24; Isa. 49.26; 60.16; Ps. 132.2, 5).[d] The Ancient of Days, the Almighty, to whom alone Israel's rise was due, will certainly arise to avenge the broken covenant (cf. Ps. 94.1) and to destroy his enemies in the midst of his people. The metaphor of v. 22a is taken up again; it shows the close connection between the prophetic lament and reproach, and the actual divine oracle. The silver which has become impure must go into the furnace of God's anger (v. 25, cf. Ps. 21.9). As a result of the severe blows that are to come, the eyes of the leaders of the nation will be opened to the ultimate cause of its ruin. The holy seed which God has in mind in carrying out his judg-ments (cf. 6.13; 7.3) is not yet separated from the chaff. Here again, it is clear that according to biblical belief, God's judgment is not simply a punishment.[e] It is a division between the devout and the godless. God rejects the base metal in order to preserve the pure silver. The destruction of the godless is followed by the renewal of the congregation (v. 26). Whereas the irresistible destruction has been provoked by the breakdown of justice (cf. 5.7), the time of salvation will be characterized by righteous rule. As in the days of David and

[a] Cf. A. Alt, 'Der Anteil des Königtums an der sozialen Entwicklung in den Reichen Israel und Juda', *Kl. Schriften* III, Munich, 1959, p. 353; R. Knierim, *ZAW* 73, 1961, p. 159.

[b] Cf. the comment on 10.2.

[c] Cf. the comment on 6.3.

[d] Cf. Weiser, *The Psalms*, on Ps. 132.2.

[e] On the motivation cf. E. Troeltsch, *Logos* 6, 1916/17, pp. 12f.

Solomon, Jerusalem will once again have true judges, who follow
God's guidance, so that it can once again bear the title of honour
which it has lost. Then its inhabitants will exclusively follow Yahweh,
and submit wholly to his will.[a]

[27–28] *The twofold judgment.* In a passage of liturgical solemnity,
a redactor living during the exile, at the earliest, emphasizes the
validity of the prophet's word for his own time. God's promise and
God's threat are still in force. The remnant who have turned to God[b]
may hope that Yahweh will set free the enslaved city of God by his
advocacy (cf. Deut.9.26; Jer.31.11; Ps.44.26), while all who have
fallen away from him and transgressed his commandments will be
subjected to his punishment (cf. Deut.28.20; Isa.58.2). For only
those who fear God may dwell upon Yahweh's holy hill of Zion (cf.
Ps.15) and rely upon his help. Thus the Israel of the writer's own
time is meant to see itself as in the furnace of God (v.20), and, trusting
in God, who can forgive not only the sins of those who are repentant
but also their consequences (vv.18ff.), the people are to turn to him
with total seriousness, as to their only helper.[c]

Chapter 1.29–31

The End of the Idolaters

29 Yes, ⟨you shall be⟩[d] put to shame because of the terebinths in
    which you delighted;
    and shall be ashamed because of the garden
    which you have chosen.
30 Yes, you shall be like a terebinth
    whose leaf withers;
    and like a garden without water.

[a] On the wide connotation of 'righteousness' cf. 11.6–8.

[b] On *šûb* cf. H. Wolff, *ZThK* 48, 1951, pp.129ff.; cf. 7.3; 30.15; 10.21.

[c] On this form of words cf. Ps.68.2f.; Judg.5.31; I Sam.2.6ff. On the idea of a
twofold judgment cf. Weiser, *The Psalms*, pp.46ff., and in the New Testament
Matt.3.12; 13.30; I Cor.4.5; II Cor.5.10; Rev.21.7f.

[d] Cf. *BH*.

31   And then the strong shall become tow
and his work a spark,
and both of them shall burn together,
with none to quench them.

[29–31] In an oracle of judgment which perhaps lacks the taunt
which introduced it and gave a reason for it, the prophet[a] attacks
those among his compatriots[b] who believe they can make themselves
safe from all misfortune by taking part in nature worship. They
gather under trees which have grown in a striking way, for Canaanite
fertility cults, with rites which in Israel's eyes are obscene.[c] Holy
terebinths of this sort were venerated in Palestine as late as the Christian era. Relics of tree worship in a changed form can still be seen
at the present day among the Arabs. The 'gardens' are sanctuaries
for the cult, in which the alternation between death and life, between
the summer heat and the spring, is meant to be made present and
brought about. In them the Egyptian and Phoenician divinities
Osiris and Adonis may have been venerated (cf. 65.3; 66.17).[d] Terebinths are deciduous trees and consequently provide a striking
symbol of the progress of a god, his journey into the kingdom of the
dead and his resurrection in the spring.[e] The prophet accepts these
views, but only in order firmly to oppose them: those who worship
these gods will themselves wither (v. 30). But this withering will not
be followed by a resurrection; they will ultimately be like trees and
gardens whose water supply has dried up (cf. Pss. 1.3; 52.8; 90.5ff.;
Isa. 40.6; Ps. 92.12f.; Job 15.30ff.; 18.16; Isa. 53.2). Probably with the
current conception of Yahweh's fire of judgment[f] in mind, the
prophet concludes with a further comparison: the mighty, who at

[a] Against Marti and Guthe, who regard the passage as post-exilic. Tree worship
must have existed in Israel at every period.

[b] Whether the prophecy can be taken with Duhm as directed against the whole
of Israel and composed at least before 722 is uncertain; but cf. 2.6ff.

[c] Cf. J. P. Asmussen, *StTh* 11, 1958, pp. 167ff. The reproaches of vv. 29–31 are
often regarded as being directed against measures taken against the socially
deprived, which is supported by the emphasis on the 'strong' in v. 31; cf. Fohrer,
ad loc.

[d] Cf. R. de Vaux, *RB* 42, 1933, pp. 31ff.

[e] Cf. Dalman, *Arbeit und Sitte* I, p. 66 and figs. 5, 6 and 8. Nötscher, *Altorientalischer und Alttestamentlicher Erlösungsglauben*, Würzburg, 1926, pp. 91ff., considers
that 1.29f. refers solely to the cult at the high places.

[f] Cf. Pss. 18.8; 50.3; 79.5; 11.6; 21.9; Ex. 19.16.

the present time believe that they are not subject to God's ordinances, will recognize how much they have fallen prey to error. Just as the spark sets the tinder on fire, their own deeds will ultimately rebound against them and destroy them without mercy (v. 31).

CHAPTER 2.1

A Second Heading

1 The word which Isaiah the son of Amoz saw
concerning Judah and Jerusalem.

[1] The heading of ch. 2 once again gives the prophet's name and that of his father, as well as those to whom his preaching was addressed. It is therefore evidence that the Book of Isaiah as we possess it was not originally a unity, since it repeats the facts already given in 1.1. It shows that this is the beginning of what was previously an independent collection of sayings of Isaiah, which was not joined to ch. 1 until later. The extent of the roll which it introduced is uncertain. In any event, the so-called 'Testimony of Isaiah', 6.1–9.6, was only embedded in it at a later stage.[a] While it is widely accepted that 2.1 is the introduction to a short collection which only extends as far as 4.6, it is more probable, from the agreement in their content, that this collection also contains 5.1–7; 5.8–24; 10.1–4; 9.8–21; 5.25, 26 30.[b] There are even serious grounds for supposing that it also contained the substance of 10.5ff. and 13–32.[c] 2.2–5 and 4.2–6 seem to have been interpolated in a later, probably post-exilic redaction, for the sake of their use in worship, so that the word spoken by the prophet in the past might be kept alive for the contemporary congregation.

[a] Cf. the comment on 6.1–13.
[b] Cf. Mowinckel, *AcOr(L)* 11, 1933, pp. 275f.
[c] *Ibid.*, pp. 276ff.

CHAPTER 2.2–5

The Consummation of History

2   It shall come to pass:
     in the course of days shall be established
     the mountain of the house of Yahweh
     as[a] the chief of the mountains,
     and it shall be raised above the hills.
     Then all nations will flow to it,

3   And many peoples shall come and say:
     'Come, let us make pilgrimage to the mountain of Yahweh,
     to the house of the God of Jacob,
     that he may teach us his ways
     and that we may walk in his paths.'
     For out of Zion shall go forth instruction
     and the word of Yahweh from Jerusalem.

4   Then he shall judge between the peoples
     and shall decide for many peoples.
     Then they shall beat their swords into ploughshares,
     and their spears into pruning hooks.
     Nation shall not lift up sword against nation,
     and they shall not learn war any more.

5   O house of Jacob, come and let us walk
     in the light of Yahweh.

This oracle of salvation is also given in Micah 4.1–4. The present passage differs from the other principally in a few inversions and in a different conclusion. If one compares the two texts with each other, the impression made by the text in Micah is of a greater unity of rhythm and content. This might suggest that it should be regarded as more original. But it is not methodologically correct to take a text handed down in two different versions and in two different places, and to emend one on the strength of the other, when it cannot be proved that the differences came into being only in the course of the tradition of the text.[b] Our exposition will show that the content of this oracle of salvation was decisively formed by cultic traditions. For reasons of language and content, the passage cannot have been com-

a *b-essentiae*; cf. Grether, *Hebr. Grammatik*, §89 k.
b Against H. Wildberger, *VT* 7, 1957, pp. 63f.

posed by Micah, while the double tradition and the use of the theme of the battle between the nations, which differs from that in passages of Isaiah which are clearly authentic, show that it is improbable that the passage is by Isaiah himself, in spite of emphatic arguments in favour of this view which have recently been advanced.[a] Both in the Book of Isaiah and in the Book of Micah interpolations have been introduced by a later hand, in order to give new hope to the congregation, which is living under the judgment of God upon his people. It may be, then, that the variations between the two versions of the one prophecy of salvation can simply be explained by assuming in both passages the copying down from memory of an oracle which originally formed part of pre-exilic worship, but which was placed in its present position in the Book of Isaiah during or after the exile.[b] This assertion of literary criticism does not imply any value judgment about its content. The significance of a biblical text is decided not by authorship, but by what it says.

This passage, which from its content is clearly an oracle of salvation, can be divided into four parts. It begins at once with a description of the miraculous exaltation of Mount Sion in the future (v. 2a); this is followed by the description of the effect of this event among the nations (vv. 2a–3b). The reason given for this in v. 3b leads in its turn to an account of the rule of God which shall end all discord, in v. 4. Finally, in v. 5, there is a demand to the audience to draw from the oracle the consequence for their own lives.

[2a] The prophecy is introduced by an expression of time, which

---

[a] Against von Rad, *The Problem of the Hexateuch and other Essays*, tr. E. W. Trueman Dicken, 1965, pp. 233ff.; Wildberger, *VT* 7, pp. 65ff.; R. Martin-Achard, *Israël et les nations*, CT 42, 1959, pp. 57ff.; J. J. Stamm, in Stamm/Bietenhard, *Der Weltfriede im Alten und Neuen Testament*, Zürich, 1959, p. 61 n. 86; Eichrodt, BAT 17.1, p. 48; H. Junker, TThSt 15 (*Bischof Wehr-Festschrift*) 1962, pp. 26ff.; with T. H. Robinson, HAT 14, ²1954, pp. 139f.; Weiser, ATD 24, ²1956, p. 262; R. H. Pfeiffer, *Introduction to the Old Testament*, New York, 1948, pp. 590f.; Eissfeldt, *The Old Testament: an Introduction*, tr. P. R. Ackroyd, 1965, p. 318. Cf. the theme of the battle between the nations in Isaiah in 10.28–34; 14.24–27; 17.12–14; 29.1–8; 30.27–33; 31.4–5, 8–9.

[b] Cf. A. Kapelrud, *VT* 11, 1961, pp. 395ff.; J. Gray, *VT* 11, 1961, p. 15, tries to explain the occurrence of the passage in both Isaiah and Micah by supposing that both prophets made use of a passage which had become part of the liturgy in the eighth century. A similar view is taken by H. Junker, TThSt 15, pp. 27ff., who supposes that an ancient promise concerning the temple from the time of Solomon was reapplied in the last days of King Ahaz.

since the LXX has usually been rendered 'in the latter days'.ᵃ This is
an adaptation of the actual expression to the late Jewish conception
of the absolute end of the present world era, which is alien to the
characteristic thinking of the Old Testament. The Hebrew phrase
which is rendered above by 'in the course of days' must be literally
translated 'in the back of the days'. This expression reflects an orien-
tation with regard to time which is contrary to the logic of our language. For the Hebrew, what has already taken place lies in front of
him, while what is to come lies behind him.ᵇ That the expression 'in
the course of days' originally refers to a moment within history follows
from Gen. 49.1; Num. 24.14; Deut. 31.29 and Jer. 23.20. Thus the
unknown prophet is in accord with the pre-apocalyptic expectations
of Israel and of Judaism in looking forward not to the end, but to the
consummation of history. At that time, by an act in which the existing
earth is transformed, God reveals to all nations the true central point
of the world of mankind, the place where he is to appear as judge, and
where his word and his will will be proclaimed. Mount Zion, on the
peak of which the temple stands, will tower over all other mountains
and hills (cf. Isa. 40.3–5; Ezek. 40.2; Zech. 14.10). There is a remi-
niscence of the conception of Paradise located upon the mountain of
God, cf. Ps. 48.2; Isa. 14.13f.,ᶜ as well as that of the 'navel', the middle
point of the world.ᵈ Just as at the beginning of world history God
founded the earth above the seas of the primeval ocean, so that from
henceforth it could no longer be shaken (cf. Pss. 24.2; 93.1; 96.10;
I Chron. 16.30),ᵉ he will one day create for the temple in Jerusalem a
place which shall not be shaken for all time to come.

[2b–4] The nations require no further enlightenment. They understand at once the meaning of this powerful convulsion and trans-

ᵃ Cf. G. W. Buchanan, *JNES* 20, 1961, pp. 188ff. As in the Accadian *ana
aḥrat ūmī, beʾaḥᵃrīt hayyāmīm* is a neutral expression of time signifying the future
without any special eschatological meaning. Its rendering in the LXX is probably
due to an attempt to give a literal translation. Gray, *loc. cit.*, discusses whether it
originally came from the cult (from the last day of the New Year feast), but there
is not as yet any real certainty about this.

ᵇ Cf. T. Boman, *Hebrew Thought Compared with Greek*, tr. J. L. Moreau, 1960,
pp. 123ff.

ᶜ Cf. H. J. Kraus, BK XV. 1, p. 345; idem, *Worship in Israel*, pp. 201ff. For the
recurrence of this theme in apocalyptic, cf. W. Bousset and H. Gressmann,
Religion des Judentums, HNT 21, Tübingen, ³1926, pp. 283f.; P. Volz, *Die Eschatologie
der jüdischen Gemeinde im neutestamentlichen Zeitalter*, Tübingen, 1934, pp. 412f.

ᵈ Cf. H. W. Hertzberg, *JPOS* 12, 1932, pp. 40f.

ᵉ Cf. Herbert Schmid, *ZAW* 67, 1955, p. 191.

formation of the earth: Yahweh has revealed himself before the eyes of all mankind as the true creator and Lord of the world. Consequently, they set forth spontaneously. The great pilgrimage of the nations to Zion begins.[a] Just as Israel once travelled in the desert to the mountain of God, in order to receive the law there (cf. Ex. 19ff.), the nations now travel on pilgrimage to the sanctuary of the people of the twelve tribes, to the house of the God of Jacob. For they know that this is the only place where they can find guidance for a life through which they can endure before the judgment of God. This is the only place in which one can know the way of Yahweh, which he follows in the history which he has determined through his promises and commands, and so it is only here that man can learn the way he must follow in order to respond with a right attitude to the promises, commands and chastisements of God.[b] 'For out of Zion shall go forth instruction, and the word of Yahweh from Jerusalem' (v.3b). The word translated 'instruction', tōrāh, means in this passage not merely the legal ordinances given in the five books of Moses, but, in the same way as the 'word of Yahweh', also the words of God that at various times are uttered by priests and prophets, and guide and interpret the existential life both of individuals and of nations.[c] Ordinary mortals are unable to bear God speaking to them directly. They need the chosen mediators (cf. Ex.19; Deut.18.15). The unnamed prophet does not promise the end but the consummation of the worship at the Jerusalem capital.[d] For centuries Israel had hoped that all the nations of the world would turn to Yahweh.[e] The meaning of Israel's election, its privileged position among the nations, did not lie in the existence of the people of God as such, but in the task which God had accorded them.[f] This hope was originally associated with the conception, kept alive in the harvest festival, of the city of God, before the gates of which Yahweh would manifest himself as a victorious judge

[a] On the survival of the concept of the pilgrimage of the nations in apocalyptic, cf. Volz, Eschatologie, pp.171f.

[b] On the Old Testament concept of the way of man and the way of God cf. A. Kuschke, StTh 5, 1952, pp.106ff.

[c] On the linguistic usage of tōrāh cf. Hos.8.12; I Chron. 16.40; 22.12; Ecclus. 41.4; Hos.4.6; Zeph.3.4; Jer. 18.18; Isa. 1.10; 8.16, 20; 30.9f.; on that of the word of God in the sense of the written law, cf. Ex.20.1; 24.3; 34.1–27.

[d] Against Wildberger, VT 7, p.80.

[e] Cf. Pss.22.7f.; 87.1; I Kings 8.41—43; Isa.45.22–25; cf. also 25.6; Jer.3.17.

[f] Cf. Martin-Achard, CT 42, pp.13ff.; 31ff.; Kaiser, Der königliche Knecht, FRLANT 70, Göttingen, 1959, p.136.

over the chaotic disorder of the nations surging towards it.ᵃ The powers of chaos, which God conquered at the creation of the world, as it were celebrated their resurrection in the other, insubordinate nations of the world. The prophet who speaks here has omitted the theme of the battle, and has replaced it solely by faith in God's power as creator. Thus in spite of the continued expectation of the consummation of God's works of salvation within history, this reflects a knowledge that humanity as a whole can be converted only through the total revelation of God associated with a new creation.

Just as in the creation of the world, and then repeatedly at the great harvest festival, with its entry into the temple, God revealed himself as the ultimate Lord and judge of the whole world,ᵇ so he will finally appear in the consummation of the world's confused history as the one who alone can give enduring peace to humanity through his word, which judges men and forgives their sins. The nations, inwardly convinced of God's deity by the new creation, will willingly submit to his decision. This means that the constant readiness of them all to take up arms against any of the others has become meaningless. The nations will voluntarily renounce their arms, by forging their weapons into agricultural implements, which will help to bring about peace and further the real task which man has been set, of making the earth serviceable (cf. Gen. 26.28; Ps. 8.5–7). Swords will be turned into ploughshares, and spears into pruning hooks. The variant text in Micah probably preserves an original feature of the passage when it adds a further detail to the description of the state of peace: 'They shall sit every man under his vine and under his fig tree.' Fear of enemies is no more. Peaceful work will no longer be interrupted by military service (cf. I Kings 4.25; II Kings 18.31). Others before and after this prophetᶜ held the view that peace came through God's victories in war, but he knows that it depends solely upon man's being inwardly convinced of the deity of God. He trusts his God in his

---

ᵃ Cf. Pss. 46.6–10; 48.4ff.; 76.2f.; 87; Zech. 14.2ff.; Isa. 41.1–5; 21–29; 43.8–13; 22–28; Zech. 8.20–23; Isa. 60.3ff.; 63.1ff.; Wildberger, *VT* 7, pp. 68ff.; Weiser, *The Psalms*, pp. 37f., 49f., 60ff.; Schmidt, commentary, pp. 168ff.; Kraus, BK XV, pp. 197ff., 342ff.

ᵇ Cf. Ps. 50.1–7; 96.10ff.; 97; 98; 99; Isa. 51.9ff.; S. Mowinckel, *Psalmenstudien* II, Kristiania, 1922, pp. 44ff.; Weiser, *The Psalms* pp. 37ff.; Kraus, BK XV, pp. 200, 647ff., 664ff.

ᶜ On the biblical images of universal peace cf. H. Gross, *Weltherrschaft als religiöse Idee im Alten Testament*, BBB 6, Bonn, 1953, pp. 118ff. and J. J. Stamm and H. Bietenhard, *Der Weltfriede im Alten und Neuen Testament*, p. 61.

lovingkindness to bring men to the point where they will give up war voluntarily and of themselves. The expectation that men who truly know God will bring war to an end means that wars are unequivocally characterized as the consequence of human sin. In modern exegesis there has been a continual dispute whether expectations such as are expressed here should be considered to be eschatological or not. If the concept of eschatology is understood in terms of its etymology, so that it is the doctrine of the end of the world and of human history, then it must be seen as inappropriate to apply it to the pre-apocalyptic literature of the Old Testament. But if eschatology is understood as referring to expectations of a fundamental change in earthly conditions in the future, regardless of whether they take place within or outside history, then the prophecy we are discussing must be regarded as eschatological in the best sense.[a] In view of the vacillation of the future hope of late Judaism and the New Testament between a fulfilment within the world and within history, and a fulfilment beyond history, the wider definition, which is applicable to the prophecy we are discussing, is preferable.

[5] With v. 5 the prophet addresses himself directly to the listening congregation, knowing that he shares its position and its task. In order to comfort them and strengthen their faith, it has been necessary to refer to the promise of the future glorification of Zion and to the consummation of the saving work of God begun in the choosing of the patriarchs (cf. Gen. 12.3).[b] This, together with the placing of this oracle before the prophecies of warning of Isaiah himself, leads to the conclusion that this congregation lacks everything which is promised here. It is not possible to specify with certainty the exact time when the prophecy we are discussing was written down and joined to the scroll containing the genuine prophecies of Isaiah, in view of the complications of the history of Israel. However, the expectations exceed even those of Deutero-Isaiah, and this implies that we should think of the period immediately following the exile. The congregation is to rise up and walk in the light of its God. In the light of the sun, the world lies revealed before man. He can walk safely and deliberately. In the sight of the presence of God, the powers that make him afraid lose their force (cf. Ps. 27.1). Where the light of God shines upon man,

[a] Cf. J. Lindblom, *StTh* 6, 1953, pp. 79ff.; T. C. Vriezen, *SVT* 1, 1953, pp. 223ff.; R. Hentschke, *ZEE* 4.1, pp. 47f.; H. Graf Reventlow, *Das Amt des Propheten bei Amos*, FRLANT 80, Göttingen, 1962, pp. 106ff.

[b] On the interpretation of Gen. 12.3 cf. Martin-Achard, *CT* 42, pp. 32ff.

he knows his own place, and is aware of what is demanded of him (cf. Pss. 36.9; 119.105). Thus v.5 is an appeal to the congregation to recognize and accept through the word of hope that the present situation is brought about by God. The concrete significance of this for the exilic and post-exilic community is that they should understand the catastrophe of the exile and its consequences as God's judgment (cf. Micah 7.8)[a] and not as the abolition of the election of Israel or of the promise, but as a step towards their fulfilment. This demand naturally also requires that the congregation should respond in their concrete acts and obedience to the will of God which has been made visible and has uttered its demand in judgment, and has been revealed and given its promise in prophecy.

Christians cannot simply take over these expectations in the concrete forms in which they are expressed here. The conceptual material of this promise is based upon a belief in the enduring significance of Zion as the sole place of the revelation of God (cf. Ps. 132.13f.), and this belief has been superseded by John 4.19–24 and Heb. 13.14. For Christians, there is no other manifestation of God within time than in the preaching of the crucified and risen Christ (cf. I Cor. 2.2). But this prophecy and what it affirms has not lost its significance for the believer. It testifies that if man is seized by the reality of God, he realizes that he is called not to violence and suffering, but to a peaceful and just life with other men, in which alone human life can be fulfilled. Consequently, it becomes a pronouncement of judgment upon the Christian church, which loses itself in the law of the present world, and is not ready to suffer in imitation of Jesus Christ; it is also a judgment upon the world, which seeks to live its life by its own resources, and consequently makes repeated use of violence.[b] But it looks beyond all the conflicts of the present time towards the moment when God will bring to completion the work of new creation which he began on Easter morning. In this respect, the Christian church, as the new people of God, can see itself as addressed in the last verse of this prophecy.[c]

[a] Cf. Weiser, ATD 24, *ad loc.*

[b] This does not imply any attempt to answer the question much discussed at the present day, whether soldiers can be in a state of grace. It is not possible to answer such a question in biblical terms, but only on the basis of theological reflection undertaken as a personal responsibility and in obedience to the law and the gospel. Cf. on this problem W. Elert, *Das Christliche Ethos*, Tübingen, 1949, pp. 148ff.; H. Thielicke, *Theological Ethics* II, ed. W. H. Lazareth, 1969, pp. 519ff.

[c] On the question of the evaluation and validity of Old Testament texts cf.

CHAPTERS 2.6–22 AND 5.15f.

The Great Day of Yahweh

6 Surely, thou has rejected thy people, the house of Jacob;
   because they are full ⟨of divining⟩ᵃ from the East
   and of soothsayers like the Philistines,
   and they abound with foreigners.

7 Their land is filled with silver and gold,
   and there is no end to their treasures;
   their land is filled with horses,
   and there is no end to their chariots.

8 Their land is filled with idols;
   a man ⟨will bow down⟩ᵇ to the work of his hands,
   to what his own fingers have made.

9 So man has been humbled
   and men have been brought low –
   forgive them not!

10 Enter into the rock and hide in the dust
    before the terror of Yahweh and his glorious majesty,
    ⟨when he rises to shake the earth⟩.ᶜ

11 ⟨   ⟩ And the haughtiness of man shall be
    ⟨humbled⟩,
    and the pride of man shall be ⟨brought low⟩;ᵈ
    and Yahweh alone will be exalted
    in that day.

12 For (there will be) a day for Yahweh Sebaoth
    against all that is proud and lofty,
    and against all that is lifted up and ⟨high⟩;ᵉ

13 and against all the cedars of Lebanon ⟨   ⟩ᶠ
    and against all the oaks of Bashan;

14 and against all the high mountains
    and against all the lofty hills;

F. Hesse, 'Die Wertung und die Geltung alttestamentlicher Texte', in *Festschrift F. Baumgärtel*, Erlanger Forschunger, Reihe A. 10, 1959, pp. 74–96.

  ᵃ Add *miqsām* in front of *miqqedem*. But H. Junker, TThSt 15 (*Bischof Wehr-Festschrift*), 1962, p. 22, does not make this addition, and sees here an allusion to trade with the East.

  ᵇ Cf. *BH*.

  ᶜ Add with vv. 19b and 21b *beqūmō laʿarōṣ hāʾāreṣ*.

  ᵈ Read as in v. 17a.

  ᵉ Cf. *BH*.

  ᶠ Cf. *BH*.

15   and against every high tower
    and against every fortified wall;
16   and against all the ships of Tarshish
    and against all the beautiful craft.
17   And the haughtiness of man shall be humbled,
    and the pride of men shall be brought low.
    And Yahweh alone shall be exalted
    in that day.
18   But the idols are ⟨like the night⟩[a]
    which passes away.
19   And they shall enter the caves of the rocks
    and the holes of the dust
    from before the terror of Yahweh,
    and from his glorious majesty,
    when he rises to shake the earth.
20   In that day man will cast forth
    his idols of silver and his idols of gold,
    which ⟨he made⟩[b] for himself to worship,
    to the ⟨shrews⟩[c] and the bats,
21   to enter the caverns of the rocks
    and the clefts of the cliffs,
    from before the terror of Yahweh
    and from his glorious majesty,
    when he rises to shake the earth.

5   15   Then man ⟨shall be[d] humbled⟩ and men ⟨shall be[d]
    brought low⟩,
    and the eyes of the haughty shall be lowered.
16   But Yahweh Sebaoth shall be[d] exalted in justice
    and the Holy God ⟨shall⟩[e] show himself holy in
    righteousness.

2   22   *Turn away from man*
    in whose nostrils is breath,
    for of what account is he?

Because the prophecy of salvation 2.2–5 has been set in front of it, the beginning of the great poem on the day of Yahweh has been so distorted that all attempts at restoration are conjectural. Thus the intro-

---

[a] Read k*e*layil with Hans Schmidt. But cf. 1QIsa.
[b] Cf. *BH.*
[c] Cf. *BH.*
[d] Read *perfectum consecutivum* as in 2.17.
[e] Read *yiqqādeš* instead of *niqdaš.*

ductory *kī*, 'for', 'indeed', can be attributed at once to the redactor, who intended it to make a link between the content of 2.2–5 and 2.6ff. He regards the association of ideas as being established by the instruction in 2.5: the promise of salvation is only valid for Israel when it is obedient. A disobedient Israel – and it appears that the time in which he lived justified this rebuke – would remain under the anger of God, which would break forth on his day of judgment.[a] But the hand of the redactor can also be seen at work within the passage. Verses 18–21 and 5.15f. are particularly suspicious. Verses 18f. and 20f. are parallel in content. Both the latter give the impression of being a subsequent commentary on what precedes them. Thus the whole conclusion appears to have been added later at different stages in the redaction. We can no longer tell how far authentic fragments of Isaiah's prophecy have been used in it. Verse 22 forms a final exhortation addressed to the listening congregation and was probably added at the same time as the interpolation of 2.2–5 and 4.2–6.

The question of the literary form of this poem must be answered by taking into account the fact that in vv.6a and 9b God himself is addressed, whereas v.10 is clearly addressed to another entity, the people. This double audience is best explained by supposing that the prophet uttered his speech during a festal gathering in the temple of Jerusalem, where he could speak both before God and to the solemn assembly. It may be that he was expected to make a petition on behalf of the people (cf. Amos 7.1ff.; Isa.6.11; Jer.14.1–15.4), and was unable to do so because of the guilt and impurity of his people, of which he had become conscious at the moment of his vocation.[b] Instead of pleading for his people, he called upon God to judge the house of Jacob, the holy people of the twelve tribes. Thus one can regard 2.6–11 as a petition which has changed its form because of this refusal, with a certain similarity to a prayer for vengeance and prophecy of warning, and 2.12–21 + 5.15f. as a warning. But the way the whole passage has obviously undergone redaction means that even the determination of its literary category must be conjectural, since we cannot exclude the possibility that even vv.6a and 9a owe their present wording to the redactor. Since v.7 assumes that the riches of the country are still great and have not yet been reduced by

---

[a] Cf. H. Junker, TThSt 15, pp. 19ff., who, however, argues that Isaiah is the author of 2.2–5.
[b] Cf. below on 6.5.

war, the passage must be dated in the early period of Isaiah's career, that is in 735.[a]

[2.6–11] *The great apostasy and the coming judgment.* In the hearing of the solemn festal assembly Isaiah addresses himself to his God. It is impossible for him to pray for his people, because the signs of their unfaithfulness are obvious.[b] The people, who have violated God's claim to be their sole Lord (cf. Ex. 20.2ff.), have broken the covenant and squandered the privilege of their election; they have been rejected by God. All forms of prophecy and divination not strictly associated with faith in Yahweh were forbidden in Israel at an early period. Even during his short reign, Saul opposed the mediums who brought up the dead (cf. I Sam. 28.9). In the Law of Holiness, Lev. 19.26, augury and witchcraft are forbidden, immediately after the prohibition of eating flesh with blood in it. In Deuteronomy, the renunciation of all magical practices is actually regarded as a mark distinguishing Israel from the nations (cf. Deut. 18.9ff.). Trying to peer into the future with the aid of the powers of the underworld is to be replaced by obedience to the will of God and trust in his promises. But Israel is trying to by-pass God through the techniques of divination (cf. Ezek. 21.21), and by conjuring up the spirits of the dead, who were held to have special knowledge concerning the future. From Mesopotamia, the classical country of magic and astrology, and from Philistia (cf. I Sam. 6.2), that is, from East and West, these customs were introduced to the country, probably coming with foreign traders who were attracted by the economic prosperity of Israel; and they threatened the faith of the people of the covenant through the attitude they implied. Here we can see something more than a narrow and intolerant provincialism in the vigilance of the prophets, who have the people's spiritual health and loyalty to their faith more at heart than a cosmopolitan outlook.

In the verses (vv. 7–9) that follow Isaiah goes further into the hidden relationship between human self-assurance and the attempt to obtain metaphysical certainty, by making a powerful contrast be-

[a] H. Junker, TThSt 15, pp. 29f., would date this passage, like 2.2–5, in the last days of Ahaz, and would regard 2.6–9 as a description of the decadence that began in the time of Solomon, since the content of these verses goes beyond what is said in II Chron. 26.5–15 concerning the reign of King Uzziah. In answer to this I would point out with regard to 5.8–24 and 10.1–4 that the account in I Chronicles is hardly exhaustive. Idolatry may have been widespread among the people in spite of II Kings 15.3.

[b] Cf. below on 8.19.

tween economic and political prosperity and the increasing idolatry which accompanied it. The land of Jacob is full of treasure and chariots. It is rich and well-armed, and enjoys a deluded feeling of self-attained security. This description of the circumstances accords best with what we know of the situation of the northern and southern kingdoms in the days of Jeroboam II and Uzziah (Azariah) and his successor Jotham. Both states were able to enlarge their territory, and achieve an increase in economic prosperity comparable to the period of Solomon (II Kings 14.25; II Chron. 26.7ff.; 27.3ff.). This general prosperity was accompanied by the weakening of the traditional organs of faith. The people turned to the cults of Canaanite fertility religion. Isaiah speaks with contempt of the idols, the 'non-entities' (cf. Ps. 96.5). The description of the setting up of images is meant to show the powerlessness of the forces which are supposed to have come to dwell among them: man cannot seek protection from his fate in the work of his own hands. It is possible that v.8 may once also have continued: 'and there is no end to their idolatry'.[a] The classical description of worship of the work of man's own hands is found in Ex. 32. The form of the idols changes with the course of history, but the attitude of man remains the same. Man seeks to assert himself within his own world by means of his works, and tries to escape through them from the grip of the ominous future, of fate, behind which stands the living God.[b] But man, who will not let God be his master, falls into the power of transitory things and becomes subject to the elemental forces of the cosmos, and so loses the position of dominance intended for him by his creator (cf. Rom. 8.21; Gal. 4.3; Gen. 1.28; Ps. 8.5ff.). He will not lower himself before his creator, and yet bows down to the work of his own hands.[c] Isaiah knows that God responds to this attitude on the part of man with his anger, and that he has resolved to judge Israel. Just as at the moment of his vocation he stood on the side of God, by acknowledging that God's judgment upon himself was just, and by declaring his readiness to serve God,[d] so now he calls upon God to judge his own people. It would, however, be quite wrong to ascribe to the prophet here an interest in the destruction of his people, as it were as a reaction to the lack of response which his

[a] Duhm, *ad loc.*

[b] Cf. Gogarten, *Der Mensch zwischen Gott und Welt*, Heidelberg, 1952, pp. 424ff.; [2]1956, pp. 388ff.; H. Thielicke, *Der Glaube der Christenheit*, Göttingen, 1947, pp. 391ff.

[c] H. Junker, TThSt 15, pp. 22f., now also agrees.

[d] Cf. below on 6.5 and 8.

preaching received: 'The emotion of the prophet is not a desire for the threatened annihilation of the people, but is aroused by the disappointment of God, his transcendental sorrow.'[a] Here comes the violent turning-point in the oracle (vv. 10–11): the prophet turns directly to the assembled people and proclaims to them the inexorable judgment of God. In extreme contrast to their own feeling of security, the people are ordered to hide in clefts in the rock and holes in the ground, out of reach of God's anger. This advice is ironical. It is meant to make the people conscious that there is no way out of the position they are in. For man cannot hide from his creator and Lord. His hand reaches from heaven to the depths of the underworld (cf. Ps. 139.9ff.; Amos 9.2ff.; Job 26.6). When the terror of God comes upon the people (cf. I Sam. 11.7; Job 13.11; 11.23) and shatters every protection they have, and when God reveals his majesty in the thunderstorm and in the catastrophes of history (cf. Job 37.4; Ex. 15.7), then, consciously or unconsciously, man must give God the honour due to him.

[2.12–17; 5.15f.] *The Day of Yahweh.* With constant new turns of phrase, the verses that follow describe the shattering of everything which can impress man by its greatness. The prophet suggests to the minds of his hearers the violent storm of God which rages over the world and brings crashing to the ground the proud cedars of Lebanon and the firm oaks of Bashan, the area south of Hermon and north of Gilead. The storm rages from the extreme north of the country, from the Lebanon, to the furthest south, the gulf of Akaba, with its harbour Elath (cf. II Chron. 26.2). Its progress from north to south is no coincidence, but probably derives from the conception of the mountain of God in the north (cf. Isa. 14.13).[b] Isaiah is undoubtedly thinking of a storm accompanied by an earthquake, and also includes elements of the concepts of the theophany (cf. the comment on 6.4). Even the hills collapse; the towers and walls, as it were the expression of the power and security of the cities, are brought down. The ships of Tarshish,[c] whether they lie hidden in the harbour or sail proudly over

---

[a] A. Heschel, *Die Prophetie*, Cracow, 1936, p.85, in H. Junker, TThSt 15, p. 23 n. 7.

[b] Cf. Fohrer, *ad loc.*

[c] According to Koehler (*s.v.*), the ships of Tarshish must be regarded as sea-going ships bound for Tunis. Others think in terms of vessels called after the Spanish city of Tarsessos. In any case, it was a generic term for sea-going ships. The Hebrew *śekiyyā*, however, is identical with the Egyptian *śk.ty*, a kind of ship the exact nature of which is not known.

the sea, are seized by the powerful storm and capsized.[a] Trade and commerce are fatally stricken by the divine judgment. Before this severe onslaught the proudest and most self-confident of men must bow; for they no longer possess anything on which they can base their self-reliance. God's judgment reveals man's impotence.

[18–21; 5.15f.] The final passage brings nothing new in terms of content. It merely draws the consequences of what has already been said. The idols, understood as metaphysical guarantees of man's own future, are revealed in the judgment as what they are, nothing. What man now credulously honours and worships, he will then cast away as a mere burden in his flight. The idols will end up among the impure animals, the shrews and bats (cf. Lev. 11.18; Deut. 14.16). There is no need for a special act of judgment against the idols; if man, who has created them, is crushed, then their impotence is made obvious.[b] The suspicion voiced above, that this group of verses was added later, need not be repeated here. It may be that vv. 8f. come from the same period, probably after the exile, although it is impossible to be certain about this.

[22] In the final verse the redactor draws the consequences of the prophet's warning for the people of his own time, who are in outwardly altered circumstances, and at the same time prepares for the transition to the following prophecy of warning (3.1–15) against the nobles.[c] The idols have been unmasked in verses reminiscent of Isa. 40.18–20 + 41.6f. and 44.9–20, and convincingly shown to be contemptible as human works. Moreover, the history of previous years has confirmed the emptiness of their works. One danger, however, survives through the ages, and that is that man may set up himself and his kind in the place of God, and so bring down the judgment of God upon himself and his people. So the redactor adds a comment on the transitoriness of man: he is nothing of his own power; he is dust, to which God's breath gives life for a short while (cf. Pss. 104.29; 90.3; 39.4–6).

The background of these words of the prophet was formed not only

---

[a] Cf. Dalman, *Arbeit und Sitte* I, p. 245. There, however, a winter storm is being described. In antiquity, sailing at sea was interrupted from the onset of the autumn storms until the spring; cf. *ibid.*, p. 155.

[b] Cf. Junker, TThSt 15, pp. 24f.

[c] A. Bruno, *Jesaja. Eine rhythmische und textkritische Untersuchung*, Stockholm, 1953, pp. 60 and 247, consequently links this verse with the passage that follows. Steinmann, *Le prophète Isaïe*, Lect. Div. 5, Paris 1950, sees the author of the gloss as a wisdom writer.

by the experience of the consuming holiness of God which was accorded him at his calling, but also by the expectation of the day of Yahweh, which originated in the worship of the covenant. When he speaks in vv. 11 and 12 of 'that day', he could assume a quite definite conception in the minds of his audience. In the great harvest festival at which Israel recalled God's acts of salvation in the past, the creation and the liberation from Egypt, the kingly rule of God and the choosing of Jerusalem and the house of David, the people were constantly made conscious of the all-inclusive power of Yahweh. They consequently could not overlook the fact that Yahweh had not yet revealed his power in such a way that all the nations were bound to acknowledge it. That which the congregation now realized in the celebration of the feast would one day become a full and manifest reality within history, on the great day of Yahweh. Israel looked forward to full salvation for itself on that day. It forgot only too easily that the manifestation of God must always bring with it a judgment upon Israel itself.[a] Amos had already uttered a warning to the people who looked forward naïvely to the final revelation of God: 'Woe to you who desire the day of Yahweh! Why would you have the day of Yahweh? . . . Is not the day of Yahweh darkness, and not light, and gloom with no brightness in it?' (Amos 5.18ff.)[b] The manifestation of the holy God must consume everything impure. This proclamation by Isaiah of the coming great day of the judgment of Yahweh stands in the same tradition.

[a] On the sources of the prophetic historical discourse in the covenant cult cf. E. Würthwein, *ZThK* 49, 1952, pp. 1ff. For a different view, Hesse, *ZAW* 65, 1953, pp. 45ff.; Rendtorff, *TDNT* VI, pp. 812f.

[b] For discussion on the origin of the future hope cf. Mowinckel, *Psalmenstudien* II, pp. 211ff.; Weiser, ATD 24, 2nd ed., p. 170; (*The Psalms*, pp. 23ff.); C. Westermann, *The Praise of God in the Psalms*, tr. K. R. Crim, London, 1966, pp. 142ff.; H. J. Kraus, *Die Königsherrschaft Gottes im Alten Testament*, BHT 13, Tübingen 1951; *Worship in Israel*, pp. 179ff.; BK XV, Neukirchen 1958f., pp. 197ff., 324ff., 647ff.; on the origin of the conception of the Day of Yahweh now cf. G. von Rad, 'The Origin of the Concept of the Day of Yahweh', *JSS* 4, 1959, pp. 97-108, which, however, lays excessive emphasis on the tradition of the holy war. Cf. also Fohrer, commentary, p. 58, n. 30.

CHAPTER 3.1–9 (11)

Anarchy

1   ⟨   ⟩ᵃ Behold, the Lord, Yahweh Sebaoth,
     is taking away from Jerusalem and from Judah
     stay and staff: ⟨   ⟩ᵇ
2   The soldier and the levy,
     the judge and the prophet, the diviner and the elder,
3   The captain of fifty and the man of rank,
     the counsellor and the wise man ⟨   ⟩ᶜ and the expert
     in charms.
     Then I will make boys their princes,
     and capricious persons shall rule over them.
5   And the people shall be oppressed,
     one man by another,
     and everyone by his neighbour,
     And the youth will be insolent to the elder
     and the base fellow to the honourable.
6   When a man takes hold of his brother
     in the house of his father:ᵈ
     'You have a mantle;
     You shall be our leader,
     and this heap of ruins
     shall be under your hand';
7   in that dayᵉ he will speak out, saying:
     'I am not a healer;
     and in my house there is neither bread nor mantle.
     Do not make me leader of the people.'
8   Yes, Jerusalem stumbles
     and Judah falls;
     because their speech and their deeds are against Yahweh,
     defying the eyes of his glory.
9   The look on their faces witnesses against them,
     and they proclaim their sin like Sodom;

ᵃ Delete *kī* with Budde, *ZAW* 49, 1931, p.202, as a gloss.
ᵇ 'The whole stay of bread and the whole stay of water' has been generally
recognized as a gloss since the time of Duhm.
ᶜ Delete *ḥᵃrāšīm*; an exilic gloss, cf. II Kings 24.14.
ᵈ Marti and Kissane punctuate differently and translate: 'When a man takes
hold of his brother, in whose father's house is a mantle: "You shall be. . . ." '
ᵉ 'In that day' should possibly be regarded with Steinmann as an interpolation
introduced under the influence of 2.11, 17, 20.

> they do not hide it.
> *Woe to them!*
> *For they create evil for themselves.*[a]
> 10 〈*Blessed are the righteous*〉[b] *for it is well with them.*
> *For they shall eat the fruit of their deeds.*
> 11 *Woe to the wicked, for it shall be ill with him,*
> *for what his hands have done shall be done to him.*

The common theme of the judgment on the ruling class has caused the two prophetic oracles 3.1–9a and 3.12–15 to be placed together. An analysis of their formal features nevertheless shows that they were originally independent.[c] The oracle, 3.1–9a, is a proclamation of judgment consisting of two parts, vv. 1–7, the proclamation, and vv. 8–9a the reason behind it, God only being spoken of in the third person. Thus a prophet is not simply the instrument through whom God speaks, but has considerable responsibility for the form taken by the message committed to him. In vv. 9b–11, a later voice is heard in words which individualize the idea of judgment for pastoral purposes, whereas in the poem that comes from Isaiah himself, the anger of God ultimately falls upon the whole people (cf. 3.12; 5.13). The question of the occasion on which Isaiah pronounced this oracle cannot be decided with certainty. One may think either of an assembly of the ruling group in the royal palace (cf. Jer. 36.20ff.), or of a cultic occasion, at which, since church and state formed a unity, the ruling circles would naturally be present. The understanding of the text is not essentially affected by this uncertainty. Since the judgment of God which is being proclaimed still lies in the future and does not seem to have given any sign of its coming, this passage also can be taken as belonging to the prophet's early period.

[3.1–7] *The total collapse of the state.* The prophet appears before the ruling class of the Davidic kingdom of Jerusalem and Judah, gathered either for a religious feast or for an official occasion. A favourable oracle or helpful counsel might be expected from him, but he comes with his message of doom. The more the times appeared peaceful and free from the threat of enemies without and within, the greater the astonishment and recoil this message must have caused

---

[a] Driver, *Textus* I, 1960, p. 120, agrees with Perles in regarding *lāhem* as a *Tiq. soph.* for *lēlōhīm*.

[b] Cf. *BH* and Driver, *Textus* I, p. 115, who takes *ṣaddīq* as an abbreviation for *ṣaddīqīm*.

[c] Cf. also the comment on 3.12–15 below.

among those who heard it. Isaiah takes no account of their state of mind, but proclaims to his audience what God has commanded him: everything that provides security and order in the present structure of the state, stay and staff, will be shattered by the intervention of Yahweh (v.1). By the title 'Sebaoth'[a] the prophet characterizes God as the Lord who makes all things possible. What appears to men as totally improbable and impossible, he can do at any time, as Lord of all things. He will strike down both the professional soldiers who are in full possession of their powers, and the free citizens levied in time of war, and so deprive the country of its protection against external attack. Judges and prophets, the guardians of human and divine law, will disappear.[b] Neither occult nor legitimate counsel will be available: the diviners (cf. 2.6) will be as inaccessible as the elders who are capable of giving information and instruction in difficult situations because of their long experience (v.2). Isaiah emphasizes once again that neither[c] military nor political leaders,[d] nor advisers endowed with natural or supernatural powers, will be available (v.3). The country will be so completely deprived of its ruling class, men distinguished by descent and education, that it will only be possible to procure inexperienced young people who are ignorant of tradition and therefore act capriciously, in order to set up a new government (v.4). The result can only be total chaos, in which both the natural order of the relationship between old and young (cf. Lev.19.32) and the social structure will be turned upside down (v.5). The young will rebel against the old, and those without name or possessions against aristocratic and previously influential property owners. In this description, Isaiah no doubt has in mind not a revolution, but a complete military collapse with all its military consequences, which, however, would be exactly the same as a revolution in its effects. The situation will be so confused, and the desolation of the countries so complete, that even the possession of a garment suitable for the representation of the authority indispensable to every state, a sleeve-

---

[a] Cf. on 6.3.

[b] That the judges also possessed a sacral legitimization is shown by the fact that they are coupled with the prophets. The omission of the priests is remarkable. Perhaps it is due to a later alteration of the text. Cf. also Micah 3.11.

[c] šar haḥmiššīm, the 'captain of fifty', may refer to a royal official who possessed both judicial and military duties; cf. Ex. 18.25 and R. Knierim, ZAW 73, 1961, p.170.

[d] On the word translated above by 'man of rank', which really means one whose countenance has been raised up, cf. II Kings 5.1.

less mantle decorated with borders and fringes,[a] is seen as a sufficient authentication for calling on someone to take a leading position (v. 6). But the person who is appointed on these grounds will refuse the promotion which in normal times he would long for – a further indication of the extent of the catastrophe (v. 7). The wounds that have been made are so great that no one knows where the reconstruction is to begin. Whoever may be accorded a leading position will make the excuse that he does not possess sufficient knowledge[b] or supplies to be able to lead the way towards a general solution. It is astonishing how realistically the prophet is here able to describe the consequences of a total collapse of the state. Anyone who remembers the months that followed May 1945 in Germany will have the sensation in reading this passage of being carried right back to those days.

[8–9a] *The coming collapse as a consequence of sin*. In v. 8 Isaiah begins once again to set out the basis of his previous words. Because the holy city and the holy people have fallen away from their God, and because in their words and deeds they consciously offend against the will of God, there is no salvation for them. God's power and glory have been clearly revealed to the people of the covenant in his historical saving acts and judgments.[c] But the people have not adopted the only possible consequence of this, the course of faithfulness, but have visibly rebelled against their Lord. As the continuation shows, the prophet is thinking here less of despairing mockery than as in 5.19, of the easy way in which the ruling and property-owning classes accept the practical acts of unfaithfulness which are evident in their daily life. It is obvious from their conceited and defiant self-satisfaction that they care little for God's commandments. They admit this without the least prevarication and so go beyond the attitude condemned in Ps. 14, of the fools who deny the deity of God only in their hearts. This public flaunting of their own outlook provides the *tertium comparationis* with the Sodomites, who proclaimed their unnatural desires to Lot's face, and called down upon themselves the judgment and intervention of God (Gen. 19.5). This human hybris, which was also seen as the source of evil by the Greeks, can be found

---

[a] Cf. *AOB*, 2nd ed., pl. 125; *BRL*, illustrations, col. 333f.; G. E. Wright, *Biblical Archaeology*, 1957, pp. 187ff.

[b] It might be possible to take the word translated above by 'healer' as a participle with the meaning 'bind on a head-cloth' (cf. Ex. 29.9) and to translate: 'I do not bind on (a turban)'; cf. the Greek.

[c] Cf. on 6.3.

in all ages. Isaiah knows from the sacral tradition and from his own experiences in the hour of his call that the Holy One cannot be mocked; if this is the attitude of the ruling class, God's judgment cannot be withheld. It must come. 'Woe to them' (v.9b)[a] when it does come, is the didactic edition of a later writer. Sinners have no right to complain of a blind and unjust destiny. They should recognize that they have prepared ruin for themselves through their own deeds. Because God is judge, the deed rebounds upon the head of the guilty.[b]

[10–11] The content of the blessing and curse uttered in vv.9b–11 shows that it is interpolated from a quite different tradition, that of the wisdom literature.[c] Whereas Isaiah soberly recognizes and declares that the whole people will share in the suffering when its leaders fail, the teacher of wisdom tries to encourage his hearers to do good, because good and evil are unconditionally requited in this world in the life of the individual. That this doctrine inevitably led its adherents into severe difficulties is shown equally clearly by the Book of Job and the sayings of the Preacher. It ignores both the ultimate irrationality of the acts of God, and also the personal nature of the relationship between God and man.[d]

CHAPTER 3.12–15

Against those who Lead the People Astray

12 My people – everyone of their governors is a tormentor[e] and usurers[f] rule them.

---

[a] *nepeš* here, as in 53.12, is a strengthened personal pronoun.

[b] For discussion on the Israelite belief in retribution cf. K. Koch, *ZThK* 52, 1955, pp. 1–42; H. Gese, *Lehre und Wirklichkeit in der Alten Weisheit*, Tübingen, 1958, pp.42ff.; E. Würthwein, *Die Weisheit Ägyptens und des AT*, Mitteilungen des Universitätsbundes Marburg, 1959, pp. 7ff.

[c] Cf. von Rad, *Old Testament Theology* I, tr. D. M. G. Stalker, 1962, pp. 383ff.

[d] Cf. Würthwein, *Die Weisheit Ägyptens und das AT*, pp. 10ff.

[e] *meʿōlēl* should be regarded, following Marti, and Driver, *JTS* 38, 1937, p.38, as the *pōʿēl* of *ʿll*, 'to maltreat someone, to behave wantonly towards someone, to act wrongly'.

[f] Cf. *BH*.

> O my people, your leaders lead you astray ⟨from the⟩ª way,
> they confuse your paths.
> 13   Yahweh has taken his place to contend,
> he stands to judge ⟨his⟩ people.ᵇ
> 14   Yahweh enters into judgment
> with the elders and princes of his people:
> 'And you, you have devoured the vineyard,
> the spoil of the poor is in your houses.
> 15   What do you mean by crushing my people,
> by grinding the face of the poor?'ᶜ
> Oracle of the Lord Yahweh Sebaoth.

This poem begins with an accusation in v. 12, and is followed in vv.
13–15 by a pronouncement of judgment in the form of a speech on the
part of the accuser (vv. 14b–15a). Both in v. 12 and in vv. 14b–15a the
speaker is God. Since v. 12 is addressed to 'my people', the *Sitz im
Leben* may be taken to be an assembly of the people either on a cultic
occasion, or – perhaps less probably – a 'secular' occasion. Like
3.1–9a, the passage belongs to the prophet's early period.

[12] The governors of the people – in the whole Old Testament the
Hebrew equivalent carries the negative suggestion of a taskmaster
(cf. Ex. 3.7 etc.) – are tormentors. They use their position to their own
advantage, and so offend against the sacred ordinance of God, which
lays down that rulers should care for the poor and unprivileged, for
widows and orphans (cf. Pss. 72.12; 101). 'Usurers' rule the people of
God.ᵈ The leaders of the people have led them astray in a double
sense: by their attitude they have destroyed the social order, the
covenant ordinance given by God to their people, over the maintenance of which he watches inexorably; and at the same time they
provoke many among the people to imitate them.

[13–15] In a dramatic climax the prophet brings his poem to its
culmination and bitter conclusion: he shows God himself rising up as
the accuser of the upper class. The whole scene seems to suggest that

ª Following Bruno, *Jesaja*, p.61, read *midderek*, and take it as part of the preceding line.
ᵇ Cf. *BH*. H. D. Hummel, *JBL* 76, 1957, p.100, suspects that the Massoretic
text contains an enclitic *mem*; but cf. E. Hesse, *ZAW* 65, 1953, p.48.
ᶜ The expression 'to grind the face of the poor' may, according to A. Schreiber,
VT 11, 1961, p.455, contain a hidden allusion to the phrase 'to lift up the face'
i.e., 'to make an exception' of someone; cf. Lev. 19.15; Deut. 10.17.
ᵈ Cf. Ex. 22.25; Lev. 25.26f.; Deut. 23.20f.; Neh. 5.7; Ps. 15.5.

Isaiah spoke this prophecy at the great autumn festival, at which Yahweh was believed to be present and manifested as judge, if his holy name was called upon and his will proclaimed.[a] In any case, he takes up these conceptions, which originated in the cult, and assumes that his hearers are already acquainted with them. Yahweh had set the elders, the representatives of the tribal structure of the people, and the princes, those who held political and military power,[b] to work in the vineyard of his people. This metaphor seems to anticipate the song of the vineyard, 5.1–7. The workman does not work for himself, but for his lord.[c] But they have regarded the vineyard as their own property, and shamelessly plundered it. They were called to protect and care for the poor, but have carried out every form of economic oppression upon them (cf. 5.8; 10.1f.) and deprived them of human dignity. These are the words of the prosecutor, who also possesses full powers to carry out a sentence. His accusation will be followed inexorably by action. It is an accusation, a sentence and the beginning of the execution of the sentence, all in one.[d]

The prophet is content to proclaim the fact of the matter. How it is to be carried out is not yet disclosed. He leaves this to the decree of his Lord. At first sight, the prophet's whole oracle of warning asserts no more than the general observation of experience, that the dissolution of the social order by the misuse of power brings disaster to the people. If this were so, the term 'God' would merely be a paraphrase for the immanent order in the structure of human society. It becomes clear that this is a misunderstanding, when one bears in mind that the prophet is obviously thinking of a destruction of the state through external intervention behind which the hand of God the judge is concealed.

[a] Cf. Weiser, *The Psalms*, pp. 30ff., 45ff.; *Bertholet-Festschrift*, 1950, p. 519.
[b] Cf. R. Knierim, *ZAW* 73, 1961, p. 160.
[c] That the labourer is worthy of his hire is taken for granted in the thought of the Old Testament, but is not part of the thought of the present passage.
[d] Cf. Isa. 55.10f.

Chapter 3.16–24

The End of the Proud Daughters of Zion

16 And Yahweh said:
Because the daughters of Zion are haughty
and walk with outstretched necks
and ogling with their eyes,
mincing along as they go,
tinkling with their feet,

17 the Lord will make scabby the scalp of the daughters of Zion
and Yahweh will lay bare their forehead.[a]

18 In that day the Lord will take away the finery of the anklets,
the headbands and the crescents; [19]the pendants, the bracelets
and the veils; [20]the headdresses, the pacing-chains, the sashes,
the perfume boxes and the amulets; [21]the signet rings and nose
rings; [22]the cut-away robes, the mantles, the cloaks and the
handbags; [23]the garments of gauze[b] and the chemises, the
turbans and the shawls.

24 And thus it shall be:
Instead of perfume there shall be rottenness
and instead of a girdle, a rope;
and instead of well-set plaits, baldness,
and instead of a rich robe, a girding of sackcloth;
a brand instead of beauty.

The unity and the interpretation of 3.16–4.1 are matters of dispute
among modern exegetes. The majority regard vv. 18–23 as a later
interpolation,[c] but there are still some who defend its authorship by
Isaiah himself. Some see the lengthy catalogue of the dress and
adornments of Hebrew women as a certain sign of secondary origin,
whereas others see it as the sign of a preference on the part of the
prophet for unbridled accumulation which cannot be attributed to
the zeal of a later theologian.[d] While such a discrepancy in the evaluation of the material can be used as an argument in favour of the
traditional attribution, the break which the catalogue causes in the

[a] For the translation cf. Driver, *JTS* 38, 1937, p. 38.

[b] Cf. Procksch, commentary, p. 80; Galling, *ZDPV* 56, 1933, pp. 211f.

[c] Since Duhm.

[d] Cf. Budde, *ZAW* 50, 1932, pp. 38f.; Feldmann, Fischer, Herntrich and
Ziegler *ad loc.*

connection between v.17 and v.24 argues just as strongly for its excision, as does the observation that a later hand can also be detected in the catalogue in 3.3. Moreover, the opening words of v.18, 'in that day', give the impression of a link placed there by a redactor, the purpose of which is presumably to link the whole passage with the great poem on Yahweh's day of judgment, 2.6–22. The point at which the passage ends is also disputed. Hans Schmidt makes the suggestion[a] that 3.25–4.1 should be regarded as a fragment of an independent prophecy of warning, because there Zion itself is addressed as the mother, and the women are discussed from a completely different point of view. Duhm wanted to exclude only vv.25 and 26 as a later interpolation. Although the unity of the passage may be defended by attributing the change of metre that takes place in v.25 to the effect of the prophet's speech, the considerations advanced by Schmidt carry more weight. The prophetic elegy, of which probably only a fragment has been preserved, and which functions as a prophecy of warning, has probably been attached to 3.16–24 by a later collector or redactor because he rightly regarded vv.25 and 26 as a supplement to the statements made in vv.17 and 24 about the proud daughters of Zion. Verse 24 describes one possibility awaiting the women, and 4.1 another.

The occasion on which this prophecy of warning was uttered cannot be stated with certainty, since it is possible to think of many circumstances in which the prophet could have encountered the women of Jerusalem whom he describes. But it would be particularly effective if it had been uttered at a feast, to which the women would have come in all their state. Since the prophecy assumes a period of undisturbed economic prosperity and outward security, the passage must have been composed before the war between Syria and Ephraim.

[16] The content of the whole passage can be summed up in a single sentence: the hollow world of the women of Jerusalem, concerned only with finery, bodily adornment and the enticement of men, is destined by God's decree to certain ruin. The biting and pertinent words of the prophet picture them to the reader as prancing through the streets, their necks stuck out like giraffes and their minds on their stately appearance, casting alluring glances towards the men. The sophistication of the women of the ancient East was hardly less than that of modern society. From Jer. 4.30 we know that Israelite women

[a] He is followed by Procksch, Fischer, Steinmann, Balla, Fohrer and Eichrodt.

also used make-up. Unlike the modern fashion, however, they did not adorn their lips, but their eyes, in order to make them seem larger and more shining.[a] It must be noted that the prophet is not attacking female beauty culture as such, but the pride of those who practise it, and who allow themselves to be led by their sensual desires, with a brazen display of ill-founded arrogance. It is evidence of Isaiah's acute perception of the inner relationship between the attitude of women and the future of the nation, that he pays them this observant attention. The men must pay for the desires of the women (cf. Amos 4.1). The more extravagant they are, the more they lead the men on into illegal profiteering at the expense of those who are socially weaker. In various ways, either by their own attitude to the ordinary man in the street, or by the consequences for the economic behaviour of their husbands, they are undermining the internal unity and health of the people of the covenant. They are judged not because they adorn themselves, but because they break down the order of the people of God through their whole attitude. [17] Nothing of their magnificence shall remain: as a consequence of the deprivations associated with the coming disastrous judgment, their heads will be covered with revolting scabs. The locks of hair covering their foreheads will be cut off by their conquerers, a sign of profound humiliation and punishment practised on both men and women in Babylon.[b] In ancient times, long and carefully tended hair was a sign of a free man. When they are dishonoured, marked by deprivation and carried off to be slaves in a foreign country, no man will turn to look at them any more.

[18–23] A later hand lists everything which will then be taken away from the women.[c] It is a lengthy catalogue, which has repeatedly captured the imagination and ingenuity of commentators.[d] Thus, for example, in 1745 and in 1809–10, there appeard two pieces on this passage, their titles reflecting the spirit of their times, and aimed in part at satisfying mere curiosity: Nicolaus Wilhelm Schröder wrote a *Commentarius de vestitu mulierum Hebraearum* ('Commentary

---

[a] On the technique cf. H. Guthe, *Palästina*, [2]1927, p. 110; the eyebrows and eyelids are painted black, to produce 'doe-like eyes'.

[b] Cf. Driver, *JTS* 38, p. 38.

[c] If this passage is also regarded as the work of the prophet himself, the unrestrained length of the catalogue will be due to the seething anger with which it was uttered.

[d] The matter has now been dealt with at length by H. W. Hönig, Die Bekleidung des Hebräers (thesis), Zürich 1957, esp. pp. 116ff.

on the Dress of Hebrew Women'), and Anton Theodor Hartmann wrote *Die Hebräerin am Putztisch und als Braut* ('The Hebrew Lady at the Dressing Table and as a Bride').[a] There are anklets, which those who wore them could rattle to attract gallants' attention to themselves.[b] There are diadems, plaited and woven headbands of wool in their simplest form, and in their most elaborate form, costly golden plates held in place by ribbons.[c] From ornamental necklaces, worn by both men and women, and even by camels (cf. Judg. 8.26), there hung amulets in the form of a moon or a half moon, meant in the first place as a protection against evil spirits, but later as pleasing ornaments.[d] From the lobes of the ears drop-shaped pendants were suspended by rings (Judg. 8.26).[e] Bracelets of bronze shone on their arms, embellished with every device, including bright and costly inlay work.[f] Some wore 'veils', a brightly coloured cloth draped artistically round the head and hanging low down the back,[g] while others simply wore a band of cloth laid upon the head, which was also worn by men (cf. Isa. 61.10; Ezek. 24.17).[h] Chains on the ankles limited their pace and made the women walk with a coquettish tripping (cf. also Judith 10.4).[i] A girdle about the hips (Prov. 31.17), or here perhaps a breast band (cf. also Jer. 2.32) gave a further opportunity of following the fashion.[j] Little bottles of perfume in handbags were also carried. Israelite women wore rings on their fingers as much as modern women. Even their noses might be adorned with a ring (cf. Ezek. 16.12).[k] Their actual fashions in clothes seem to have been particularly sophisticated. Here there seem to have been deeply cut-away clothes leaving both breasts free,[l] full robes not drawn in at the waist,[m] and possibly also ornate garments wound around the body.

[a] According to Herntrich, commentary, p. 58.
[b] Cf. Galling, *BRL*, col. 168.
[c] *BRL*, cols. 125ff.
[d] *BRL*, cols. 27ff. fig. 15; Nötscher, *Biblische Altertumskunde*, p. 68.
[e] *BRL*, cols. 399f. figs. 11–14.
[f] *BRL*, cols. 30ff. figs. 1–8.
[g] Israelite women usually went unveiled, cf. Gen. 24.15ff.; Nötscher, *op. cit.* pp. 59f.
[h] *BRL*, col. 333ff. fig. 2; Nötscher *op. cit.*, p. 56.
[i] Nötscher, *op. cit.* pp. 67f.
[j] Cf. Koehler, s.v.; Nötscher, *op. cit.* p. 59.
[k] Nötscher, *op. cit.* p. 67.
[l] *BRL*, col. 335 fig. 7.
[m] *BRL*, col. 335 fig. 6; Nötscher, *op. cit.* fig. 32.

Other garments could be close fitting and made of transparent material.[a] The precise meaning of many of the objects mentioned in this list is still not known. While on the one hand they reflect the whole delight of oriental women in bright colours and pretty clothes, the accumulation points to the immoderate desire of these women for finery. Women are referred to here in the plural: 'One must not imagine that each individual woman wore all these together or actually at the same time'.[b] All these things, by which women set so much store, will disappear in the hour of judgment.

[24] The prophet sums up the consequences of the judgment for the women in a few telling words: they shall have no further opportunity to use their costly perfumes. They will be so ill cared for that they will stink. The ornate girdles will be replaced by the most primitive means of keeping a garment together, a rope. The beautiful hair arrangements, prepared even at that period with curlers and hair clips, with a rich use of oils and pomades,[c] will be replaced by baldness, which is particularly disfiguring and degrading to women. The costly clothes will be replaced by sackcloth, a rough material of hair, which used to be worn for mourning and penance (cf. Gen. 37.34; II Sam. 3.31; I Kings 20.32; Isa. 22.12; Lam. 2.10; etc.).[d] On their brow they will be branded, as was done to slaves as a sign of recognition and ownership: the figures which are now so radiantly beautiful will stagger into slavery, so disfigured as to be unrecognizable (cf. Amos 4.1–3).

[a] Cf. Galling, *ZDPV* 56, 1933, p. 211.
[b] Dillman, *ad loc.*
[c] Cf. Nötscher, *op. cit.* pp. 62ff.
[d] Cf. Nötscher, *op. cit.* p. 60.

CHAPTERS 3.25–4.1

The Lot of the Widows

25 Your men shall fall by the sword
   and your mighty men in battle.
26 And her gates shall lament and mourn;
   ravaged, she shall sit upon the ground.
4 1 And seven women shall take hold
     of one man *in that day*,
     saying, 'We will eat our own bread
     and wear our own clothes,
     only let us be called by your name;
     take away our reproach'.

[25] Having in mind the terrible fate which is awaiting Jerusalem, Isaiah begins with this passage, which is only preserved in fragmentary form,[a] his funeral elegy upon Zion. He uses the metre of the *qīnā* or funeral elegy with three and two stresses. The more solemn the occasion on which he spoke, the more strange and terrifying must have been the effect of the warning uttered in this way. Here, as so often in the Old Testament, the city of Jerusalem is presented as a woman. As a mother mourns her children, Jerusalem will mourn over her young men who have fallen. [26] The city gates, similarly personified, will lament and mourn, that is, they will lie abandoned for ever (cf. Lam. 1.1, 4). All the riches of the city will be destroyed by the victors, or carried away. [4.1] The fate of the women who remain in Jerusalem will not be any more desirable than that of those who are driven into foreign lands. With regard to what we have learned from 3.16–24 about the attitude to the women of Jerusalem, we can say that the period of pretentious high living will finally come to an end. After the women have been widowed, and deprived of the protection of their own tribe, they will have to be content with finding any male protector at all. Setting aside all womanly modesty, the daughters of Zion who are now so proud will have to look on their own account for one surviving man, and attach themselves to him as concubines, as additional wives. They will be so abandoned and broken down, that they will themselves give up the right to be maintained which a master and husband owed to Israelite women who were his additional wives and bondwomen (cf. Ex. 21.10). They will find their

---

[a] Cf. above pp. 46f.

own food and clothing, if only the name of the man can be pronounced over them. This pronouncing of the name is not anything like the changing of a name associated with marriage, but was a legal act, by which the woman passed into the possession of the man. Thus this is the ultimate meaning of this verse: the pride of the daughters of Zion will be so broken that as the final way out of their distress they will voluntarily give themselves to a man as his additional wives, as bond-women and slaves.[a]

Unjust rule (3.1–15), the misuse of power, and a pleasure-seeking and sensual attitude on the part of women are destroying the inner order of the people of the covenant and calling down the stern judgment of God, who expects obedient loyalty in justice and brotherly love from his people. – Looking back upon 3.16–4.1, one cannot fail to realize that the ferocity of the prophet's criticism of the attitude of the woman implies that he recognized them as responsible persons, who, although endowed with fewer rights than men, nevertheless in their own way shared responsibility before God for the destiny of the people.[b]

[a] K. Galling, *ThLZ*, 1956, cols. 67f.
[b] Cf. Eichrodt, commentary, p. 62.

CHAPTER 4.2–6

The Life of the Holy Remnant

2 In that day what Yahweh causes to sprout up shall be beauty and glory, and the fruit of the land shall be pride and adornment for the escaped of Israel.
3 And it shall be: He who is left in Zion and remains in Jerusalem will be called holy, everyone who has been recorded for life in Jerusalem. 4When the Lord has washed away the filth of the daughters of Zion and cleansed the blood-guiltiness of Jerusalem from its midst by the breath of judgment and the breath of devastation,a 5then Yahweh will create over every site on Mount Zion and over her assemblies a cloud by day, and smoke and the shining of a flaming fire by night;b *for over all glory is a cover.*c 6And it will be a booth for a shadow by day from the heat and for a refuge and a shelter from the storm and rain.

The question of the date and origin of this prophecy of salvation can no longer be answered with certainty. Although at first it gives the impression that Isaiah meant it to sound a final note of reconciliation for the circle of the faithful after his warnings, a closer study reveals objections to this view. However close its connection is at first sight to the previous passage (3.16–4.1), its scope extends beyond the fate of the women to that of the whole congregation of Zion. It looks as though this prophecy was meant to provide a conclusion to the present short collection 2.1–4.1 (or 4.6). God's last word concerning his people is not judgment, but his purpose of salvation. Through his judgment he is proceeding directly towards his saving work of redemption. A later writer might feel himself even more justified in making an addition of this sort, since Isa.6.13 and 7.3 already contained an indication of this hope. A break in the rhythm, which ceases to be recognizable from v.3 on, suggests that these verses are a supplement, almost giving the effect of having been written by a 'scribe', as do the conceptions of the book of life and the divine cloud appearing as a protective canopy. Its date cannot be elucidated with any certainty. Verse 3 assumes that the great and purifying judgment of God has not yet begun. While this might be held to suggest that it is pre-exilic, for

a 1 Q Isa reads 'spirit of the storm' instead of 'spirit of devastation', probably under the influence of 2.12ff.

b LXX reads 'he will come' instead of 'he will create'. The Massoretic text can be maintained as the *lectio difficilior*.

c Cf. Duhm, *ad loc.*

the reasons mentioned above a post-exilic origin is more probable. For that was a time when the most far-seeing figures in the congregation of the second temple already recognized that the great and decisive crisis in the destiny of the people had not been brought about either by the catastrophes of the years 597 and 587, nor by the rebuilding of the temple, and that the congregation still did not form the holy remnant which the great prophet had proclaimed. A date even as late as the third or early second century BC is not excluded. Thus there was to be yet another judgment, a decisive judgment, in which God would consummate his work in Israel. Consequently, the historical occasion of this prophecy of salvation is likely to have been the reading of the book of Isaiah in the worship of the congregation of the second temple.

[2] The author of this addition links his statement, which draws upon the traditional material of the faith of Israel, with what preceded it by means of the words 'in that day . . .'ᵃ The great future judgment which will come upon Israel, because the sins named in 2.6ff.; 3.1ff, and 3.15ff. have still not disappeared from its midst, will purify Israel, so that Yahweh can reveal the fullness of his grace upon those who have escaped.ᵇ The latter will no longer glorify their own vain works and acts, but the great works of God in creation, which now visibly glorify his name before all the world. In spite of the messianic interpretation of the 'branch of Yahweh', which begins with the Targum,ᶜ the phrase does not refer here, as in Jer. 23.5; 33.15; Zech. 3.8 and 6.12, to the messianic and Davidic king of salvation,ᵈ nor to the holy remnant of Israel itself,ᵉ but quite simply to what Yahweh will cause to grow in the period of salvation following his judgment.ᶠ The parallelism to the 'fruit of the land' in the same verse is unequivocal evidence of this. For the thought of the Old Testament, this expectation is not to be distinguished from a moral perfecting of the people. According to Ps. 72 the land will bear salva-

---

ᵃ Cf. 3.18; 4.1.

ᵇ For the expression 'the escaped of Israel' cf. Isa. 10.20f.; 37.31f. = II Kings 19.30f.; Ezek. 14.22; Obad. 16; Ezra 9.8, 13ff.; Neh. 1.2; Joel 2.32.

ᶜ Targ.: 'In that time the anointed of the Lord shall be for joy and for glory and those who keep the law shall be for splendour and for praise for those who have escaped of Israel.'

ᵈ Against Herntrich, etc.

ᵉ With Reuss.

ᶠ With Duhm, Marti, Budde, Gray, Hans Schmidt, Procksch, Fischer, Ziegler and Fohrer.

tion and righteousness under a righteous king, and in concrete terms this means a rich harvest of corn, and numerous progeny for the people (cf. Ps. 72.3, 16). The Deuteronomic writer promised his people that if they were perfectly obedient to the commandment of God, they would have a blessing which would extend to food and drink (cf. Ex. 23.25ff.[a]; Deut. 7.12ff.). The assumption behind this expectation is the understanding of the world as *one* creation, all the parts of which, in nature and in history, are related to one another. Every transgression of man against the will of God is reflected in nature (cf. Ex. 7.1 – 12.30; Amos 4.6ff.; Jer. 14.1ff.; Joel 1.1ff.; etc.). Because the time of salvation which is awaited will be a time of perfect righteousness, it will be fruitful like Paradise. This theme is a permanent element in prophecies of salvation.[b] Corn and wine, oil and honey, cattle and sheep, will be found to increase with such abundance in those days that Israel will thereby acquire standing and respect among the nations.

[3] Verse 3 continues in the same direction, which is wholly that of Israel's prosperity. At the same time it confirms what was said above about the automatic association made between the well-being of nature and the inward renewal of man. Just as the burning coal has purified Isaiah, the remnant will also be purified and sanctified by a cleansing judgment of God. Israel will not be able to boast of this holiness as of its own work, for it will be created by God's elective judgment. The saints are those whose names are recorded in the book of life. The concept of the great book preserved in heaven and containing the deeds of men probably derives from two different sources, the memorandum book of ancient Eastern rulers, in which the reports of messengers coming in from their empire were recorded,[c] and also the Babylonian tables of destiny,[d] and in fact it contains two quite separate emphases. The first can be represented in the words of the psalm: 'Yahweh knows the way of the righteous, but the way of the wicked will perish' (Ps. 1.6),[e] and the other in the words of Ps.

[a] Cf. Noth, *Exodus*, tr. J. S. Bowden, 1962, pp. 192f.

[b] Cf. Isa. 30.23ff.; Jer. 31.12; Ezek. 34.29; 47.1–12; Amos 9.13ff.; Isa. 41.17–20; 43.16–21; 51.3; 55.12f.; 65.25; Zech. 9.16f.; 14.8; Mal. 31.11.

[c] Cf. Esth. 6.1ff.; Elliger, ATD 25 on Mal. 3.16.

[d] Ps. 139.16; cf. Weiser, *The Psalms, ad loc.*

[e] Cf. Ex. 32.32f.; Ps. 69.28. To be recorded in this book means in the first instance that one's earthly life is maintained for as long a time as possible; cf. Nötscher, *Altorientalischer und Alttestamentlicher Auferstehungsglauben*, Würzburg, 1926, pp. 163f.

139.16: 'Thy eyes beheld my days (rsv: "unformed substance"); in thy book were written, every one of them, the days that were formed for me, when as yet there was none of them.' The complete dependence of man upon God and his complete responsibility in the sight of God can equally be described in this image. Just as both these conceptions, which are based on man's experience of God, cannot be thought of together in conceptual terms, but in fact point to the ultimate mystery of God,[a] similarly here the image emphasizes the belief in predestination which was in fact growing stronger in Judaism, the belief that only those who do the will of God will be saved, and that at the same time these righteous persons, as a result of God's decree, are becoming what they are already are.[b] In any case, what God has created, and what man has made of it, will be intimately associated with what God is going to create (cf. II Cor. 5.10).

[4–6] Verse 4 alludes to the guilt of the daughters of Zion (3.16ff.) and also to the lawless and violent attitude of the men (cf. 3.1ff.; 1.15). In the judgment Yahweh will purify his holy seed from all unrighteousness.[c] In translating $r\bar{u}^a h$, one may hesitate between 'spirit' and 'breath, wind'. There is evidence for the conception that Yahweh uses particular spirits for his purposes as early as I Kings 22.21ff. Since close connections in content have been recognized between this passage and the preceding oracles, the second alternative must be chosen (cf. 2.12ff.; also 59.19). The storm wind is one of the traditional accompaniments of Yahweh's theophany (cf. I Kings 19.11). The judgment is followed by Yahweh's gift of total salvation. What he will then create over Mount Zion, the cloud during the day and the pillar of fire at night, is a sign of his gracious and guiding presence (v.5). Just as clouds and the pillar of fire led the people of God

---

[a] Cf. Gogarten, *ZThK* 47, 1950, pp. 227ff.; Martin Buber, *Tales of the Hasidim: The Early Masters*, tr. Olga Marx, New York, 1947, p.92, 'The Fiftieth Gate'.

[b] Cf. also Luke 10.20; Rev. 13.8; 17.8; 20.12, 15. Here those who are destined for eternal life are recorded in the heavenly book. A similar view is found in Dan. 12.1. The conception of a heavenly book, in which the deeds of men are listed for judgment, is also found in the religion of Zoroaster, cf. *Yasna* 31.14: 'I ask you, O Ahura, for what is true and will come. What demands will be made of the righteous on the basis of what has been written down, and what, O master, to the liars – what will they be like, when the end comes?' From F. König, *Die Religion Zarathustras*, CRE II, Freiburg 1951, p. 649.

[c] For cultic purification by washing cf. Ex. 29.4; 40.12; Lev. 8.6; for rinsings cf. Ezek. 40.38; II Chron. 4.6.

through the wilderness after their flight from Egypt (cf. Ex. 13.21),[a] he will now set up both over the holy hill of the temple. God will no longer separate himself from his people. The time of temptations and judgments is past. A later reader makes the scholarly observation that a cover is drawn over every reflection of the divine presence (cf. Ex. 34.33; I Kings 8.12). The guidance of the holy congregation is carried out through the word (cf. 2.3). Consequently the ancient signs of the presence of God, which are understood as created by him, take on a new meaning: they will protect the temple hill and the assembly gathered there for feasts from heat and cloudbursts (cf. also Ps. 121.5f.). Where God is present, all the terrors of the world have lost their power.[b] He protects those who are his own in all dangers.[c] What is now experienced only by faith will then have a full reality.

The book of Revelation (21.23) takes up again the conception of the tabernacle of God among men. Among the men of the new heavenly Jerusalem[d] there will be neither death nor suffering nor crying, for the former things will have passed away. But even there the promise is not true simply of the whole world of mankind, but reads: 'He who conquers shall have this heritage, and I will be his God and he shall be my son' (Rev. 21.7). The prophecy of salvation which we have here preserved in the book of Isaiah, and its expectations, remain within the known world. Its thought extends to the coming of the time of salvation and to the marvellous, prosperous life of the righteous in that time. It has still nothing to say about eternal life.

CHAPTER 5.1–7

The Song of the Vineyard

1 I will sing for my beloved
   a song of my friend concerning his vineyard:
   My beloved had a vineyard

[a] On the symbolization of God's presence in the sanctuary by means of a cloud cf. Ex. 40.34; Num. 9.15ff.; I Kings 8.10f.; Ezek. 43.5.
[b] Cf. Buber, *Tales of the Hasidim: The Early Masters*, p. 212, 'The Song of "You"'.
[c] Cf. Pss. 46; 48.3; 91.1ff.; 23; 84.12.
[d] On the changes in the symbolism of the city in the language of the Bible cf. J. Hempel, *WZ-Greifswald* V, 1955/56, pp. 123ff.

on a fertile hill.

2   He digged it and cleared it of stones,
    and planted it with choice vines;
    he built a watchtower in the midst of it,
    and hewed out a wine vat in it;
    and he looked for it to yield grapes,
    but it yielded wild grapes.

3   And now, inhabitant of Jerusalem,
    and man of Judah,
    judge now between me
    and my vineyard.

4   What more was there to do for my vineyard,
    that I have not done in it?
    Why did I look for it to yield grapes,
    and it yielded wild grapes?

5   And now I will tell you
    what I will do for my vineyard.
    Remove its hedge,
    so that it is destroyed;
    break down its wall,
    so that it is trampled.

6   I will deliver it to plunder[a];
    it shall not be pruned
    and shall not be hoed,
    and briar and thistle[b] will grow up.
    And I command the clouds
    that they rain no rain upon it.

7   Yes, the vineyard of Yahweh Sebaoth
    is the house of Israel,
    and the man of Judah
    is the planting in which he delights.
    And he looked for justice,
    but behold, bloodshed;
    for righteousness,
    but behold, a cry[c]!

---

[a] Driver, *JTS* 38, 1937, p. 38, refers to the Accadian verb *batū*, 'I. to turn into ruins, II. to destroy utterly' and regards *bātā* as a *nomen abstractum* from the root *bth*.

[b] According to Sa'adya, quoted in Dalman, *Arbeit und Sitte* II, p. 321, *šāmīr* is the wild carrot (*dacus aureus*), which rises to nearly five feet, and *šayit* a plant similar to yarrow, which also grew to about three feet. Because of their white flowers it was natural to mention both together.

[c] Duhm reproduces in German the play of words in the Hebrew as follows:

The song is clearly sub-divided: it consists of a brief introduction, v. 1a, the song proper in three stanzas, vv. 1b–2; 3–4; 5–6, and the interpretation of the parable it contains in v. 7. Fohrer has drawn attention to the fact that the structure follows that of a speech of accusation, the themes of which include 'the affirmation of a relationship in society imposing an obligation between the accuser and the accused, the account by the accuser of the way in which he has fulfilled his own duty, a complaint at the failure of the accused to fulfil his duty, and an appeal to the court for a decision'.[a] The choice of the material for comparison and the presence of the inhabitants of Jerusalem assumed in v. 3 suggests that the universally observed harvest and vintage festival was the actual occasion on which this prophecy was uttered (cf. Lev. 23.34–43; Deut. 16.13–15).[b] This was the same festival at which the election of the people, the temple and the dynasty was remembered.[c] We must not imagine that on this occasion the assembly was concerned only with the serious consideration of the saving acts of God in history. The book of Deuteronomy emphatically enjoins that Israel is to rejoice at it (Deut. 16.14). But there would have been no need for such an exhortation, since everyone had just completed a strenuous year of work. And if the harvest had only been moderately successful, then everyone's hopes were set upon the coming year which was now being begun anew. On the first and eighth day of the feast, the congregation gathered in the temple. Through the week of the feast they lived in huts of branches, which according to Neh. 8.14ff. were erected upon roofs, in the courts of houses, in the courts of the temple, and in public places.[d] The effectiveness of the song presupposes a period of undisturbed outward peace and consequently belongs to that period of Isaiah's activity which preceded the war with Syria and Ephraim.

[1a] The prophet appears in the midst of the turmoil of the feast, and is apparently seized by the general rejoicing and boisterousness. On this day, as one man among others, he does not seem to have the

---

Und er harrte auf gut Regiment,
doch siehe da: Blutregiment!
Auf Rechtspruch,
und siehe da: Rechtsbruch.

[a] Cf. Fohrer, commentary, p. 76, esp. n. 39.
[b] Cf. H. Schmidt, Fohrer and Eichrodt.
[c] Cf. Weiser, *The Psalms*, pp. 27ff.; H. J. Kraus, *Worship in Israel*, pp. 183ff.
[d] Cf. Nötscher, *Biblische Altertumskunde*, pp. 358ff.

intention of uttering divine oracles loaded with doom, but of adding to the general merriment. As the best friend of a bridegroom, who after the strict custom of ancient times had the task, as a messenger, of maintaining communication between the bridal pair and then of leading the bride home (cf. John 3.29), he begins the words of a love song.[a] For the 'vineyard' was a metaphor for the bride which was familiar to all his hearers (cf. S. of Sol. 2.15; 4.16f.; 6.1f.; 8.12). What sort of song can the friend sing about his vineyard, his bride? [1b–2] However, after the promising opening, it seems at first that it is only a small farmer who is speaking: the friend possessed a fine vineyard, to which he had not failed to give proper care and attention. Being on the peak of a hill it lay isolated, and received the sun unhindered from every side. In order to prevent the ground from cracking and caking in the baking heat of summer it was thoroughly hoed and loosened.[b] The stones were cleared. Then, in the ground which had been worked in exemplary fashion, vines were set.[c] In the middle of the vineyard the friend built a tower in order to keep watch against thieves and birds, and as a place to keep tools. He also dug out a vat in which to press the grapes, a simple tub press hewed into the stone, from which the raw juice ran down into troughs set on a lower level, in order to settle.[d] Everything was prepared in the best way possible, so that the owner could rightly expect a good harvest of fine purple grapes. But at harvest time came bitter disappointment: the vines bore only wild grapes, small bitter fruit, unpleasant and unusable. The hearers would have accompanied this lament over a faithless lover with unrestrained and perhaps even malicious observations.[e]

[3–4] Suddenly it is no longer the prophet who is speaking, but his friend himself. He turns directly to the assembled congregation, to the men of Jerusalem and Judah, to demand a judgment from them. A rhetorical question that follows makes it clear once again that the guilt is in no sense that of the 'owner of the vineyard'. The audience can scarcely still be following the prophet's words with the same naïve

[a] H. Junker, 'Die literarische Art von Is. 5.1–7', *Biblica* 40, 1959, pp. 264f.

[b] According to Dalman, *Arbeit und Sitte* I, p. 264, the time for hoeing was January and February, while pruning took place later, in March.

[c] *śōrēq* is related to the Accadian *sarāqu* 'to be red'. Consequently these were fine purple grapes. – According to Ezek. 17.6 it was not usual to prop up the vines. In so far as they did not twine up between fig trees, they lay on the ground; cf. H. Guthe, *Palästine*, Leipzig, ²1927, p. 88; Dalman, *Arbeit und Sitte* I, p. 69.

[d] Cf. Procksch, *ad loc.*

[e] Cf. Eichrodt, *ad loc.*

assumption. If the bride had been unfaithful, then she would have had to be punished by stoning to death (Deut. 22.23f.). So this was no taunt sung about a deceived bridegroom to amuse them. Neither, however, was this the occasion to utter a lament, quite apart from the fact that the bridegroom would have had to take up his case himself. It is quite clear that the prophet had a purpose different from that which they had supposed at first. Today of all days, in the midst of the joy of the feast, was he giving them yet another warning? Those to whom the question was put would be displeased and would remain silent.

[5–6] But Isaiah is already continuing with his song. Once again it is really the 'friend' who speaks. In brief impressive phrases he describes the consequences which he draws from the failure of the 'vines': the 'vineyard' must be abandoned to complete destruction. The hedge planted as a protection against wild beasts and grazing animals will be cut down and the wall itself pulled down. Then anyone who wishes can break into the plantation. The vineyard is free to be plundered. Anyone may go into it to cut off grapes or cut off vines, perhaps to use as fuel. It is no longer cultivated: the remaining vines may grow how they please. In any case, without attention, they are abandoned to certain ruin. Briars and weeds will come up and smother them. And then it is revealed who the friend is: if he has the power to command the clouds, then he is God himself. With great artistic power, the prophet leads his reader step by step to an understanding of the meaning of his parable.

[7] Thus the conclusion would hardly be a surprise to an attentive hearer: the house of Israel, the sacral community of the people of God, is the vineyard of Yahweh, and Judah is his favourite plantation. The comparison between the vineyard and the bride, which remains unspoken from v. 1 on, remains valid until the end. One ought not, on the basis of the closing words, to misunderstand the parable as an allegory, by interpreting the individual steps in the cultivation of the vineyard, described in v. 2, in terms of the history of salvation, associating the hill with the land of Canaan, the vines with the Israelites, the hoeing and the clearing with the driving out of the Canaanites, and the setting up of a tower with the foundation of the Davidic dynasty, and so forth. The people of God is the faithless bride of God! Like Hosea (cf. Hos. 2) and Jeremiah (cf. Jer. 2.2), Isaiah emphasizes in this parable the direct and intimate relationship between God and his chosen people, which ought to be expressed in

mutual love and loyalty. But the people have broken this covenant of love. In a play on words which impresses itself firmly on the memory, the prophet gives the reason: in choosing and faithfully guiding his people through the centuries, God expected a response of faithfulness and righteousness. Instead of this, the corruption of the law is a daily occurrence, so that the piercing cry of the oppressor and the oppressed rings in his ears (cf. 5.8–24 and 10.1–4). The prophet, whose fate it is to meet rejection (cf. 6.9ff.), is by contrast the friend and the true advocate of his God.[a]

Isaiah goes no further. His song comes to an abrupt end. He leaves it to his hearers to draw the consequence that Israel and Judah will be subject to the judgment of the Lord of all things, who watches over the keeping of his covenant ordinance. No word contains a call to repentance: the people are proceeding ineluctably to a just judgment. With this stern proclamation, the prophet consciously or unconsciously provokes a reaction of impenitence in his hearers. In its structure, and by the double meaning of the parable, the song is a masterpiece of literature: it first fixes the attention by the interest of its theme, and then deepens and reveals it step by step, until its sudden end. The meaning of the song is so obvious that lengthy exposition is superfluous. When God turns to his people, his congregation, he expects them to respond to his choosing and protection with righteousness, with action which derives from the acceptance of his will (cf. Matt. 5.20; Rom. 12.1ff.; Gal. 5.13f.; Phil. 4.8f.; II Cor. 5.10). Even under the new covenant, a faithless congregation faces his judgment (cf. Rev. 2.1–3.22).[b] The New Testament has taken up the parable into the allegory of the wicked husbandmen (Mark

[a] Cf. Junker, *Biblica* 40, p. 266; on the use of *yādīd* cf. Pss. 127.2; 60.5; 108.6; Deut. 33.2.

[b] Cf. also Calvin, CR 64, p. 107: *Eadem apud nos doctrina hodie valere debet. Testatur Christus se vitem esse, in quam insita excolimur a patre, quum munus agricolae erga nos obire dignetur Deus, ac sedulo praestare quae se in populum veterem contulisse exprobat, non mirum est graviter excandescere, si frustra et inutiliter operam consumat. Hinc illa comminatio, Omnem palmitem in me non ferentem fructum avellet, ac in ignem proiiciet (Joann. 15.2).* 'The same teaching is true for us today. Christ testifies that he is the vine, on to which we are grafted and cared for by the Father (John 15.1). If God condescends to carry out the task of the husbandman with regard to us, and diligently to provide everything which he reproaches himself with having heaped upon the people of the Old Covenant, it is not surprising that his anger is so furious, if his work is spent in vain and to no purpose. That is the reason for his warning: "Every branch of mine that bears no fruit he takes away . . . and throws into the fire" ' (John 15.2).

12.1–9). It may also have influenced the parable of the labourers in the vineyard (Matt. 20.1–16).

CHAPTERS 5.8–24 AND 10.1–4

The Sevenfold Woes

8 Woe to those who join house to house,
   who add field to field,
   until there is no more room,
   and you remain to live alone
   in the midst of the land.

9 In my ears [cries] Yahweh Sebaoth:
   'Surely many houses shall become a desolation,
   beautiful houses, without inhabitants.

10 For ten acres of vineyard shall yield but one *bath*
   and a *homer* of seed shall yield but an *ephah*.

11 Woe to those who rise early in the morning and run after strong drink,
   who tarry in the evening; wine inflames them.

12 There is lyre and harp, timbrel and flute ⟨   ⟩ᵃ at their feasts.'
   But they do not regard the deeds of the Lord
   and they do not see the work of his hands.

13 Therefore my people go into exile without knowledge,
   their nobles starving, and their multitude parched with thirst.

14 Therefore Sheol has enlarged its appetite,
   and opened its mouth beyond measure,
   and itsᵇ nobles and itsᵇ multitude go down,
   and her throng and he who exulted in her. ⟨   ⟩ᶜ

17 Then shall the lambs graze as in their pasture,
   in the ruins of the destroyedᵈ sheepᵉ shall feed.

ᵃ Delete *wāyayin*, for the sake of the metre.
ᵇ Cf. below on v. 14.
ᶜ Verses 15f. probably belong after 2.21; cf. *ad loc.*
ᵈ Read with Driver, *JTS* 38, 1937, pp. 38f., *meḥuyīm.*
ᵉ Read with Driver, *loc. cit.*, *gerāyīm.*

18   Woe to those who draw guilt with ⟨sheep cords⟩
     and sin with ⟨calf ropes⟩,[a]

19   who say: 'Let his work make haste and be speedy,
     that we may see it.
     Let the purpose of the Holy One of Israel draw near and come,
     that we may know it!'

20   Woe to those who call evil good and good evil,
     who put darkness for light and light for darkness,
     who put bitter for sweet and sweet for bitter.

21   Woe to those who are wise in their own eyes,
     and shrewd in their own sight!

22   Woe to those who are heroes at drinking wine
     and valiant men in mixing strong drink!

23   Who acquit the guilty for a bribe
     and take away the right of the righteous![b]

24   Therefore, as the tongue of fire devours the stubble,
     and as dry grass sinks in the flame,
     so their root will be as rottenness,
     and their blossom go up like dust;
     for they rejected the instruction of Yahweh Sebaoth
     and despised the words of the Holy One of Israel.

10   1   Woe to those who decree iniquitous decrees and write regu-
         lations[c] of suffering,

     2   to ⟨turn aside⟩ the ⟨cause⟩ of the weak[d]
         and to rob the poor of my people of their right,
         that the widows may be their spoil
         and that they may plunder the orphans.

     3   What will you do on the day of punishment,
         in the storm which comes from afar?
         To whom will you flee for help,
         and where will you leave your wealth?

     4a Nothing remains but to crouch among the prisoners and
         fall among the slain.

[5.8–24 and 10.1–4a] There are considerable differences of opinion
among commentators as to whether all the woes originally belonged
together. Whereas some see in them merely a concatenation of oracles

---

   [a] Read with Dahood, *CBQ* 22, 1960, p. 75, *beḥabelē haššā'ā* and *weka' abōt hāʿēgel*
haḥaṭṭā'ā; cf. Gordon, *Ugaritic Manual* 49. II. 28–30.

   [b] Delete *mimmennū*.

   [c] Read with Ginsberg, *JBL* 69, 1950, pp. 53f.; *ūmiktebē-ma* with an enclitic *mem*.

   [d] Read with Ginsberg, *JBL* 69, pp. 53f., *leḥaṭṭōt-ma* with an enclitic *mem*; cf. Gk,
Syr.

pronounced on various occasions, others see them either as an original
unity, or even as an interpretation by the prophet of the song of the
vineyard. In spite of numerous attempts to produce closer coherence
by rearranging the text, it is better to retain the order as it stands,
since all attempts of this kind suffer from the fact that they have been
unable to advance decisive reasons for the rearrangements suggested.[a]
It is certain, however, that 5.8–24 and 10.1–4a originally formed a
literary unity. The two associated passages were separated as a result
of the interpolation of the collection of prophecies 6.1–9.7. The
common refrain also shows that 5.25 and 9.8–21 formed a unity.
Their content, however, reveals that 5.25 formed the conclusion of
9.8–21. Probably the redactor wanted to link the warning directed
against the northern kingdom (9.8–21) more closely to the words
aimed against it in 6.1.[b] This led to the separation and inversion of
sayings which originally occurred together. Traces of the redactor's
work are also to be found in the displacing of vv. 15 and 16, which
belong after 2.21, although it is also possible to understand them as a
secondary comment on 2.11, 17, meant to increase the effect of the
latter. Further, v. 24, which is out of harmony with the rest, and was
only linked to it by the *tertium comparationis* of general disaster,
possibly comes from the hand of a theologian who derived his inspiration from the poetry of the prophet. The woes may be dated in
Isaiah's early period.

[8–10] *The first woe: against the great landlords and property owners.* The
first woe gives us an insight into the primitive capitalist conditions of
the kingdoms at the period of the prophet: the rising monetary
economy was obviously leading to a crisis among small house-
owners and landowners (v. 8). As a result of the success of Uzziah's
foreign policy, the tributes of neighbouring countries and the lati-
fundia economy practised by the king brought ready money into the
country (II Chron. 26.7f.).[c] The prophet sees how the new rich set up
house after house on the land they have obtained, and buy up one
farmer after another. Inevitably, in so far as the latter are unable to
find a new living as traders, they become totally dependent upon
large capitalists. In Israel such a change in the ownership of property
represented an attack on the sacred ordinance of the people concerning the land. Everything the Old Testament has to say about the

[a] Cf. Duhm, *ad loc.*; also the attempt by Budde, *ZAW* 50, 1932, pp. 57ff.
[b] Cf. Mowinckel, *AcOr(L)* 11, 1933, p. 275; Porteous, *RGG³*, III, col. 602.
[c] Cf. Procksch, *ad loc.*

possession of land is summed up in the affirmation of Lev. 25.23b: '. . . the land is mine; for you are strangers and sojourners with me'.[a] The land between the wells of Beersheba and Mount Hermon was given in fief by God to Israel. Yahweh himself remained the real owner of the whole country. The Israelite landowner was like a stranger and sojourner, like one who possessed the right to use the land, but did not own it. A natural consequence of this sacral under-standing of land law was the prohibition of the sale of land (cf. Lev. 25.23). For Israel, possession was primarily and ultimately an act of grace and not a right. In the view of Deuteronomy, the effect of this ought to be that an owner ought to take account of the need of those who were without land. In this way brotherly love was to be main-tained within the people of the covenant. The prohibition of the sale of land was meant to keep in being the sound economic and social structure of the people of the twelve tribes.[b] If the owner fell into poverty or died, then the nearest male relative on the father's side had the right of pre-emption, or else the property reverted to the direct heirs. The intention was that the hereditary property of the tribes should not be reduced. Ideally, land which had gone to an alien purchaser was intended after fifty years to return into the possession of the family (cf. Lev. 25.8ff.; also Ezek. 46.16–18). Pre-sumably during the early period the agricultural land was regularly redistributed by means of a lot. Whether the whole of the land that was held or only certain fields common to the community were shared out in this way, is not certain from the surviving references in the Old Testament (cf. Micah 2.5; Ps. 16.6; Num. 36.2 and Josh. 14).[c] Both customs, distribution by lot and the year of jubilee, seem to have lapsed in the course of time in the face of human acquisitiveness, which Isaiah is attacking here. The position seems to him so threaten-ing that he sees the time coming when all ownership will be accumu-lated in the hands of a few. The result of this development was bound to be that the inner coherence and legal security of the people of the covenant would collapse. A deep gulf would be opened between poor and rich, into which the poor were in danger of sinking.[d]

This breach of the covenant cannot go unpunished: Isaiah hears

---

[a] Cf. von Rad, *Old Testament Theology* I, p. 299.

[b] Cf. H. J. Kraus, 'Das Eigentum als Problem evangelischer Sozialethik', *Kirche im Volk*, vol. 2, Essen 1949.

[c] Cf. von Rad, *Old Testament Theology* I, p. 299; Weiser, ATD 24 on Micah 2.5.

[d] Cf. the similar warning in Micah 2.1ff.

Yahweh's proclamation of judgment ringing in his ears (vv. 9–10). Everything that is now being built up through the transgression of the sacred ordinance of the people of God is condemned to destruction. The numerous magnificent new houses will one day become deserted ruins. They have been built to receive the expected record harvest. But this will not take place: Yahweh will respond to this self-conscious effort with a total failure of the harvest. Ten acres, 'yokes', of vineyard, an area which ten yoke of oxen could plough in a day, will produce only one *bath*, that is, about eight gallons. A donkey-load of seed, a *homer*, or about ten bushels, will bring in precisely one *ephah*, one bushel.[a] Instead of the yield being at least forty-fold, it is reduced to a tenth. There is no blessing upon ownership which is not morally justified. The Lord of man and of nature will make sure of that.

[11–17] *The second woe. Against the debauched and godless life of the nobility.* The second woe paints a severe picture of the lives of men in the ruling class. It is made perfectly obvious that their principal concern was the satisfaction of their pleasures (v. 11). In the early morning they are already drinking strong drink, a beer probably made from various kinds of corn.[b] Anyone who drinks early in the day is naturally, and particularly in the East, incapable of any serious work (cf. Eccles. 10.16; Acts 2.13–15). And when evening comes, they are still sitting over their tankards. So long as they have everything which makes their carousing pleasant, music played while they drink,[c] and wine, they no longer ask what Yahweh has to say about their activities, and what he is about to do as a judgment on his people, decadent and inwardly sick (v. 12). But God is not mocked (cf. Gal. 6.7). His hand will fall violently upon them: he will send his people into exile (v. 13). Isaiah foretells a great political and military disaster. Because the people will not hear, and because they will not show any understanding of the position, they are to be made to feel what it is. The rich lords, who are now never satisfied with the extent of their debauchery, will suffer bitter hunger. The people form a unity in the sight of God. Since the men of power and responsibility have sinned, the whole people must suffer as a result. Parched with thirst, the masses will be carried off into exile, together with their former lords. The appetite of the underworld, the realm of shadows, on the day of

[a] For the quantities cf. Galling, *BRL*, col. 367.
[b] Cf. Nötscher, *Biblische Altertumskunde*, p. 41.
[c] For the instruments used cf. Galling, *BRL*, cols. 390ff. figs. 2 and 3. Cf. also Amos 6.3–6.

judgment, is contrasted with the present unbridled appetite of men
(v. 14). With its powerful jaws, it is conceived of here as a violent
animal, which will swallow both upper and lower classes. A difficulty
arises from the third person singular feminine possessive pronoun in
v. 14b. It has given rise to frequent suggestions that the verse has
undergone a later rearrangement, although no certainty has been
reached.[a] The opening words and content of v. 14 show that we are
dealing here with a fragment of a woe aimed at the magnificence and
the turmoil of the capital.[b] Those who today are rejoicing throughout
the land will disappear tomorrow into the abyss. The divine woe is
pronounced over every nation which sets pleasure and profit above
the common interest and the law. Isaiah prophesies the total collapse
of his country: the sheep will graze over the ruins of cities, villages and
estates (v. 17).[c]

[18–19] *The third woe: against frivolity and mockery.* Isaiah turns
against those who frivolously and consciously treat God's demands
with contempt, and reply to unpleasant warnings with the comment
that if they are true God should carry out the judgment he has proclaimed.[d] Just as a tethered cow must follow its rope, God's punishment must follow their actions. This prophecy shows that during the
period of the nation's economic prosperity, unbelief was becoming
widespread, leading to contempt and indifference to God's commandments in the interests of the unlimited extension of personal
power, and treating these commandments as outdated human ordinances. When man reverses the proper sequence of faith in God and
proof of God, he is judged. Only someone who stakes his life, in
faithful obedience, on the word of those who bear witness to God, is
given assurance of the help and presence of the living God (cf. Luke
5.5f.). It is not by chance that Isaiah refers to Yahweh as the Holy
One of Israel; for his judgment is no less than the emanation and
consummation of his holiness (cf. 6.3ff.).

[20] *The fourth woe: against the perversion of truth.* The background
of this proclamation of judgment is formed by the attitude of the
same persons against whom Isaiah directed the preceding woe, the
perversion of moral standards on the principle that whatever is

----

[a] The suggestion of Steinmann, that v. 14 together with vv. 15 and 16 should
be placed after 2.17, is worthy of serious consideration.
[b] Cf. Eichrodt, *ad loc.*
[c] Cf. Lam. 5.17f.
[d] Cf. Jer. 17.15; 20.8.

pleasurable is permitted. This principle has been a permanent destructive element in every society and every individual life. What is wrong becomes right. Then God intervenes as the ultimate guardian and advocate of what is right. A classical expression of this conception is found in the confession which Shakespeare places in the mouth of Claudius in *Hamlet*:

> In the corrupted currents of this world
> Offence's gilded hand may shove by justice;
> And oft 'tis seen the wicked prize itself
> Buys out the law: but 'tis not so above;
> There is no shuffling – there the action lies
> In his true nature; and we ourselves compelled
> Even to the teeth and forehead of our faults,
> To give in evidence. . . .[a]

[21] *The fifth woe: against those who are wise in their own eyes*. True wisdom, the beginning of which is the fear of the Lord (cf. Prov. 1.7; 9.10; Job 28.28), is contrasted with the pretended wisdom of the world, at which man's unfaithfulness masquerades. Whereas the former attempts to base life on the will of God, the latter looks down in contempt upon the fear of God as a means of educating children. This saying of the prophet should not be regarded as a special reproach against those who relied upon Egypt from 713 onwards, against the advice of the prophet, and with false self-confidence carried out an anti-Assyrian policy,[b] for all the woes probably belong to the prophet's early period. Marti rightly describes the outlook of those who are attacked here: 'Not merely "parsons", but even the prophet can teach them nothing, and they regard "religion" as good only for women and children; they are able to look after themselves.' That is why they are judged.

[22–24] *The sixth woe: against the impotent judges*. Even the men appointed to maintain the law have been infected by the corrupt spirit of the times. This passage does not apply merely to the citizens with full rights who formed the local courts, and sought a verdict in common, but also to the professional royal judges in Jerusalem.[c]

[a] Act 3, scene 3. – Fohrer's suggestion that here Isaiah is attacking adherents of wisdom does not seem convincing to me, since the wisdom of both Israel and the rest of the Ancient East remained associated with religion. On the other hand it is possible to agree with Fohrer that such an attack is to be found in the taunt that follows.

[b] Against Fichtner, *ThLZ* 74, 1949, col. 77.

[c] Cf. Fohrer, *ad loc.*

They demonstrate their manliness not in inflexible verdicts, made with regard only to the truth, but in drunken excess. They are experts in drinking wine and mixing strong drink. The drink referred to was not weakened in its effect, for example, by adding water, but was strengthened by the addition of herbs. The mixing itself was carried out in a special vessel (cf. Amos 6.6; S. of Sol. 8.2; Prov. 23.30). Driven by the pursuit of pleasure, the judges of Israel had become venal tools of those who exercised power and authority. It may have been a redactor of the book of Isaiah who added v. 24 as a conclusion to the whole of the woes gathered in ch. 5: all who now feel themselves unassailably strong and in need of no advice will be swept away into nothingness by the almighty and holy God, when he comes to punish the transgression of his word and his will.

[10.1–4] *The seventh woe: against those who make laws to suit their own purposes.* In this final woe, Isaiah attacks the state officials and judges, who in their own interests promulgate new laws and statutes, which contradict the sacred ordinance of the covenant. In this way they were creating not merely for themselves but also for the other members of their class, the rich landed nobility and the leading citizens of the towns, a legal basis for the abuses attacked in 5.8. The prophet was probably thinking of the new provisions concerning purchasing and property, which justified serfdom, and particularly affected small property owners and the landless.[a] As examples of the latter, he makes particular mention of widows and orphans, who, relying as they did upon legal assistance given by others, had a right to special protection from society (cf. Ex. 22.22). If men should fail, then God, as the father of orphans and judge of widows, must take up their neglected cause (cf. Ps. 68.5). With his own questions, Isaiah attempts once

[a] The suggestion of C. A. Keller that Isaiah is here attacking an excessive output of laws which was harmful to the proper exercise of law, *ThZ* 11, 1955, p. 90, does not seem to me to have sufficient support in the text and the context. With the greed condemned here, and for a censure upon it, cf. also the Elegy of Solon: 'But the citizens themselves, driven by the desire for money, / are blinded and seek the fall of our mighty city. / For the leaders of the people are wicked and evil-minded, / and thereby only bring painful suffering upon themselves. / Their greed is insatiable, they do not know how to enjoy / with order and sobriety the pleasures of the feast. The riches they heap up come from violence and wrong; / neither what the gods possess nor what belongs to man / is spared by their appetite; they are not ashamed of open robbery, / have no regard for *dike* and her sacred commandment, / for her who, without our hearing, knows past and future, / and surely punishes evil at the appointed time.' M. Pohlenz, *Gestalten aus Hellas*, Munich, 1950, p. 70; cf. K. Freeman, *The Work and Life of Solon*, Cardiff, 1926, pp. 207f.

again to make clear to the legislators and judges the senselessness of their whole attitude. When God rises up to give his judgment within history, and when his storm destroys the flimsy structure made by man, they will not have anyone to help them, nor will the riches they have illegally acquired be of any use to them. The 'storm from afar' is a metaphor with two meanings here. In the first place it recalls the conception that Yahweh will come to his day of judgment accompanied by a storm (cf. 2.12ff.; 59.19; I Kings 19.11); secondly, the prophet seems to be thinking of warriors descending upon the land like a whirlwind, and he probably has the Assyrians in mind. The mythical features of the theophany of the judgment characterize and interpret earthly events as acts of God. – Then those who are now so self-confident will be able to choose between only two possibilities, imprisonment and death.[a]

In the seven woes, the prophet is attacking the general dissolution of the sacred ordinances of Israel by capitalists without conscience, profligates seeking only pleasure, conscious and cynical transgressors of God's commandments, and perverters of the truth and the law. These form such a complete picture that it is not unlikely that Isaiah himself conceived and uttered them as a unity from the first. Since if they are so regarded they all assume a period of undisturbed peace and economic prosperity, then like most of the sayings of Isaiah collected in chs. 2–5 and 9, they belong to the prophet's early period. They proclaim with compelling force that all material well-being obtained at the expense of the people as a whole and in defiance of the law is precarious, because God loves what is right.

[25–30] See after 9.8–20.

CHAPTER 6.1–13

The Call

1 In the year that King Uzziah died I saw the Lord sitting upon a throne, high and lifted up; and his train filled the temple. 2Seraphim

---

[a] Many scholars follow Lagarde and read here: 'Baaltis crouches, Osiris is broken.' The verse would then mean that they will find no help in the hour of danger from the Phoenician and Egyptian gods. But for a contrary view cf. Budde, ZAW 50, 1932, pp.69f., and the suggestions of Kissane and Bruno.

stood above him; each had six wings. With two he covered his face,
with two he covered his feet, and with two he flew. ³And one called to
the other and said:

>   'Holy, holy, holy, is Yahweh Sebaoth,
>   his glory is the fullness of the whole earth.'

⁴Then the pivots of the doors in the foundation stones shook at the voice
of him who called, and the house was filled with smoke. ⁵And I said:

>   'Woe is me; for I must be silent,ᵃ
>   for I am a man of unclean lips
>   and I dwell in the midst of a people of unclean lips.
>   For my eyes have seen the King, Yahweh Sebaoth!'

⁶Then flew one of the seraphim to me, a burning coal in his hand,
which he had taken with tongs from the altar. ⁷And he touched my
mouth and said:

>   'If this touches your lipsᵇ
>   your guilt is taken away, and your sin covered.'

⁸And I heard the voice of the Lord saying:

>   'Whom shall I send,
>   and who will go from us?'

Then I said:

>   'Here am I! Send me.'

⁹And he said: 'Go and say to this people:

>   Only hear, but do not understand,
>   only see, but do not perceive.
> 10   Make the heart of this people fat
>   and make their ears heavy
>   and shut their eyes,
>   so that they do not see with their eyes
>   nor hear with their ears,
>   nor their heart understand,
>   and they are healed once again.'

¹¹Then I said, 'How long, O Lord?' And he said:

>   'Until the cities are waste and without inhabitant
>   and the houses without men, and the field lies fallow like the
>   wilderness.
> 12   For Yahweh will remove men far away,
>   so that the desolation will be great in the midst of the land.
> 13   And though a tenth remain in it,
>   it will be a pasture againᶜ

ᵃ Cf. L. Köhler, *Kleine Lichter*, Zürich, 1945, pp. 32ff.

ᵇ For the construction cf. Brockelmann, *Hebräische Syntax*, Neukirchen, 1956,
§164a, and Josh. 2.18; Isa. 7.14.

ᶜ For the translation cf. J. P. Seierstad, *Die Offenbarungserlebnisse der Propheten
Amos, Jesaja und Jeremia*, SNVAO, 1946, II, 2, p. 107.

like an oak[a] and like a terebinth,[a]
whose stump remains when it is felled.[b]
A holy seed springs from its stump.'

Chapter 6 is the beginning of the so-called testimony of Isaiah which extends as far as 9.7.[c] Its central message is contained in ch. 7 and 8.1–22, in which the prophet gives an account, as evidence for posterity, of his activity in the period of the war with Syria and Ephraim. Here he speaks in the first person, and this was probably originally the case in ch. 7 as well. This roll, which was first handed down separately, is introduced by the story of the call and commissioning of the prophet in ch. 6, and concluded by a prophecy of salvation extending from 8.23 to 9.7. If the testimony solemnly sealed in the presence of his disciples (cf. 8.16ff.) is opened and read with no less solemnity in the hour in which the judgment he proclaims is fulfilled, then it will serve as a witness to those who survive, to call them to repentance (7.3) and to confirm trust in God as their only helper and their only security. Thus the purpose of the story of Isaiah's call, with its restrained description of the vision of God, is neither to give rise to speculation concerning the divine world above, nor merely to legitimize the prophet himself, but to testify that God's judgment was already decreed when he called him to a task that went beyond all normal feeling and understanding. For he had not merely to proclaim judgment upon his people, but to bring it upon them by this very message, which would harden the hearts of his contemporaries. Of course, those who survived would not be able to excuse themselves thereby, but would be obliged to admit that a choice between judgment and grace was offered to them or to their fathers, and so to admit that God was justified in his judgment (cf. Rom. 3.4ff.).

[**1–4**] *The vision of Isaiah.* Isaiah opens his account by giving an exact date (v. 1). In the year in which King Uzziah died, the last calendar year of his official reign, 736/35 (cf. the comment of 1.1), Isaiah was called by God.[d] Since the details given in 1.1 are not entirely reliable, it is no longer possible to tell whether what is recorded here actually took place before the death of Uzziah. Accord-

[a] Unlike the English, the Hebrew has a definite article here.
[b] Probably read *miššaleket* with 1Q Isa.
[c] Cf. K. Budde, *Jesajas Erleben*, Gotha, 1928, pp. 1ff.
[d] Morgenstern suggested that the calling is set on New Year's Day, *HUCA* 5, 1928, pp. 42ff.; cf. *VT* 10, 1960, p. 159.

ing to II Kings 15.1 the official throne name of the king seems to have been Azariah, 'Yahweh is help.' The reason why he appears here under the name of Uzziah ('my strength is Yahweh') is perhaps that as early as the year 758/57 he had been obliged to hand over active rule to others for reasons of health. By giving this date Isaiah emphasizes that his prophetic activity was not a consequence of his own meditation and decision.[a] God's hand had reached out for him in time and space. One is involuntarily reminded of the beginning of the story of the Nativity in Luke 2.1, which firmly links the birth of Christ to world history.[b] With understandable brevity, the prophet introduces his vision of God, which even to Israelite sentiment was a monstrous conception: he has seen the Lord. He does not reflect upon the mode of seeing. Everything is concentrated upon the content of the vision and no account is taken of the mental process. Isaiah sees the Lord enthroned (for the expression used cf. Amos 1.5, 8; Isa. 40.22) as the heavenly king in the full exercise of his rule. But it is of great importance to notice that the prophet does not actually describe Yahweh himself, but only the hem of his garment and the seraphim. Thus he has not actually seen God himself, but 'has only been aware of His presence in what he has seen'.[c] God's power is emphasized by the mention of the loftiness of the throne and the dais, and his greatness and dignity by the cloak flowing down into the hall of temple.[d] As vv.4 and 6 show, there is no doubt that the prophet saw his God in the earthly sanctuary, the temple of Jerusalem. Of course, God's permanent dwelling is in heaven;[e] but he appears to those who seek him in the earthly sanctuary.[f] There he manifests himself above all at the great harvest festival held at the turn of the year, when he ascends his throne, the Ark, in order to judge his people.[g] The view based on I Kings 8.6–8, that the Holy of Holies formed a pedestal, on the highest step of which stood the Ark, would explain why Isaiah

[a] Cf. M. Luther, WA 31.2, p.47. 29f.

[b] E. Jenni, *ThZ* 15, p.329, points to the authenticating function of the mention of the 'official' year.

[c] E. Brunner, *Revelation and Reason*, tr. Olive Wyon, London, 1947, p.97.

[d] Seierstad, SNVAO, 1946, II, 2, p.97.

[e] Cf. Pss.2.4; 11.4; 103.19; 115.3; Isa.40.22; 66.1; Micah 1.2f.

[f] Cf. Ps.11.4; Hab.2.20; Pss.46. 4; 68.35; Isa.1.12; 8.18. For the significance of the temple as the place of Yahweh's appearance in Isaiah cf. M. Schmidt, *Prophet und Tempel*, Zürich, 1948, pp. 32ff.; R. Hentschke, BZAW 75, 1957, pp.57ff.

[g] Cf. S. Mowinckel, *Religion und Kultus*, Göttingen, 1953, pp.76f.; Weiser, *The Psalms*, pp.37ff.; Pss.50.1ff.; 24; 47.5ff.; 96.10ff.; 97; 98.9; 99.

emphasizes the height of the throne in this way: the whole of the Holy of Holies formed a single throne in a series of steps.[a] One can already recognize how the content of the prophet's vision is determined by conceptions current in his time.[b] At the same time it would be a mistake to deny that the experience was authentic. By the whole way in which he describes it, Isaiah leaves no doubt that this vision came upon him, without any contribution on his part, as a strange event.[c]

Moreover, though it cannot be proved conclusively, it is most probable that Isaiah was also present in the temple, either in the temple building[d] or in the forecourt.[e] Many exegetes in fact put forward the suggestion that he may have been carried into the temple in his vision like Ezekiel (cf. Ezek. 8–11).[f] His familiarity with the cultic traditions of his people could also suggest that at the time of his calling he already belonged to the temple personnel in some way.[g] It is even conceivable that he was previously intended to be a prophet.[h] The name 'the prophetess', given to his wife (8.3.),[i] may imply that apart from his prophetic activities he exercised no other calling. On the other hand, he may have worked as a free farmer.[j] But because of our fragmentary knowledge of the institution of prophecy it is not yet possible to be certain about this. In any case, it is clear that Isaiah exercised his office in a different way from the official prophets of salvation (I Kings 22). One may perhaps see the clouds rising from the altar of incense as the reality behind the trains which fill the

[a] K. Galling, *JPOS* 12, 1932, pp. 44f.; also R. de Vaux, *Ancient Israel*, tr. J. McHugh, 1961, pp. 318f.

[b] This has been convincingly shown above all by I. Engnell, *The Call of Isaiah*, UUÅ 1944, 4, though not without overemphasis. Cf. also J. Gray, *VT* 11, p. 14.

[c] Jenni, *ThZ*, 15, p. 325.

[d] Cf. K. Galling, *JPOS* 12, pp. 44f.; Hertzberg, *ad loc.*; also Luke 1.11.

[e] So M. Buber, *The Prophetic Faith*, tr. C. Witton-Davies, 1949, p. 127.

[f] Cf. Kissane, Feldmann, *ad loc.*; Engnell, *The Call of Isaiah*, pp. 2/f., similarly Eichrodt, *ad loc.* Delitzsch had in mind an assumption in a vision into the heavenly temple; cf. Pss. 8.6; 29.9.

[g] So also A. H. J. Gunneweg, *Mündliche und schriftliche Tradition der vorexilischen Prophetenbücher*, FRLANT 73, 1959, p. 103.

[h] Cf. I Sam. 3. This story perhaps shows how people conceived of the vocation of a prophet. Cf. H. J. Kraus, *Die prophetische Verkündigung des Rechts in Israel*, ThSt(B) 51, 1957, p. 23.

[i] Cf. the comment on 8.3.

[j] Cf. p. 2 above.

actual temple building. They surround God, enthroned in the Holy of Holies, with a twilight which obscures all details.[a]

The heavenly king does not appear alone to the prophet. Yahweh is surrounded by the seraphim (v.2), ministering spirits, in considerable numbers,[b] just as an earthly ruler is surrounded by his followers and courtiers. They shut him off from the gaze of man. According to Isa.14.29; 30.6 and Num.21.6; Deut.8.15, the seraphim must be thought of as naked winged serpents with human faces and hands (cf. v.6), and according to the meaning of the word as glowing beings of light, on whose wings forked flashes of lightning may have appeared.[c] Man is not able to conceive of supernatural beings independently of his experience. The seraphim reverently conceal their faces and private parts[d] with their wings. Even the heavenly beings, who day and night surround their God and serve him, are similar to men in that they cannot and may not look upon the face of God. The sight of him would be fatal for them as well. Their covering of their private parts expresses the immensely ancient experience of a connection between sex and the feeling of guilt. The attitude of the angelic beings emphasizes the infinite distance between God and every creature, and recalls the holiness of God to Isaiah.

The prophet paints an impressive picture: in the darkened temple at night, where only the coals of the altar of incense glow mysteriously, a blinding and flashing blaze of light suddenly shines out. In the midst of it, Yahweh is enthroned in sublime majesty and power, on his raised throne. His royal cloak flows right down into the temple building. Around him, in blinding splendour and constant movement, are the heavenly hosts. And the vision is at once extended to the hearing: Isaiah hears – perhaps as the echo of a hymn which was actually sung on New Year's Day in the temple – the thunderous note of the seraphim's song of praise, at which the doors shake in the foundation stones. One calls it out to another, in a mighty fugue: 'Holy, holy, holy, is Yahweh Sebaoth, his glory is the fullness of the whole earth'

[a] On the structure of the temple of Solomon, cf. F. Nötscher, *Biblische Altertumskunde*, Bonn, 1940, pp. 28off.; G. E. Wright, *Biblical Archaeology*, pp. 132ff.

[b] Verse 6 shows that in any case there were more than two.

[c] *śārāp* is related to the verb *śārap*, 'to burn'. Cf. Budde, *Jesajas Erleben*, p. 10, and Procksch *ad loc*. Since the flashes of lightning belonged to the phenomena which accompanied the theophany (cf. Ex. 19.16; 20.18; Ezek. 1.13) it is obvious that the vision has been influenced by tradition in this feature

[d] Cf. Ex. 4.25 and Isa. 7.20. In both passages 'feet' is used as a euphemism for the genitals.

(v. 3).[a] Here appears one who alone is worthy of adoration, and who alone is holy.[b] The threefold attribution emphasizes that he is the source of all holiness.[c] Whereas his glory, his *kābōd*, lies behind every reality in the world as an invisible force, which is revealed to the man who has eyes to see it (cf. Rom. 1.19f.), 'his holiness signifies his hidden and innermost being'.[d] Man has become aware of this, and still does so, when he encounters the God who is vigilant to see that his will prevails (cf. Ex. 15.11ff.; Lev. 10.1ff.; 19.2ff.), and when he sees that there is a power and a will ruling over him, before which he cannot endure as a naturally existent human being. The Holy One is the wholly other, whom man cannot reach by himself, who remains far away and terrible, unless each man turns to him in his free grace, which cannot be forced and cannot be merited. By contrast to the modern feeling, which consciously or unconsciously depends upon the Christian belief in God's power permeating the whole world (cf. I Cor. 8.4–6), men in ancient times also encountered the holy as an impersonal power, proceeding from God, in objects which were consecrated to his service and therefore partook of his holiness (cf. Ex. 29.37; 30.29; I Sam. 5; II Sam. 6.6f.).[e] That in the Old Testament one conception cannot be regarded as superseded by the other is shown by the present chapter, in which Isaiah tells how he was shattered by the personal presence of the Holy God, and sanctified by a cultic purification. For him, the Holy One is the perfect and mighty God, who is not under human control, and who is capable of establishing his claim to rule throughout the whole world.[f]

This all-embracing power of God, the Lord over all lords, is also emphasized by the title Yahweh Sebaoth which is given to him, and which may be translated as 'surrounded by hosts' (perhaps the closest rendering of the Hebrew word, and following Buber's German rendering *der Umscharte*[g]). Its meaning has been variously explained. On the basis of I Sam. 17.15, many scholars think of the host of the Israelite

---

[a] Cf. also the passage in Ethiopian Enoch 39.12 which echoes this verse.

[b] Cf. the conclusion of the Gloria, *Tu solus sanctus*, in the liturgy.

[c] For centuries this was regarded in the church as an allusion to the Trinity, God the Father, God the Son, and God the Holy Spirit.

[d] Procksch, *TDNT* I, pp. 93f.

[e] Cf. H. Ringgren, *The Prophetical Conception of Holiness*, UUÅ 1948, 12, pp. 14f.

[f] Cf. Seierstad, SNVAO II, 2, p. 100.

[g] Cf. his translation, *Verdeutschung der Schrift* (1925ff.), 1956ff., begun in collaboration with F. Rosenzweig.

armies, in which case it would refer to Yahweh as the Lord of the earthly armies of Israel. Others think of the stars, and others again of the heavenly host of spirits and angels. But the two latter explanations are not strictly speaking opposed, since the ancients thought of the stars as animate beings (cf. Judg. 5.20; Isa. 40.26). A recent suggestion has been to interpret the word as an abstract noun in the sense of 'mightiness'. But the fact that the divine title becomes less prominent during the exilic and post-exilic period implies that Sebaoth should be regarded as an ordinary plural, and that these hosts should be understood as the gods of the ancient Canaanite pantheon, reduced to the status of Yahweh's servants. At that period, those Israelites whose religious syncretism was under attack considered themselves justified by the assertion that Yahweh was the Lord of all gods.[a] This divine title seems to have come into use when Israel consciously recognized Yahweh's cosmic power and opposed it to the claim of the old gods, that is, during the period of the judges.[b] The Greek Bible correctly interprets the title in its translation of II Sam. 6.2 and Amos 9.5 as 'the Lord of the powers' and 'the Lord, the ruler of all'. The holy God, the Lord over all the powers and forces which form and control this world, possesses the power to make his will prevail in this world.

Whereas the first part of the heavenly song of praise hymns God's inner, hidden being, which is nevertheless powerful and strong in will, the second half praises the power by which he sustains and underlies the world, his kābōd, his honour and glory. Whereas in his innermost being God remains hidden from man in profound concealment for all but a few moments, in the everyday world man is not without a testimony to his presence. God's 'weightiness', God's glory, fills the whole earth with a living power.[c] All reality proclaims him who created, sustains and governs it. Thus heaven and earth, and day and night, tell of his glory (Ps. 19.1f.). Even the destiny of the Gentile nations points towards him as the true ruler of history, and so maintains his glory, which excludes every other claim (Isa. 42.8). Yet there can be no greater misunderstanding of this hymn than as the expression of a rationalist natural theology. For man is blind to the

---

[a] Cf. B. Maag, *Schw. Theol. Umschau* 20, 3/4, 1950, pp. 27ff.; O. Eissfeldt, *Misc. Acad. Berolinensia* II, 2, 1950, pp. 128–50; esp. W. Kessler, *WZ-Halle* 7, 1958, pp. 767–72.

[b] Cf. Eissfeldt, *SVT* 4, 1957, pp. 138–47; K. Galling, *ThLZ* 81, 1956, cols. 68f.

[c] Cf. Ps. 24. For the tradition history cf. R. Rendtorff, *BKD* 1, 1961, pp. 28f.

glory of God to which all reality bears witness, until he is convinced
of his holiness. Both God's glory and God's holiness are always recognized simultaneously. Only someone who knows of his holiness also
recognizes his glory. Consequently, one can follow Herntrich's comment on the passage, which in its turn follows the Württemberg
divines Oetinger and Bengel, in saying that God's 'holiness is his
hidden, concealed glory . . . But his glory is his holiness revealed'.
Here again we encounter the mystery of revelation, which is always,
at one and the same time, both the unveiling and the affirmation of
the mystery of God. For God 'can be glorified aright only when He is
known as the Holy One, when He, the Mysterious One, proclaims
His mystery'.[a] The revelation of the holiness of God means at the
same time the realization of our own sinfulness – Isaiah underwent
this experience of being overpowered in the form of the Old Testament theophany. The experience of being set free to know the true
deity of God and his own creatureliness comes to a Christian in hearing the word of Christ who is crucified for him. There is therefore
good reason for the Christian church to sing the hymn of the seraphim
before hearing the words of institution in the eucharist, in order to
praise the coming of him whose glory fills and sustains the whole
world, and from whose grasp man cannot find any place to hide. The
Holy One is always ready to reveal his glory, but sustains and per-
meates the earth, to slay everything that is unholy, and to consummate his judgment. It is the goal of history that every knee should
bow before him (cf. Isa.45.18, 23f.; Phil.2.10f.). God's visible rejection contains a hidden acceptance offered to man; his judgment
brings about his grace. 'Nothing is said in heaven about the nature
of the world, but the earth is claimed for the purpose of its consummation. This means that v.3 is the most powerful affirmative of the
earth that can ever be spoken.[b]

Just as in the view of the Old Testament the heavens dropped rain,
the mountains shook, clouds of smoke rose up and lightning flashed
down when Yahweh appeared, because the cosmos proclaimed the
coming of his glory (cf. Ex.19.9, 18; 24.15ff.; Judg.5.4f.; I Kings
8.10; Ezek.44.4; Hab.3.3–6; Pss.18.7ff.; 50.1ff.; 104.3f.), Isaiah
experienced a realistic emphasizing of the song of praise of the seraphim, as even their voice forced a response from the cosmos: from the
very foundations a shudder passed through the whole temple, so that

[a] E. Brunner, *Revelation and Reason*, p. 45.
[b] Herntrich, *ad loc.*

the doors, with their pivots set in the foundation stones, trembled (v.4, cf. also Amos9.1). And the clouds of smoke concealed the countenance which is both heavenly and earthly.

6.5–7. *The Preparation for Service.* Into the darkness which once again surrounds him, the prophet cries out his confession, with which he acknowledges the holiness of God and draws from it the consequence for himself: he knows that as a sinner he must be struck dumb before God and is lost (v.5).[a] He and all his contemporaries were certain that no man can survive the vision of God (cf. Ex.33.20; 19.21; [Gen. 32.20]; Judg.6.22f.; 13.22).[b] But he has seen Yahweh the King! The designation of Yahweh as king must have come into use as early as the period of the judges, when he was venerated in Shiloh as enthroned upon the cherubim.[c] It provides an excellent description of the relationship between God and man: God is the Lord who can demand obedience and the loyalty of vassals from his worshippers, and because of this ensures them of his protection.[d] Isaiah knows that he himself is as unworthy of this claim as his whole people. They are both of unclean lips. He hears the voices and the message of the seraphim, in whose unceasing hymn of praise is reflected their life, wholly consecrated to service. This in itself warns him of his own unworthy condition and that of his people. Sinful man cannot join in the praise of the angels; the presence of the Holy One 'silences' him, and destroys him.[e] Thus his inability to speak becomes a symbol of his own remoteness from God. Here the part stands for the whole (cf. John

---

[a] Cf. Job 42.5f.

[b] Cf. also Ethopian Enoch. 14.30–22.

[c] Cf. I Sam.4.4; Eissfeldt, *SVT* 4, 1957, pp.143f.; Alt, *Kl.Schriften* I, pp.345ff.; von Rad, *TDNT* I, pp.568; now also B. Maag, *SVT* 7, 1960, pp.129ff.; for a different view, H. J. Kraus, *Worship in Israel*, p.203f., who is certainly right in arguing that by this period the structure of earlier conceptions had now been affected by the adoption of the ancient Jerusalem cultic tradition of the Most High God.

[d] Cf. O. Eissfeldt, *Kl. Schriften* I, Tübingen, 1962, p.178. The cosmic theme of the battle with chaos, which is associated with the coronation of Yahweh in a whole series of psalms (cf. Pss.93.3f.; 98.7f.) is not mentioned by Isaiah. The judgment of God in his epiphany purifies the prophet, who in his turn becomes the instrument of the judgment of the sinful people. Cf. J. Gray, *VT* 11, 1961, p.14. Of course the liturgical material is not slavishly followed by the prophet, but is used with a freedom appropriate to the situation; Gray, *VT* 11, p.28; Ex.33.20; 19.21; Gen.32.30; Judg.6.22f.; 13.22.

[e] Cf. L. Köhler, *Kl. Lichter*, pp.32ff.; E. Jenni, *ThZ* 15, 1959, p.322; Eichrodt, *ad loc.*

13.10). With this confession Isaiah acknowledges that God's judgment upon sinners is just. He knows that as a transgressor of the will of God, he has deserved death.

At once, however, one of the seraphim flies to the prophet to cleanse him from his sin (vv. 6–7). That he acts at God's command is not expressly stated, but is naturally understood. With tongs he has taken a burning coal[a] from the altar of incense. On this altar the incense sacrifice burns, the clouds of which protected the priests against the risk of death from the close presence of God (cf. Lev. 16.12f.). Because the coal comes from the consecrated altar, it possesses in itself an atoning and purifying force for the congregation (Num. 16.46f.).[b] The action is both interpreted and given effect by the words of the seraphim: 'See, if this touches your lips, your guilt is taken away, and your sin covered.' The Hebrew equivalent for sin and guilt are virtually the same in meaning. They originally signify a departure from the norm which is demanded. By sin, man departs from the form of existence which is his as a creature. On his creatureliness is based the fact that by trust in God's unceasing presence he opens himself in service to the claim and obligation of the fellowship of God. Since every departure from this is guilt, there is no intermediate neutral position with regard to the demand of the will of God. At all times man stands either in the grace of God or under judgment. To 'cover' is a sacral, cultic word, which in the first instance signifies the process of atonement for removing blood-guiltiness.[c] If God does not cover sin, then every human attempt to remove it is without effect (cf. Isa. 22.14; Jer. 18.23). Isaiah, cleansed from sin and blessed against every expectation, can now hear the voice of God and answer it in the right way. He can take part in the heavenly council, which he now witnesses.[d] Only one who has recognized his sin and has been set free from it can do the will of God.

[8–11] *Calling and sending*. By the extraordinary purification which has taken place, the prophet has been prepared to learn that God has some extraordinary purpose in mind. Consequently, when his God

---

[a] Cf. Gk.

[b] Cf. Nötscher, *Biblische Altertumskunde*, pp. 322f. and 296f.; J. Köberle, *Sünde und Gnade*, Munich, 1905, pp. 162f.; cf. also, with Eichrodt, Num. 31.22ff.

[c] Cf. Procksch, *TDNT* IV, p. 329; J. Herrmann, *TDNT* III, pp. 301ff.; J. J. Stamm, *Erlösen und Vergeben im Alten Testament*, Bern, 1940, pp. 61ff.

[d] Cf. I Kings 22.19ff.; Seierstad, SNVAO II, 2, p. 103.

asks: 'Whom shall I send, and who will go from us?'[a] he replies
without hesitation: 'Here am I! Send me' (v.8). This answer forms an
extreme contrast to Jeremiah at his call. This is a willing declaration of readiness on the part of a man who announces that he is ready
for service in answer to a question that was not even addressed
directly to himself; in Jeremiah's case, a young man tries to avoid the
task God intends for him by pointing to his youth (cf. Jer.1.6; 20.9
and Ex.3.11). Isaiah recognizes that as a sinner he had forfeited his
life in the sight of God. Consequently, his call seems to him an un-
merited grace, to which he is obliged to be faithful throughout his life
(cf. I Cor.15.8–10).[b]

With astounding brevity the dialogue between God and his chosen
one proceeds. Isaiah has scarcely declared his readiness, when his
task is given to him: 'Go, and say to this people . . .' (vv.9–10). It is
customary to regard the description of Israel as 'this people' as an
expression of contempt, although this view is not corroborated by
biblical usage in general.[c] At the same time, it is notable that God
does not use the solemn sacral names 'Israel' or 'the house of Jacob'.
The task itself is so unusual, and so paradoxical to normal human
thought, that the suggestion has been made that the prophet first formulated it retrospectively, on the basis of his apparent failure.[d] But
this explanation ignores the Old Testament belief in the creative
prophetic word: it does not merely foretell events, it brings them
about (cf. the comment on 9.8). Verse 9 sums up not the content of

---

[a] Many scholars translate not 'from us' but 'for us' and assume a *pluralis
majestatis*, cf., for example, Buber, *The Prophetic Faith*, pp.128ff. The nature of the
scene seems to me to imply the former view. Engnell, *The Call of Isaiah*, p.42, points
to the parallel in an Accadian text of the calling of a priest to the service of the
heavenly god Anu. What we have here could be a traditional element. C. Westermann, *Basic Forms of Prophetic Speech*, tr. H. C. White, Nashville and London, 1967,
p.115, draws attention to the fact that v.8 consciously uses a circumlocution for the
office of messenger, 'because a man cannot be designated as the messenger of God'.

[b] Seierstad, SNVAO, 1946, II, 2, p.105. For the connection between theophany
and prophetic inspiration cf. also I Kings 19. I am grateful to Ernst Würthwein
for drawing my attention to the possibility that this passage derives from the tradition of the Jerusalem cult.

[c] Cf. Ex.3.31; 5.22; 17.4; 18.18; Num.11.14; Deut.5.28; Josh.1.2; Micah
2.11; Hag.1.2; etc.; cf. Boehmer, *JBL* 45, 1926, pp.134ff.

[d] Cf. F. Hesse, *Das Verstockungsproblem im Alten Testament*, BZAW 74, 1955,
pp.83ff.; for the opposite view, cf. K. Elliger, *ZAW* 53, 1935, p.9 n.1; von Rad,
Old Testament Theology II, pp.152ff.

Isaiah's public preaching, but the effect intended from it by God.[a] The word of God is not merely withdrawn from the sinful people. It continues to be uttered through the prophet, but only in order to speed the coming judgment. 'Every word of the prophet will merely make them (his hearers) even wiser in their human thoughts, and will make them more determined not to abandon their human attitude, in which they consider they are so firm and unassailable.'[b] Their heart, which for the Hebrew was not so much the site of physical life, but rather the centre of man's plans and desires,[c] would not draw the obvious consequences from what was heard and seen. If the people can be described metaphorically as already sick, a prophet will not only not heal them, but make them more and more like a sick man, whose fatty heart only beats slowly, whose ears are deaf and whose eyes are closed up with a cataract. At the very moment of his call, Isaiah is consecrated to the purpose of hardening the heart of the people, a purpose God intends to pursue in sending him; and this is done in order to preserve the prophet himself, and his adherents also, from the temptations which the apparent failure of their ministry was bound to bring them.[d] It ought also to be noted that this passage, in the version of the Greek Bible, is taken up again in Mark 4.10–12, in order to describe the mysterious presence of the kingdom of God.

The meaning of the question then posed by the prophet is disputed (v. 11a). It can be taken to refer either to the duration or to the effect of the task imposed upon him.[e] It probably refers to both.[f] The prophet's question forms a short lament (cf. Pss. 13.2; 74.10; 79.5; 80.4; 89.46; 90.13; Hab. 1.2). It is as though he were taking on immediately the exercise of his prophetic office, which also included

[a] Cf. E. Jenni, *ThZ* 15, 1959, pp. 335ff.

[b] Herntrich, *ad loc*. On the psychology of the hardening of the people's hearts cf. F. Haeussermann, *Wortempfang und Symbol in der alttestamentlichen Prophetie*, BZAW 58, Giessen, 1932, p. 79; cf. Seierstad, SNVAO, 1946, II, 2, p. 126: 'It is the consciousness of guilt that from the human point of view provokes a defensive reaction, and sets up the barriers which prevent the holy God from being given genuine attention and obedience.'

[c] Cf. Baumgärtel, *TDNT* III, pp. 605ff.

[d] Jenni, *ThZ* 15, p. 338.

[e] On the first possibility cf. König, Fischer, Kissane, Buber, Herntrich, *ad loc*.; S. H. Blank, *HUCA* 27, pp. 82f.; on the second cf. Budde, *Jesajas Erleben*, p. 20; Seierstad, SNVAO, 1946, II, 2, pp. 105f.; Engnell, *The Call of Isaiah*, pp. 44f.; Ziegler and Eichrodt, *ad loc*.

[f] Cf. Delitzsch, *ad loc*.

petition for his people (cf. Amos 7.2, 5; Jer. 15.1). Isaiah begs for mercy. His preaching of judgment is not a consequence of the hatred, reinforced by religion, of one who is an outsider in his society, but of his unconditional obedience towards the God who has revealed his overwhelming holiness to him in the hour of his call. In spite of his manly severity he sympathizes with his people, even though this means that he must once again be subdued by God (cf. 8.11; 22.14).[a] God's answer is a decisive negative. There is no reflection here on the possibility that God's rejection may conceal a hidden affirmative, and that his judgment is a purification of his congregation. A fearful punishment for its godless behaviour awaits the people of God. Its cities and houses will fall into ruins and ashes, its men will fail, its fields will be laid waste, and lie fallow and unused (v. 11). All this can only be the consequence of extensive wars and utter defeat. But how this will come about is not at the moment important; all that matters is that it will be so.

[12–13] Verse 11 concludes the original account of the prophet's vision. The transition from v. 11b, where God is the speaker, to v. 12, where he is the object of what is said, the change of metre, as well as the difference in content between vv. 11 and 12, all show that vv. 12 and 13 were not joined to 6.1–11 until later. But the conclusion of v. 13 is also secondary, because it gives a positive sense to the comparison between the survivors and the growth that springs up after the felling of the tree, which serves as food for the cattle and wild beasts, while its original sense was negative.[b] It is no longer possible to define the history of this supplement with certainty. In the light of Amos 5.3 and 6.9, it seems better not to take the reduction of the people by nine-tenths literally as referring to the deportation of the population of Israel, but to regard it as a proverbial expression, used to declare the severity of the coming destruction. Consequently, it ought to be regarded rather as a fragment of a genuine saying of Isaiah than as a corroborative addition by a disciple, or by an even later hand.

[a] Cf. S. H. Blank, *HUCA* 27, pp. 85ff. For the idea of the remnant cf. also J. Fichtner, *ZAW* 63, 1951, pp. 29f.
[b] Delitzsch, Bredenkamp, Orelli, Dillmann, Kittel, Budde, Feldmann, König, Hertzberg, Fischer, Seierstad, Engnell, Ziegler, Buber, Bruno and apparently also von Rad, *Old Testament Theology* II, p. 65, have all argued that vv. 12f. are original. On the interesting variant of v. 13 in 1Q Isa. cf. H. W. Brownlee, *VT* I, 1951, pp. 296ff.; Hvidberg, 'The Masseba and the Holy Seed', *Mowinckel-Festschrift*, Oslo, 1955, pp. 97–99; cf. also M. Burrows, *More Light on the Dead Sea Scrolls*, 1958, pp. 147ff. On the text of the LXX cf. Engnell, *The Call of Isaiah*, pp. 13ff.

In spite of the different ways in which it may be translated – it is disputed whether it is the land or, as we suggest, the remaining tenth of the population which is compared to the stump of a tree; and again, because of the similarity of the Hebrew verb concerned, it is doubtful whether a destruction of the stump by a clearing through fire, or by being eaten by wild beasts or cattle is intended[a] – its meaning is clear: the prophet proclaims to his country that it will be totally depopulated through successive visitations. – When the prophet's oracle had been fulfilled in the catastrophe of the exile, an unknown hand added a confession of hope after the original prophecy of judgment, the latter being entirely in accord with the tendency of 6.1–11: '. . . a holy seed springs from its stump.' The judgment is not the end of the history of God's dealings with his people. The congregation of the second temple is called to be the holy seed, set apart by God, of a new people of God, in which all the great promises given to the people in the fathers will ultimately be fulfilled. Those who return home are the remnant who have repented.

If one asks how Isaiah's prophcy of judgment was fulfilled, one must point to the blows which fell upon the northern kingdom in the years 734–21, leading to the destruction of the state, the severe defeat of the southern kingdom in 701, and finally to its collapse in 587, in the course of which the holy hill of the temple (cf. 8.18) became a place for jackals to prowl over (Lam. 5.18). Whereas those who had escaped could confess: 'We have transgressed and rebelled, and thou hast not forgiven' (Lam. 3.42),[b] this did not take place without the previous ministry of the prophets, who time and again proclaimed God's judgment, and of whom Isaiah was one of the greatest (cf. Isa. 48.3ff.; 42.9). Although we cannot look into the divine reason for what took place on earth, we cannot overlook the fact that ultimately there did in fact arise one from out of the people of God who had so often been subject to destruction, whose preaching at first aroused as little faith among his people as that of the prophet Isaiah (cf. John 12.37ff.), but who was nevertheless called to found, from Jews, Greeks and Gentiles, the church of those who believe, and whose words, death and resurrection are valid for all men throughout all ages. The story of the call of the prophet Isaiah is a constant reminder to the Christian church that the holy God is an inexorable judge of everything that is unholy, a warning against falling under the

[a] For the translation of *b'r* cf. Isa. 3.14; 5.5; Ex. 22.4.
[b] Weiser, ATD 16/3, *ad loc.*

punishment of God in unrepentant reliance upon themselves (cf.
Rom. 11.22). But the preacher of the gospel, who faces the apparent
failure of his ministry, and who is therefore tempted to despair, may
recognize from the example of Isaiah that he is required to be wholly
on the side of God in his heart, and to let himself be used by him as a
tool, in whatever way God pleases (cf. Mark 4.1–9). In the readiness
which is expressed in the twofold 'Here am I!' of the prophet (cf.
6.8 and 8.18), there are revealed in the hour of grace a peace and a
freedom which are independent of outward success or failure.

CHAPTER 7.1–9

The Hour of Faith

1 And it happened in the days of Ahaz the son of Jotham, son of
Uzziah, king of Judah, *that Rezin the king of Aram and Pekah the son of
Remaliah the king of Israel came up to Jerusalem to wage war against it, but
they could not conquer it.* 2And the house of David was told: 'Aram has
made a treaty with Ephraim.'ᵃ

Then his heart and the heart of his people shook as the trees of the
forest shake in a storm. 3Then Yahweh spoke to Isaiah: 'Go out to
meet Ahaz, you and Shear-jashub, your son, to the end of the conduit
of the upper pool, to the highway to the Fuller's Field, 4and say to him,
'Take heed, be quiet, do not fear, and do not let your heart be faint
because of these two smouldering stumps of firebrands, ⟨before⟩ᵇ *the
fierce anger of Rezin and Aram and the son of Remaliah.* 5Because Aram devised
evil against you, *Ephraim and the son of Remaliah*: 6'Let us go up against
Judah to tear it apartᶜ and break it up for ourselves and set up the son
of ⟨Tabe-el⟩ᵈ as king in the midst of it.'
7Thus says the Lord Yahweh:
             'It shall not stand and it shall not (any longer) be,

ᵃ For the meaning of *nāḥāh*, 'to join in a treaty', cf. O. Eissfeldt, *Schw. Theol.
Umschau*, 20, 3/4, 1950, pp. 23–26.
ᵇ Cf. *BH*.
ᶜ Derived from *qūṣ* II, 'strike apart', tear apart'. Cf. Koehler, s.v.
ᵈ Cf. *BH*. The Massoretic text makes the tendentious alteration into 'Good-for-
nothing'; cf. H. W. Wolff, BSt 23, 1959, p. 6 (35, 1962, p. 9) note i.

8 that Damascus is the head of Aram
and Rezin the head of Damascus,
(*within sixty-five years*
Ephraim will be broken to pieces, without a people)
9 and Samaria the head of Ephraim
and the son of Remaliah the head of Samaria.[a]
If you do not believe, you shall not endure.'[b]

Chapter 7 is a central part of the 'testimony' of Isaiah concerning his activity in the period of the war with Syria and Ephraim, which extends from 6.1 to 9.6. What was promised to the prophet at his call (cf. 6.9f.), the outward failure of his activity, he is now to experience in the decisive encounter with his king. The precise position of the chapter within the whole composition makes its exceedingly probable that this passage too was originally told in the first person, but was changed by a redactor, whose work can be perceived in vv. 1, 4, 5, 8 and 17, into the third person, by means of small alterations in vv. 3 and 13. It can be divided into three sections, vv. 1–9; 10–17 and 18–25, of which the first two are consecutive in content and time, while the last gathers together more short prophecies of warning, which probably belong to the same period, even though the form in which we find them is due to a redactor. The first section can be divided into vv. 1–2 with the account of the political situation, vv. 3–6, God's command to Isaiah to give a warning to King Ahaz, and vv. 7–9, the substance of this warning.

[**1–2**] *The political situation.* The prophet opens his account with a brief description of the situation; for he can assume that his readers knew the historical circumstances. It was a later writer who supplemented it with details drawn from II Kings 16.5, in order to make it more comprehensible to his contemporaries. – In view of the brevity of the original introduction, the mention of the grandfather of King Ahaz, Uzziah, is surprising. The prophet uses it to make a conscious link between what he is now describing and the story of his call, which begins his 'testimony': what God proclaimed to him in the year in which King Uzziah died, the outward lack of success of his activity, was now to be verified under his grandson, and therefore

---

[a] For the translation and general interpretation cf. M. Saebø, 'Formgeschichtliche Erwägungen zu Jes. 7.3–9', *StTh* 14, 1960, pp. 54–69.

[b] Wolff reproduces the Hebrew play of words as follows: *Wer kein Amen erklärt, der kein Amen erfährt*, BSt 23, p. 19 (35, 1962, p. 23).

this too was unable to shake his consciousness of his mission. Anyone who is on the side of God and knows his plan must not fear rejection by men.[a] Isaiah takes his readers back into the year 733 BC. In the previous year, the Assyrian king Tiglath-pileser III had crushed a movement of revolt on the part of the states of Syria and Palestine in its early stages by means of a surprise campaign, which took him as far as the borders of Egypt.[b] This made it clear to those states that their independence was at an end, unless they could succeed in bringing into being a large coalition with real force at its disposal. Thus Razon of Damascus[c] and Pekah of Israel made a treaty with each other. They probably sought at first to bring Ahaz into their alliance by means of negotiations. Only when they recognized that their efforts were in vain would they have decided to place a man who would agree with their plans on the royal throne of Judah by means of a military attack. The account in Chronicles (cf. II Chron. 28.5ff.) suggests that the two carried out their military operations separately, and severely defeated Ahaz.[d] This threat is not mentioned by the addition which supplements the account of the situation in Isaiah, for it omits the phrase contained in II Kings 16.5, 'they besieged Ahaz'. In this, it follows the tendency of the words of the prophet which follow to stress the weakness of the allies.[e] But here the campaigns have not begun. Only the news of the coalition has reached the house of David, the royal court in Jerusalem. The prophet gives a dramatic description of its effect. As the tops of the tree begin to shake before the approaching storm, trembling anxiety seizes the court, the people, and the class of responsible property owners closely connected with the royal palace.[f] In human terms this reaction is easy to understand; for the imposition of a new king, who certainly would not be descended from the house of David (cf. v.6), would be bound to result in the extermination of all the branches of the ruling dynasty.[g] The consequence was an

[a] Cf. Budde, *JBL* 52, 1933, pp.46f.

[b] Cf. the comment on 1.1 above.

[c] The name of king is so pronounced, in accordance with the *Rasōn* of the Gk and the *Raṣunnu* of the annals of Tiglath-pileser. The vocalization of M is tendentious. The similarity to *rāṣōn*, pleasure, was offensive to Hebrew ears. Following a suggestion by Lindblom, StKHVL, 1957–1958, 4, p.11, the Massoretic *reṣīn* could be understood as the passive participle of a root *rṣṣ*: 'the crushed, the annihilated'.

[d] Cf. Rudolph, HAT 21, 1955, *ad loc.*

[e] Cf. Herntrich, *ad loc.*

[f] Cf. Würthwein, *Heim-Festschrift*, Hamburg, 1954, p.49.

[g] Cf. Judg. 9.1–5; I Kings 16.9ff., 18; II Kings 9.7f., 24ff.; 10.1–8; 11.1.

extremely intensive effort to prepare arms and defences, in which the whole city must have taken an active part.

Since Ahaz obviously did not feel himself the military equal of his attackers, he looked round for a more powerful ally. Egypt was not available, since it had been decisively weakened by the loss of Thebais to the Ethopian kingdom. Thus the king considered the idea of making a voluntary submission to the Assyrian king and of asking his help against Damascus and the northern kingdom of Israel, a step which at that time was bound to have religious consequences, and meant the acknowledgement of the state deities of the protector nation. What from a human point of view seems to be understandable and to show political acumen, is not thereby justified in the eyes of faith: over this royal house have been pronounced the solemn promises given by the prophet Nathan, and continually recalled at the coronation of the king of Judah and at the annual harvest festival, that the house and throne of David will endure forever.[a] Thus in this attack on the royal house, the devout inhabitants of Jerusalem and Judah were not concerned merely, or principally, with the question of political power, but with a matter of faith: have men the power over the promises of God or has God power over the designs of men, which seek to bring his promises to nothing? The emphasis on the anxiety of the royal house and the nobility already implies a criticism on the part of the prophet.[b]

[3–9] *God's Message to Ahaz.* In this situation Isaiah received Yahweh's command to go to meet the king and to call him back to the ordinances of faith. Originally the beginning of v.3 must have read: 'And Yahweh said to me. . . .' The change into the third person is due to the redactor, whose hand is already visible in v.1. According to the wording of the verse the prophet does not merely learn what he must say, but also where and how he is to say it: outside the city, at the end of the conduit of the upper pool and the way to the Fuller's Field he is to meet the king, accompanied by his son Shear-jashub. This precise detail can hardly be a later casual men-

[a] Cf. with Würthwein II Sam.7.16 (I Sam.25.28); 23.5; Ps.132.11ff.; also Weiser, *The Psalms*, pp.44f.; H. J. Kraus, BHT 13, 1951, pp.30ff.; BK XV pp. 879ff.; *Worship in Israel*, pp.179ff.; von Rad, *The Problem of the Hexateuch and Other Essays*, pp.222ff.

[b] Quite apart from whether or not 7.9 is seen as a direct echo of II Sam.7.16, Würthwein should be followed in pointing to the special background of this scene in the royal ideology of Judah. Cf. also W. Vischer, ThSt(B) 45, 1955, pp.16ff.; J. J. Stamm, ThZ 16, 1960, p.442.

tion of the way in which the command was given. The measures taken by the king would have been followed and discussed with anxious tension in the city, which at that time numbered hardly more than four thousand inhabitants,[a] so that one may be sure that the prophet knew where he would find his man. God's utterances are not to be compared to the writing of a magic pen on a blank paper, but make use of human experience.

However well known the place mentioned must have been to contemporaries, it cannot nowadays be located with certainty. The upper pool must be sought in the south of the city, either in the Tyropoion or Cheesemaker's valley, or in the lower valley of the Kidron.[b] At least, the south is also suggested by the position of the Fuller's Spring (*'ēn-rōgēl*[c]), in the neighbourhood of which the Fuller's Field must be sought, and which lies north of the junction of the valley of Kidron with the valley of Hinnom. The prophet is sent here to meet the king, not of course because Ahaz would not have received him in his palace on the pretext of urgent government business, but because of the profound symbolism inherent in the whole scene. Care for an adequate water supply in case of siege was one of the most important defensive tasks of the king, for it was a particularly weak point. David himself seems to have conquered the city by means of a sudden attack on the water supply.[d] The king, who sought to save himself by his own actions, was inspecting the vital water supply for this purpose, and was no doubt taking steps to increase it on this occasion by new arrangements. At this very point he is directed towards God, who alone is capable of giving and sustaining. The accompaniment of Isaiah by his son Shear-jashub also has symbolic meaning. Whether the name should be translated in accordance with 10.21f. and the normal grammatical rules as 'only a remnant will return', or whether a more complicated syntactical construction should be adopted giving the rendering 'a remnant, it will return',[e]

[a] Cf. E. Janssen, FRLANT 69, 1956, p. 36, n. 3.

[b] Cf. the detailed discussion by M. Burrows, *ZAW* 70, 1958, pp. 221–27, with the references given there.

[c] Cf. I Kings 1.9; Marti, *ad loc.*, and Dalman, *Jerusalem und sein Gelände*, Gütersloh, 1930, pp. 163ff.; L. H. Vincent and M. A. Steve, *Jérusalem de l'Ancien Testament* I, Paris, 1954, pp. 284ff.

[d] Cf. II Sam. 5.8 and the comments of H. J. Stoebe, *ZDPV* 73, 1957, pp. 73–99, with the references given there.

[e] Cf. Lindblom, StKHVL, 1957–1958, 4, pp. 8f. The translation of the name as 'It is once again a matter of a remnant' seems rather forced. S. H. Blank argues

is not of importance for its meaning. In either case, it sets out the programme of the whole preaching of Isaiah (cf. ch. 6). The prophet was
so certain of the coming judgment of God upon the whole of Israel
that he did not hesitate to give his son a name which reminded everyone who met him that only a remnant would be saved and return
from the catastrophe. A man who had experienced God's overwhelming might and holiness in the hour of his call, could not doubt that
his people, in their present state, were proceeding inexorably towards
a divine judgment, a judgment which because of God's faithfulness to
his promises would be followed by a new period of salvation. Thereafter, he was certain, no one would have any cause to point scorn-
fully towards the child with this name, and towards his father,
because history had unmasked him as a false prophet. – The silent
witness at his father's side was meant to point out to the king the
seriousness of his decision. God's will is firm. But this will is not an
unalterable and blind destiny, exercised over men without regard for
right and wrong. It depends upon the king's decision whether the
child is to be a testimony of salvation or of doom to him. If the king
trusts the words of the prophet, Judah can be saved.[a] Thus the command to take his son out to the Fuller's Field implies the same as
Isaiah was commanded to say in v. 9.

There is no further mention of Shear-jashub. Consequently, the
king must have been in a position to understand the sign without any
explicit interpretation. One can conclude from this that the prophet
and the king were not meeting for the first time, and that Ahaz knew
the name of the child and his significance.

[4] The words that follow intervene directly in the political plans
of the king: 'Take heed, be quiet, do not fear, and do not let your
heart be faint. . . .' Their significance is disputed. Some scholars see
in them a command to make a cool and collected use of the existing
possibilities and to prepare for defence without fear,[b] whereas others
regard them as an exhortation to quietism,[c] although the concept is
not meant to be understood in the negative sense which it has acquired

---

unconvincingly that the name also contains an element of promise, *JBL* 67, 1948,
pp. 211ff.; *HUCA* 27, 1956, pp. 87f.

[a] Cf. Fohrer, *Die symbolischen Handlungen der Propheten*, AThANT 25, 1953, p. 24.
[b] Cf. Procksch, *ad loc.*
[c] Cf. von Rad, *Der heilige Krieg im alten Israel*, Göttingen, ²1952, pp. 56ff.; C. A.
Keller, *ThZ* 11, 1955, p. 83; H. W. Wolff, BSt 23, pp. 16f. (35, 1962, pp. 19f.).

in current usage. Herntrich rightly asks, against the first view, whether the counsel of a prophet was needed for this. The command, 'take heed, be quiet', must be understood in a much more fundamental sense. Quiet, peace, is a comprehensive term in the Old Testament. It takes in the normal condition of the country, without harmful activity and interference, which is guaranteed by the presence of God and the trust of the people.[a] In the earlier holy wars an exhortation was delivered before battle to call the Israelites to trust in Yahweh, who had given the enemy into their hands. In the same way, the prophet has now to appear before his king and exhort him to trust in him in whom all help is to be found.[b] Just as he later turns against the faithless policy of alliance with Egypt (cf. 30.15), he now opposes the plans of Ahaz, which are apparently so skilful, and with which he seeks to save his throne and kingdom.[c] Probably the messenger has not yet departed to offer submission to Tiglath-pileser and to beg his help. From II Kings 16.7 we learn the wording of the message which was still under consideration: 'I am your servant and your son. Come up, and rescue me from the hand of the king of Syria and from the hand of the king of Israel, who are attacking me.' Isaiah was certain of the consequences of this step: the violation of exclusive loyalty to a God who tolerates no other gods beside himself (Ex. 20.3). In fact, as a consequence of the rejection of his warning, an altar on the Assyrian pattern was set up in the temple of Jerusalem.[d] Thus the decision demanded of the king consisted of a choice between unconditional loyalty to his God, and apostasy. *Tertium non datur.* The king, who at his coronation was proclaimed the adopted son of God,[e] ought now to live as such. There is no other genuine possibility for him, nor for his people.[f]

The warning implies a promise of salvation: Ahaz has no reason to fear.[g] The prophet knows God's plan. For him, the powers who are now approaching to attack are already defeated. Their fire is already

[a] Cf. C. A. Keller, *ThZ* 11, p. 83; Gen. 24.6; Ex. 10.28; Isa. 14.7; Ps. 76.8.

[b] Cf. von Rad, *Der heilige Krieg im alten Israel*, pp. 56ff.; H. W. Wolff, BSt 23, pp. 15f.

[c] Cf. Würthwein, *Heim-Festschrift*, pp. 54ff.

[d] Cf. Kraeling, *JBL* 50, 1931, p. 279.

[e] Cf. Ps. 2.7ff.

[f] Cf. Amos 5.6.

[g] 'Fear not' is a conventional opening for an oracle of salvation: cf. *ZAW* 70, 1958, p. 111. On its occurrence in addresses before battle cf. Wolff, BSt 23, p. 15 (35, 1962, p. 18).

being extinguished. However terrifying the exertions they are making at present, they are like the charred and smoking ends of burning logs, as they go out. They will not attain their aim, because it is not the aim of God.[a] Once again, a later hand has supplemented the picture with an interpretation: the smoking brands are the kings of Damascus and Israel, burning with anger. The fact that it is always the king of Damascus who is placed first shows who was the real provoker of this war. The name of the king of Israel is not given. This silence is a sign of contempt.[b]

[5–6] The two verses that follow form the introduction to the word of God which begins in v.7,[c] for which they provide the basis (cf. 3.16f.; 8.6f.; 29.13f.; 30.12f.). In v.5b the redactor once again interpolates the names of Ephraim and the son of Remaliah. Judah is to be torn apart. This does not refer merely to its military defeat, but probably also to the partition of the territory of Judah. It is the intention of the allies to create a vassal state amenable to their will and incapable of pursuing a policy of its own. The new king, the son of Tabe-el, whose name is once again omitted with derogatory intent, would inevitably remain inseparably linked to the interests of those who had given him his position. One can only conjecture as to his origin, and to his previous public position. According to Alt he would have been 'a man not of royal descent, but in a high position, either in a neighbouring kingdom, or more probably at the court of Jerusalem itself'.[d] His name suggests that he was an Aramaean.

[7–9] The word of God comes as an answer to human action.[e] By contrast with human words, which do not accord with the will of God, it represents an unshakable reality (Ps.99.9). While the allies are setting forth to deal an annihilating blow to the Davidic dynasty, God has resolved upon their own fall: neither the kingdom of Israel nor that of Damascus will survive their revolt against the Assyrian overlord.[f] In referring to the northern kingdom simply as Ephraim

---

[a] On the precognitive element cf. Elliger, ZAW 53, p. 11.

[b] Cf. I Sam. 10.11; 20.27, 30; 22.12; Lindblom, StKHVL, 1957–1958, 4, p. 11.

[c] Cf. Wolff, BSt 35, pp. 20f.

[d] *Kleine Schriften* III, p. 213. For a different view, cf. Albright, *BASOR* 140, 1955, pp. 24f.; and cf. also Rignell, *StTh* 11, 1957, p. 104.

[e] For the formula 'Thus says Yahweh' cf. C. Westermann, *Basic Forms of Prophetic Speech*, pp. 93ff.; on the difference between it and *ne'um yāhwē* cf. F. Baumgärtel, ZAW 73, 1961, pp. 284f., 287.

[f] For the meaning of *kūm* cf. with Saebø I Sam. 13.14; 24.21; Amos 7.2; Nahum 1.6.

and not as Israel, he intends to imply that its religious consecration is no more. Probably, however, this usage also corresponded to the actual political situation, if it is right to suppose that Tiglath-pileser had already deprived it of the coastal provinces in 734.[a] In the text as it stands v. 8b awkwardly separates vv. 8a and 9a by its prophecy that Ephraim will be depopulated and shattered within sixty-five years. This note presumably refers to an event in 671. At that time, Esar-haddon settled a foreign ruling class in Samaria in the course of his war against Baal of Tyre and the Ethiopian Pharaoh Taharka (cf. Ezra 4.2).[b] This is obviously a later interpolation, which is betrayed as such by its reckless interruption of the train of thought. It has often been supposed that the logical continuation of vv. 8a and 9a could be the sentence: 'And the head of Judah is Jerusalem and the head of Jerusalem is the house of David (or: Ahaz).' Vriezen has recently suggested a concessive understanding of v. 8. But it is better regarded as the subject of v. 7: the rule of Razon and Pekah is destined to destruction.[c] Even those who are powerful upon earth are in the hand of God! Their plans are broken by his will. If Ahaz resisted this will, the same would happen to him. Therefore the prophet continues: 'If you do not believe, you shall not endure.' This saying is directed in the first instance towards the king and his royal entourage, the 'house of David'. Because these act as representatives of the whole people, the latter are also included in what is said. Verse 9 does not contradict the earlier part of the prophecy. Whichever way the king and his followers now decide, they will have no influence upon the sentence of God already pronounced. But in this case, what will be the consequences of the decision of the royal house? Is it only a matter of the inner clarity and peace which distinguish faith from unbelief?[d] To suppose so, is to fail to realize how serious a moment has in fact been reached – and this can be seen from v. 17. Faith had never been spoken of before in such an absolute sense, and therefore particular emphasis must be laid upon this saying. In Isaiah, faith refers to the particular mode of existence of the people of God, the continuance of which depends upon faith

[a] Cf. Alt, *Kleine Schriften* II, pp. 156f.

[b] Cf. Hans Schmidt, *ad loc.*; Alt, *Kleine Schriften* II, p. 321 n. 4; Rudolph, HAT 20, 1949, on Ezra 4.2; E. Jenni, *Die politischen Voraussagen der Propheten*, AThANT 29, 1956, pp. 18f., and the references there.

[c] Cf. Saebø, *StTh* 14, 1960, pp. 63f.; Vriezen, BZAW 77, 1958, p. 269.

[d] Lindblom, StKHVL, 1957–1958, 4, p. 14.

alone (cf. 28.14ff.; 30.15ff.).[a] Israel is not a people like any other. It came into being through God's act of election. Only as long as it relies entirely upon its God can it endure. Without faith, Israel does not exist. In the first instance this verse is concerned with the continuance of those who are directly addressed, the house of David. There is no other guarantee of their survival and continued rule than that which God has given them in his promises.[b] If they seek security in their own human intrigues, they will have departed from the covenant and fallen inexorably under the judgment of the jealous God (cf. Ex. 20.5); if they look for their future from God, then this very moment, in human eyes so perilous, could lead to a renewal of the empire of David (cf. 8.23–9.6). Faith is strictly related to the promises of God, who carried out his work in history, and reveals himself in the word of the prophets.[c] It does not refer to belief in general. It is related to the word which calls for a decision from it here and now. Thus Ahaz ought to abandon his faithless political plans and trust that the promises given to him and his fathers, and now renewed in concrete terms, will be authenticated in the hour of danger.[d] Against all appearances, the only hope he has is the word which reveals the will and purpose of the living God, who alone controls the future. The prophet tells only of the commission which God has given. That he has carried it out goes without saying. All that is said here about the faith to which Isaiah exhorts his king is also true of the church of the new covenant, with regard to the new situation brought about by the cross and resurrection. This too is based solely upon the word of the promise that the gates of hell will not prevail against it, and that its Lord will remain with it to the end of the world (Matt. 16.18 and 28.20).[e] This faith too is to some extent a confidence in what the

[a] Cf. Weiser, *TDNT* VI, pp. 189f.

[b] Cf. W. Vischer, ThSt(B) 45, 1955, pp. 18f.

[c] On the correlation between prophetic word and historical event as the characteristic feature of Israelite faith with regard to history cf. H. H. Rowley, *The Faith of Israel*, London, 1956, pp. 40ff.

[d] Cf. M. Luther, WA 31.2, p. 58.3f.: *Sola fides certificat et habet solidum fundamentum. Frustra autem fit promissio, nisi accedat fides.* 'Faith alone gives certainty. But the promise is given in vain, unless faith follows.'

[e] Cf. J. Calvin, CR 64, pp. 150f.: *Unde colligenda est universalis doctrina: Quum scilicet a verbo Domini recessimus, quamvis optime credamus nos esse fundatos, ruinam tandem instare. Salus enim nostra in verbo Dei inclusa est: Aut igitur acquiescendum in promissis Dei, aut frustra a nobis salus expectatur.* 'From this a general doctrine can be drawn: as soon as we fall away from the word of God, we are faced by ruin, how-

church cannot see and what is promised to it in the word alone (Heb. 11.1). The church must also daily recall these words: 'At the acceptable time I have listened to you, and helped you on the day of salvation. Behold, now is the acceptable time; behold, now is the day of salvation' (II Cor. 6.2). But these words are valid for the church and not for the world. What they signify for Christians in the reality of the state and of politics cannot simply be deduced from them in the form of a law, but must be tested and tried anew in every age. As such, they justify neither a pacifist world view nor its opposite. Faith does not take away from us our own political and secular decision. The situation of the 'ecclesiastical state' found in the Old Testament is past history to the church of Jesus Christ. The church must carry out its secular business in a secular way, with mature responsibility in the sight of God and men.

CHAPTER 7.10–17

Immanuel

10 Again Yahweh spoke to Ahaz: 11'Ask a sign of Yahweh your God. Go deep into the ⟨underworld⟩ᵃ or high into the heavens.' 12But Ahaz said, 'I will not ask, and I will not tempt Yahweh.' 13And he said: 'Hear then, O house of David! Is it too little for you to weary men, that you weary my God also? 14Therefore the Lord himself will give you a sign: if a young woman, who is now pregnant, bear a son,ᵇ she will call his name Immanuel. 15Cream and honey shall he eat, when he knows how to refuse evil and choose good. 16For before the child knows how to refuse evil and choose good, the land before whose two kings you are in dread will be deserted. 17Yahweh will bring upon you and upon your people and upon your father's house days such as have not come since the day that Ephraim departed from Judah – *the king of Assyria.*'

---

ever firm we think our foundation is. For our salvation is determined by the word of God. Thus we must either acquiesce in the word of God or wait in vain for salvation.'

ᵃ Cf. *BH*.

ᵇ *hinnē* introduces a conditional clause. Cf. Brockelmann, *Hebräische Syntax*, Neukirchen, 1956, §164a, and Josh. 2.18.

Verses 10–17 belong in content to the preceding passage. But the new
introduction in v. 10 implies that the scene which follows belongs to a
different time and place from what precedes.[a] Except for the brief
addition at the end of v. 17 and the change from the first to the third
person at the beginning of v. 13, the text has been preserved in its
original form.[b] It is clear that the promise and warning given to Ahaz
on the road to the Fuller's Field was not able to weaken his resolve to
seek help from the Assyrian empire. But Isaiah does not give up his
task, but faces the king a second time under God's command. The
situation has grown more acute in the meantime, and accordingly
the means used to win over the hearts of the king and his entourage
are intensified. In full consciousness of his prophetic authority Isaiah
offers the king a sign in order to convince him by what is before his
very eyes that God is in fact the Lord of the universe and the Lord of
the future. Under God's command, the prophet tests the king's faith
(cf. v. 9). Will he fail or endure? Will he and his family remain or fall?

[10] Isaiah knows that he is one with the will of God to such an
extent that he introduces his own words without comment as the
words of God. He thereby protects himself against the possible reproach that he sought to induce his king to sin by presumptuous acts.
Although the explicit prohibition against tempting God is first found
in Deut. 6.16, it is fully in accord with the thought of ancient Israel.
Thus according to an ancient tradition Moses reproached the people
who begged for water in the wilderness with the words: 'Why do you
tempt Yahweh?' (Ex. 17.2). On the other hand, Gideon (Judg.
6.17f.) is not censured for asking for a sign to authenticate his call.
It can be a sign of unbelief to ask for a sign, and it can be a sign of
unbelief to refuse a sign. The criterion is whether man is ready to
expose himself to the future laid down by his God and subject himself
to his will.

[11–12] The prophet seeks at all costs to draw his king from his
hesitant reserve, and to force him to make a clear decision. Conse-

---

[a] Against Delitzsch, Duhm, Marti, Budde, König, Gressmann, Herntrich,
Stamm, *RHPhR* 23, 1943, pp. 1f.; *VT* 9, 1959, p. 333; Vischer, ThSt(B) 45, 1955,
p. 20; Wolff, BSt 23, p. 22 (35, 1962, p. 26); Eichrodt, *ad loc.*; and following Kittel,
Hans Schmidt, Procksch, Lindblom, StKHVL, 1957–1958, 4, p. 15; Balla, *Die
Botschaft der Propheten*, p. 134; Stamm, *ThZ* 16, 1960, p. 440; and Fohrer, *ad loc.* Cf.
Isa. 8.5.

[b] G. Quell, *Wahre und Falsche Propheten*, BFChTh 46.1, Gütersloh, 1952, p. 171
n. 2, seeks to regard the whole passage as legendary, but in my view overestimates
its didactic character.

quently, he may and indeed must now offer him a sign. 'The sign guarantees that Yahweh's presence, power, promises and threats will be realized.'[a] With this offer Isaiah himself steps into the background and confronts Ahaz directly with 'his God'. The tiny possessive pronoun, which the Hebrew text only represents by a suffix, is an allusion to the whole royal tradition of Judah: 'You are my son, today I have begotten you' (Ps. 2.7). The prophet might also have said: 'You who are the son, turn now to your father. Just to put to the test whether the promises pronounced over you are empty words or not, and whether I have now spoken to you with authority or not.' With this offer Isaiah is not claiming any special miraculous power for himself. He appears only as the mediator between God and the king; for his own part, he withdraws behind his commission, and seeks to bring the king to faith as a part of the carrying out of this commission.[b] King Ahaz is given complete freedom: he may seek a sign from the underworld or from the heavens.[c] In the first case, what is intended is not the calling up of the dead, a practice forbidden in Israel,[d] but an earthquake or something similar. The second case could refer to lightning, rain and so forth. With the two extremes, heaven and the underworld, the king is given a choice of the whole of reality. But the king refuses: 'But Ahaz said: "I will not ask, and I will not tempt Yahweh"' (v. 12). His answer appears outwardly a pious one: it is not man's part to tempt God, but God's part to try men (cf. Gen. 22.1; Ex. 20.20). But there are situations in which outward piety and inward unbelief are identical, and where man in his egotism hides from the call of the living God, uttered here and now, behind his piety, apparently sanctified by tradition. The king here is

---

[a] Cf. Wolff, BSt 23, p. 23 (35, 1962, pp. 27f.). Cf. 8.18; 20.3; 37.30; 38.7, 22. On the sign as a means of authenticating the prophetic word cf. I Sam. 2.34; 10.2; II Kings 19.29 (Isa. 37.30); 20.8ff. (Isa. 38.7ff.); Jer. 44.29f.; Judg. 6.17, 36–40; and cf. A. R. Johnson, *The Cultic Prophet in Ancient Israel*, Cardiff, ²1962, pp. 52ff.; also G. Quell, 'Das Phänomen des Wunders im Alten Testament', *Verbannung und Heimkehr* (Festschrift W. Rudolf), Tübingen, 1961, pp. 253–300.

[b] Following Seierstad, SNVAO, 1946, II. 2, p. 159f., against Hölscher, *Die Profeten*, Leipzig, 1914, p. 244.

[c] On the conventional use of the contrast between the underworld, Sheol, and heaven, cf. Amos 9. 2; Ps. 139.8; Job 11.8.

[d] Cf. I Sam. 28; Ex. 22.18; Lev. 20.6; Deut. 18.9ff.; Isa. 2.6; against Balla, *Die Botschaft der Propheten*, p. 135; for positive demands for a sign cf. Judg. 6.17f., 33ff.; I Sam. 10.2ff.; Isa. 38.7f. Eichrodt, *Theology of the Old Testament* II, tr. J. A. Baker, 1967, pp. 221f., thinks the raising of a dead man is meant here.

acting as a shrewd tactician, who intends neither to reject the possibilities carefully discussed with his advisers because of the prophet's
word, nor to come into conflict with those groups in his country who
are unequivocally faithful to Yahweh and who could have been
offended by his political position in general, and in particular by his
ignoring the warning voice of the prophet. He obviously sees in
Isaiah no more than what Amaziah saw in Amos, a fanatic who could
have a dangerous influence upon the masses.[a] With his pious answer,
he is paying the required attention to the masses, so easily stirred up
on a religious issue. His plan is made. He is no longer prepared to
submit it to discussion, not even for God. Consequently he will not
have anything to do with the offer of a sign. If the tests had failed,
Isaiah would have been unmasked as a false prophet and his way
would have been opened before him. Clearly Ahaz had at least in the
back of his mind the feeling that God might give a sign and thereby
bring his plans to nothing. He was a half-hearted man who closed his
mind to the fact that he could then renounce them. Thus Luther
rightly accuses him of hypocrisy: *Sic hypocritae, ubi non est opus, sunt
religiosissimi, rursus ubi debeant esse humiles sunt superbissimi. At ubi Deus
audere iubet, est audendum. Nam obedire verbo non est tentare Deum.*[b]

[13] The prophet's answer stresses how determined he was to submit the offer of a sign to an authoritative trial. After his solemn opening, 'Hear then, O house of David!', with which he addresses the king
and his whole entourage, he first asks a question, in order to emphasize once again the decision that faces the king in this situation: 'Is it
too little for you to weary men, that you weary my God also?' It is

---

[a] Cf. Amos 7.10–17; A. C. Welch, *Kings and Prophets of Israel*, London, 1955, p. 215.

[b] 'That is what hypocrites are like: where it is not necessary, they are very pious;
but when they ought to be humble, they are very proud. But where God gives the
command to take a risk, one must take a risk. For to obey the word is not to tempt
God' (WA 25, p. 116.9–11). It is Wolff, *BSt* 23, pp. 25f. (35, 1962, p. 30) who draws
attention to the passage. See also WA 31.2, p. 58.31–33: *Nec tentatur deus, ubi iubet
ipse. Non est tentare deum credere in Christum, diligere proximum, quia praecepit ea deus.
Citra praeceptum autem deo servire volens tentat eum, quando nescit an illi placeat.* 'God is
not tempted, when he himself commands. It is not tempting God to believe in
Christ or to love one's neighbour, because God has commanded this. But anyone
who tries to serve God beyond what he commands tempts God, since he does not
know whether it will please him.' – G. Quell, *Verbannung und Heimkehr*, pp. 171ff.,
takes a completely different view of the attitude of the king, whom he compares to
Jesus in the story of the temptation. 'The knowledge that the criticism is of a
believer, and that consequently the two partners to the dialogue failed to make
contact, gives a tragic note to the scene' (p. 179).

difficult to say what concrete facts Isaiah has in mind in the first half of this sentence. It presumably ought not to be interpreted as the expression of his personal feelings, as though he himself were wearied at the failure of his attempt to rouse the court to faith; but rather as a criticism of the policy of vacillation between the group of nations in Syria and Palestine which were fighting for freedom, and Assyria, which Ahaz had followed in the last few years.[a] The emphasis lies on the conclusion of the question: God tolerates human activity for a time, but then his patience becomes exhausted, so that he intervenes in judgment. The prophet now consciously ceases to use the expression 'your God' or 'thy God', and instead says 'my God'. He knows that the decision has already been made. The king and his followers, with the feigned piety which they used to camouflage their own political plans, separated themselves from Yahweh as soon as they ignored his concrete command. The only way one can have God is by relying on him and using him. For the only way it is possible to accord God's deity to him is by using him, and risking one's life upon God's word by trusting his promises and obeying the revelation of his will. This is the only way in which man allows room for God to reveal himself as gracious and faithful.[b]

[14-17] The interpretation of the sentences that follow is among the most disputed in all scripture. Exegetes are not agreed either as to whether they form a promise or a warning, or who is meant by the child Immanuel (v. 14). Since Matt. 1.22f., and to some extent even up to the present day, a hidden prophecy of the marvellous birth of Jesus Christ has been seen in the passage.[c] This view is based on the Greek translation, which translates the Hebrew word *'almā*, rendered here as 'young woman', as 'virgin'. A related view is the messianic interpretation which is interwoven with numerous familiar themes from the history of religion, and which seems to prophesy here the birth of a king bringing salvation,[d] or a prince of the line of Ahaz,

---

[a] Following Wolff, *BSt* 23, p. 26 (35, 1962, p. 30), and against Procksch, *ad loc.*

[b] Cf. Kierkegaard's Edifying Discourse of 1844, 'Man's Need of God Constitutes his Highest Perfection', *Edifying Discourses*, tr. D. F. and L. M. Swenson, 1958, pp. 138-72.

[c] Cf. Delitzsch, Bredenkamp, König, Procksch, Fischer, Kissane, Herntrich, Ziegler, H. Junker, SVT 4, 1957, pp. 181-96.

[d] Cf. R. Kittel, *Die hellenistischen Mysterienreligionen und das AT*, BWANT II. 7, 1924, pp. 9ff., 64ff.; H. Gressmann, *Der Messias*, FRLANT 43, 1929, pp. 230ff.; H. Schmidt, *ad loc.* Eichrodt has put forward a variation of this interpretation which is worthy of consideration. He regards vv. 14 and 15 as a quotation, in which the

possibly even Hezekiah.[a] All we shall do here is to give a brief summary of the argument which not only makes these interpretations impossible but also prevents the identification of the child with another son of Isaiah. Against the ancient christological interpretation, it can be shown that the whole context demands an event which is shortly to come about,[b] and that the Hebrew word *'ālmā*, like its Ugaritic equivalent *ġlmt*, does not simply correspond to the word 'virgin', but signifies a young woman without regard to whether she is married or single.[c] The messianic interpretation of the verse is

---

prophet is referring to a popular expectation of a redeemer, and to which he adds an indication of time in v. 16, so that the prophecy of v. 7 remains in force, yet only with the addition of the prophecy of warning in vv. 17ff.: the expected bringer of salvation, Immanuel, will be born in the immediate future, but not in order to bring in the Golden Age, but rather as a messenger of doom. Thus the sign is the fulfilment of the hope, transformed into the very opposite; and the ambiguity of milk and honey, as the food of paradise and at the same time the frugal nourishment of impoverished peasants, forms the *tertium comparationis*. The difficulty of this interpretation seems to me to lie in the figure of Immanuel, whom I cannot regard as historically or psychologically possible in this form.

   [a] Cf. Bentzen, *ad loc.*; Buber, *The Prophetic Faith*, pp. 139ff.; J. Steinmann, *Le prophète Isaïe*, Lectio Divina 5, Paris, 1950, p. 90; E. Hammershaimb, *StTh* 3, 1951, pp. 124–42; S. Mowinckel, *He That Cometh*, Oxford, 1956, pp. 110–19; Lindblom, StKHVL, 1957–1958, 4, p. 24.
   [b] H. W. Wolff, BSt 35, 1962, p. 40, agrees with this argument, which I advanced in the first German edition of this book (p. 73), against his interpretation, so that I do not regard my interpretation here as affected by what he says. If I do not agree with his carefully argued interpretation, which sees the sign ultimately in the giving of the name within a circle of true believers in Yahweh, that is because there do not seem to me to be sufficient grounds for excluding v. 15 as a gloss. I give more weight to the difficulty caused by the fact that in vv. 15 and 16 Immanuel is spoken of only in the singular. The objection he advances on p. 35 against the collective interpretation advanced by me, that the indication of time given in v. 16 shows that it was to be a long time before the dangers were to cease, does not seem decisive, since it is possible to distinguish between the withdrawal of the enemy troops, which was to be the cause of the giving of the name, and the final devastation of the two states of Israel and Aram. Von Rad, *Old Testament Theology* II, pp. 172ff., has also given a cautious approval to Wolff's exegesis. I admit that my own interpretation is based principally on an attempt to give a meaning to the text as it stands, in view of the difficulty of denying with certainty the authenticity of v. 15 or v. 16b.
   [c] Cf. Gen. 24.43; Ex. 2.8; Ps. 68.25; Prov. 30.19; S. of Sol. 1.3; 6.8; Ugaritic texts, Gordon *Krt* 204; 77.7; 128. II. 22; cf. Goetze, *JBL* 60, 1941, pp. 357ff.; Stamm, *RHPhR* 23, p. 11; B. Vawter, *CBQ* 1952, pp. 319f.; A. E. Meyers, *LuQ* 7, 1955, pp. 137ff.; Lindblom, StKHVL, 1957–1958, 4, pp. 18ff.

refuted by v. 17, as well as by the whole content of the passage, which we shall expound below. In this content, milk and honey are sometimes interpreted as a food of the gods and of paradise, with reference to parallels from comparative religion, and are used to support this thesis, but it must be pointed out that similar examples are lacking in the Bible. For the Israelites, milk and honey are natural products of the country.[a] The specific interpretation of Immanuel as the child of the king who was expected, and who occurs in history under the name of Hezekiah, is also impossible to maintain for chronological reasons. II Kings 16.2 and 18.2 show that Hezekiah ascended the throne when he was twenty-five years old, after his father had reigned sixteen years in all. Consequently, in 733 Hezekiah was sixteen or seventeen years old, and it is quite impossible that he could be the child referred to here. Furthermore, it is wholly unlikely that Ahaz was intended to experience the fulfilment of the sign in his immediate family. This also excludes the other princes.[b] In recent times, it has repeatedly been suggested, following the interpretation of the great medieval Jewish scholars, that the woman is Isaiah's own wife and that this child a second son of his.[c] But it is quite improbable that during the war with Syria and Ephraim yet another son should have been born to the prophet in addition to the one named in 8.3; moreover, any speculation that he may have had a second wife is idle, since the texts say nothing of this. Finally, it would be remarkable for Shea-jashub in v. 3 and Maher-shalal-hash-baz in 8.3 to be expressly named as sons of Isaiah, whereas the text says nothing similar in the case of Immanuel.[d] Thus all that is left is the collective interpretation given below, which is not made impossible by the article which in Hebrew precedes the words 'young woman', for in Hebrew, as

[a] Cf. Stamm, *RHPhR* 23, pp. 15ff. According to Guthe, *Palästina*, Leipzig and Bielefeld, ²1927 the honey is wild honey, since bee-keeping was not known before the time of Alexander the Great. For the plentiful supplies of honey in the country cf. Gen. 43.11 and Ezek. 27.17.

[b] For a criticism of the various interpretations cf. Stamm, *RHPhR* 23, pp. 10ff.; *ZAW* 68, 1956, pp. 46ff.

[c] Cf. Hölscher, *Dir Profeten*, p. 229 n. 1; Gray, *ad loc.*; Stamm, *RHPhR* 23, 1943, pp. 17ff.; *VT* 4, 1954, p. 33; *ZAW* 68, 1956, p. 53; *VT* 9, 1959, p. 333: C. Kuhl, *The Prophets of Israel*, tr. R. Ehrlich and J. P. Smith, 1960, p. 78; E. Rohland, Die Bedeutung der Erwählungstraditionen Israels, Heidelberg (thesis), 1956, p. 170 n. 2; N. K. Gottwald, *VT* 8, 1958, pp. 36ff. Rignell's exegesis in *StTh* 11, 1957, pp. 112f., according to which Immanuel is the new Israel, seems to me wholly improbable.

[d] Cf. Rignell, *StTh* 11, p. 111.

opposed to German or English, the article is used both with words
for a class of person or things and also to introduce persons or
things which have not previously occurred in the story.[a] In view of
the preceding passages, I cannot see that there is any doubt that the
whole sense of the sign of God which Isaiah is proclaiming is that of a
prophecy of doom. Yet it would be too simple to see the passage as
merely a warning. Rather, the divine sign has a double aspect. On
the one hand it confirms the promise of vv.4ff., given to Isaiah with
regard to the existing situation, and in addition it serves as a warning
for the future. The structure of the proclamation of the sign is sym-
metrical: the prophecies described in metaphorical terms in vv.14
and 15 are followed in vv.16 and 17 by their political interpretation,
in the same order, so that vv.14 and 16 and vv.15 and 17 correspond.
The link between the two parts is formed by the idea of the ability to
choose found in vv.15 and 16.

A refusal of the king to ask for a sign, and thereby to place his trust
in God who gives his promise and demands obedience, does not
simply result in the abrogation of what Isaiah said previously concerning the fall of the coalition against Judah. Here, as in 8.1–4,
Isaiah holds firmly in the first instance to the view that its attack is
doomed to fail. The danger will disappear so rapidly that women who
are now with child will name their sons, in thankfulness for being
saved, 'Immanuel', 'God with us' (cf. Judg.6.16; Ps.46.7, 11).[b] (In
Israel, a name could be given at the wish either of the father or the
mother, but it seems that the will of the mother was more often
decisive.[c]) But if things had turned out thus, Ahaz would have been
able to regard it as a complete confirmation of his own foreign policy.
Only the fulfilment of the warning that follows could show him or his
successors that the prophet was in fact making his promise and his
offer with the authority of God, and that to reject it was nothing other
than apostasy from the living God: the life of the children who were

---

[a] Cf. Grether, *Hebräische Grammatik*, Munich, 1951, §§68 h–s. On the collective
interpretation cf. Marti, Guthe, Köhler, *ZAW* 67, 1955, pp.48ff.; Fohrer, *ZAW* 68,
1956, pp.54ff.; and his commentary, *ad loc.*; also Duhm, *ad loc.*; Budde, *Jesajas
Erleben*, p.53; Volz, *Prophetengestalten des Alten Testaments*, Stuttgart, 1938, [2]1949,
pp.207f. n.1; Balla, *Die Botschaft der Propheten*, p.136.

[b] Cf. the name '*immānū-yāh* found in the Elephantine Papyri, the name
'*immādī-yāhū* found in inscriptions, and *yahwēh-ṣidkēnū* in Jer.23.6 and 33.16; cf.
Stamm, *RHPhR* 23, 1943, p.22 and *ZAW* 68, 1956, p.53 n.18.

[c] Cf. Gen.4.25f.; 5.3, 29; 35.18; Ex.2.22; Judg.13.24; I Sam.1.20; 4.21;
Isa.8.3; Hos.1.4ff.; cf. Nötscher, *Biblische Altertumskunde*, pp.71 and 83.

born in what was apparently so fortunate a time will be lived in utter
contrast to what is implied by their name. When they know how to
distinguish between good and evil, when their conscious freedom of
choice based on personal experience is fully developed, which is the
case at about the twentieth year,[a] they shall eat cream and honey
(v. 15). Although even for the later Deuteronomic historian milk and
honey may have seemed splendid and desirable food for those who
lived in the desert (cf. Ex. 3.8, 17; Deut. 6.3; 11.9; etc.), they would
not have been so to anything like the same extent for children who
had grown up in a cultivated region.[b] But even before his hearers
could fully realize the significance of the saying, Isaiah added the
interpretation of the whole twofold sign. First he takes up once again
what he said in v. 14: the development which was apparently so
favourable for Jerusalem, and which led to the giving of the name
Immanuel, will first be confirmed in the fate which is to come upon
the Aramaean state and the northern kingdom of Israel. Both countries will be devastated before the children who are being born now
have reached the twentieth year of their lives (v. 16). This length of
time must not be pressed too closely. Isaiah takes it up once again, for
the sake of the play of words. The whole context leaves no doubt that
he was expecting judgment to come soon upon both states. However,
the confirmation of the prophet's promise with regard to the distress
of the present time cannot remain the last word to the king. For by
his unbelief he is bringing upon himself, his house and his whole
people times which can only be compared with those of the break-up
of the kingdom at Solomon's death in 926/25 (v. 17). The king acts
not for himself alone, but for his people. Consequently, the people are
rightly mentioned in this context, whether by the prophet himself, or,
like the mention of the king of Syria, in an interpolation by a later
hand.[c] The whole people of the covenant faces a period of the utter-
most distress. Ahaz still sees in the Assyrians only welcome liberators
in his extremity. One day he will recognize what kind of power he has
subjected himself to. In twenty years at the most, God's judgment
upon the king's unbelief will be realized in new wars and terrible
defeats. Then the population that remains will be reduced to the

---

[a] Cf. Gen. 3.5 and Deut. 1.39; H. Stern, *VT* 8, 1958, p. 415. Others, like Fohrer
and Eichrodt, think in terms of a period of two or three or four to five years.

[b] Against Stamm, *RHPhR* 23, 1943, pp. 15f.; Lindblom, StKHVL, 1957–1958,
4, p. 23; with Kissane, *OBL* 1, 1957, pp. 179ff. and Fohrer, *ad loc.*

[c] Cf. Wolff, BSt 23, p. 7 (35, 1962, p. 10), notes.

level of nomads and shepherds (cf. v. 15). Because Ahaz did not accept the offer of the God of grace, he will not escape his punishment. And therefore this is also a true sign, a proof, permeating the whole of the subsequent history, of the reality of God, in whose name the prophet now pronounces that the sinner does not escape his punishment and that God's word prevails. We are meant to observe that God's time is his own. Man may often think that God's time is finally concluded and that he has lost his control over the world or never possessed it, but he nevertheless still rules and in good or evil holds firm to the word he has once uttered (cf. Hab. 1.3; II Peter 1.19; 3.9). The reality of life and the judgment of God is so hard that there are events, the consequences of which never cease to exist. In the crisis of the Davidic kingdom the end of the old covenant is prophesied. The word of judgment upon the son who dared not be a son, receiving what was offered, arouses the expectation of one who is the Son (cf. 10.33–11.9).

Jesus rejected the demand of his contemporaries for a sign, and promised them no sign other than that of Jonah (Matt. 12.38f.) and consequently made the faith which his preaching aroused the sole legitimization of his authority. Since his resurrection is also an object of faith, we too have to rely on the word of forgiveness and hope. Only our acceptance in faith permits us to experience the might and glory of God: forgiveness in Jesus Christ sets man free to hope, and also sets him free, as surely as he hopes, from the burden of his past. But it does not simply take away the consequences, within the world, of his perverse actions. The forgiveness he is accorded does not set him above his master (Matt. 10.24). Consequently, his faith is the victory which conquers the world at the point at which it is subject to death, but is not a means which guarantees him an enduring position within the world. Thus the Christian knows only that it is better for him in every case to remain faithful to his God rather than to save himself without trust in God and in alleged self-reliance. Where and how the salvation he is promised will be realized for him, whether in this world or in the world to come, he does not know in the moment of his decision. And it is this that makes it clear that faith, as an infinite trust, demands the self-abandonment of the whole man, for in this alone can God be experienced as his helper in the struggle. Everyone must endure the reality of God objectively. For God to remain distant means simply that man is standing under his judgment. If the pattern of the story that we are discussing is close to that of Christian existential life, we must not fail to see the differences, which arise from the difference between the two covenants, and the resulting difference in the task and authority of those who hold office under them. An evangelical Christian has neither the authority nor the commission to intervene in political decisions in the manner of the prophet Isaiah; though of course he has no right to hold his peace in the face of wrong and violence. The Christian church owes as a duty to the secular community, the proclamation of the law and the gospel in concrete terms, of the wrath of God against sin and the offer of grace available to sinners; but not amateurish political preaching.

CHAPTER 7.18–25

The Great Devastation

18 In that day it will come to pass: Yahweh will whistle for *the fly from the end of the rivers of Egypt and* the bee in the land of Assyria.
19 And they[a] will all come and settle
    in the ravines of the valleys and the clefts of the rocks,
    and on all the thorn bushes and on all the pools,[b]
20 In that day the Lord will shave with the razor, which is hired beyond the River ⟨   ⟩,[c]
    the head and the hair of the feet, and it will sweep away the beard also.
21 And it will come to pass in that day that one can only raise a heifer and two goats,
22 *and because of the abundance of the milk one will eat cream.*
    Yes, whoever is left in the land will eat cream and honey.

[a] In M the verbs were probably originally in the plural because of the collective *debōrā*.

[b] A worthwhile suggestion by Dalman, *Arbeit und Sitte* II, p. 322, and which is based on Sa'adya, is that the *nahalōlīm* should also be regarded as bushes or trees. According to Sa'adya the *na'aṣūṣīm* are Christ's thorn (*Zizyphus Spina Christi*), and the *nahalōlīm* the liquorice, *prosopis stephanica*, a bush which grows to just over 1 metre (3 ft.) in height, and which provides a suitable contrast to Christ's thorn, which grows to over 5 metres (15 ft.).

[c] Cf. *BH*.

23 And in that day it will come to pass:
    Every place, where a thousand vines grew, worth a thousand
    shekels of silver –
    will become briars and thorns.
24 With bow and arrow men will come there; for all the land will
    be briars and thorns.
25 *And every hill which is now hoed with a hoe –*
    one will not come there for fear of briars and thorns,
    so that it becomes a place for cattle to forage and for sheep to tread.

The passage is frequently regarded as a secondary composition on the
part of the redactor, uniting four fragmentary Isaianic prophecies of
warning and providing them with explanatory additions,[a] in order to
fill in the details of the judgment prophesied in v. 17. But it is probable that the four short prophecies of warning originally formed part
of the prophet's memorandum, 6.1–9.7. Perhaps they were originally
pronounced directly after 7.10–17. However, they were later so
expanded that it is no longer possible to say with certainty which are
the authentic words of Isaiah. The introductions to vv. 18, 20 and 23,
the stereotyped 'in that day it will come to pass. . . .' do not argue
against their authenticity, for they are a meaningful way of linking
the short oracles. On the other hand, v. 22a breaks the continuity[b]
and no doubt comes from the editor. The greatest difficulty is caused
to critics by vv. 23–25. The inartistic threefold reference to 'briars
and thorns' does not give the impression of being the work of the
prophet, whose language is always so forceful. Although (as opposed
to Procksch) one need not regard the whole passage as a later addition, yet v. 25 is so reminiscent of the conclusion of the song of the
vineyard (5.1–7) that we can scarcely be mistaken in seeing it as the
work of the redactor. The same may well be true of v. 23b, which
anticipates the conclusion of v. 24. The passage effectively underlines
the warning of judgment pronounced over the unbelief of the king in
v. 17. His enemies will descend irresistibly upon the country and
deprive it of its glory. As a consequence of their ravages, bitter

[a] A different view is taken by Budde, *Jesajas Erleben*, pp. 58ff.; *JBL* 52, 1933,
pp. 32f.; Fohrer, *ZAW* 68, 1956, p. 56; his commentary, *ad loc.*; Rignell, *StTh* 11,
p. 116 and Eichrodt, *ad loc.*

[b] But cf. Balla, p. 137, who regards the whole verse as the work of Isaiah: 'The
saying is meant to be ironical. A young cow and two goats will have so much to
eat in Palestine, which is empty of men, and will therefore give so much milk,
that their owner will be able to live solely on the cream of their milk and a little
wild honey.'

poverty will be found everywhere. The people will be decimated to such an extent that there will not be sufficient workers to man the vineyards and fields fully.

[18–19] In a manner reminiscent of 5.26, Yahweh calls the Assyrians to exercise judgment upon the rebellious people of the covenant. Just as bees follow the whistling of the bee-keeper,[a] they are drawn on irresistibly, to descend upon the country and fill every last corner. Isaiah sees the time coming in which his homeland will be abandoned without defence to the very Assyrians by whom Ahaz and his advisers expect it to be saved from the coalition of Syria and Ephraim (cf. 7.1–9). Just as a man who is overwhelmed by a swarm of bees cannot defend himself, Judah will be totally abandoned to the enemy attack. Whatever the political issues that are prominent at that time, Yahweh will always be present in the background as the true Lord of history and of nations. Without his agreement there can be no blessing upon any human plan and action, and everyone involuntarily draws down judgment upon himself. A later writer, probably living at the time of the struggle between the Seleucids and Ptolemies, felt the lack of the name of Egypt and added it, retaining the imagery. Thus 'the end of the rivers of Egypt' would refer to the area of the Delta. Otherwise the whole passage would have to be dated, following Procksch, in the years following 725, in which the Nubian Pianchi conquered Lower Egypt, and so became a neighbour of Judah.

[20] In the next prophecy of warning, the Assyrian army is compared to a razor which Yahweh himself has hired from the other side of the Euphrates. Here Isaiah is probably not prophesying the procession of prisoners, carried off into a foreign country, shorn as a token of their shame, but is referring to the disgrace associated with conquest. Anyone whose hair was shaved from his head, private parts and face was dishonoured,[b] and like a slave was completely at the disposal of his conquerer. Thus the prophet foretells to his compatriots the total defeat which God has willed upon them. This brief oracle must also have been uttered after the rejection of the signs offered in 7.10, and with the policy of the king specifically in mind.

[21–22] In this short prophecy of warning, the misery of the conquered people is described in even greater detail. They will be so

---

[a] Cf. Delitzsch on 5.26; Virgil, *Georgics*, 4.54.

[b] Cf. II Sam. 10.4 and the comment above on 3.17. The hair of the feet is a euphemism, cf. Ex. 4.25.

poor, that it will only be possible for a man to keep a young heifer and two goats. The brevity of the prophecy does not make clear whether this inability is due to oppressive taxes or to the total devastation of the country (cf.6.11f.), but the prophecy that precedes it suggests that the latter is the case. In any case, the population of the southern kingdom is to be reduced to a nomadic level of civilization: those who escape the catastrophe will eat cream and honey instead of bread and meat. The relationship of vv.21 and 22b with v.15 is obvious. The short prophecy of warning is easily explained as coming from the same period. Verse 22a is a later addition, which attempts to turn the prophecy of warning into an oracle of salvation for the remnant.[a]

[23–24] In God's judgment upon his people, nothing is spared. The most valuable vineyards will be overwhelmed by rank weeds. The price of one shekel for a vine is astonishingly high. One could buy a ram for two shekels.[b] Thus this is a deliberate hyperbole. People will not even be able any longer to protect these valuable plantations. It will only be safe to enter them armed. This warning is also extraordinarily realistic. Isaiah notes how theft increases in the course of war, because it is nourished on all sides by the slain, and the number of those who survive is no longer sufficient to defend their own. A consequence of defeat will be a shortage of workers in a land sorely in need of cultivation. This prophecy could equally well belong to Isaiah's early or later period.

[25] The redactor completed the picture by explicitly drawing from 5.5f., of which he preserved the poetic form, the idea that it will no longer be possible to begin the cultivation of the hills, and that they will only be used for pasture. This, however, gives rise to a contradiction with v.21, which states that there will not in fact be many cattle and sheep. Thus his attempt to attain completeness led him astray.

[a] Cf. Lindblom, StKIIVL, 1957 1958, 4, p.46 and p.107 note a above.
[b] Cf. BRL, col.177.

CHAPTER 8.1–4

'Spoil-speed-Prey-hasten'

1 And Yahweh said to me, '⟨Take an ordinary⟩ᵃ sheet and
write upon it in ⟨indelible⟩ᵇ characters: "For Spoil-speed-Prey-
hasten." ' ²And I ⟨took⟩ᶜ for myself Uriah the priest, and Zechariah
the son of Jeberechiah, as reliable witnesses. ³And I had ᵈ gone to the
prophetess, and she conceived and bore a son. And Yahweh said to me:
'Call his name Spoil-speed-Prey-hasten. For before the child knows
how to cry "My father" or "My mother", the riches of Damascus and
the spoil of Samaria will be carried before the king of Assyria.'

[1–4] As v. 4 shows, this passage also belongs to the period of the
war with Syria and Ephraim. The lack of any mention of the son
Maher-shalal-hash-baz in ch. 7 implies that ch. 8 must in fact be later.
By two symbolic actions which follow one another, Isaiah emphasizes
the message he is addressing to King Ahaz concerning the imminent
overthrow of the kingdoms of Israel and Damascus (cf. 7.4ff.). When
the prophecy is fulfilled, both the writing and the name of the son will
bear witness to Isaiah as a true prophet.

Though it is not the usual view, it seems that v. 1 has suffered two
serious textual corruptions. Since in Canaan, as opposed to Egypt,
there was only a single script in Isaiah's day, the traditional reading
'a stylus of man', i.e. 'common characters', is meaningless. Rather,
the prophet received the command to use for his writing an ink which
will survive the passage of time. The material he is to use is not a
tablet, but a sheet of papyrus.ᵉ Just as Jeremiah (Jer. 32.16) received
a deed of purchase for the field he had bought, Isaiah is here as it
were drawing up a legal document, made out to the name of Maher-
shalal-hash-baz.ᶠ Under God's command, the prophet has already

ᵃ With Galling, *ZDPV* 56, p. 213 read *gōrāl*, cf. Prov. 19.19.
ᵇ With Gressmann, *Messias*, p. 239 n. 1, read *'ānūš*.
ᶜ Cf. *BH*.
ᵈ The *impf. cons.* should be understood in a pluperfect sense, following Duhm,
Marti, Galling and Rignell, *StTh* 10, 1957, p. 41.
ᵉ Accordingly *gilyōnīm*, 3.23, cf. Gk, signifies a transparent garment fabricated
from papyrus; for all the details of the exegesis put forward here cf. Galling, *loc.
cit.*
ᶠ Morenz, *ThLZ* 74, 1949, cols. 697ff., refers to a parallel Egyptian usage in
documents of the eighteenth dynasty, where both imperatives are used as sub-
stantives to describe an easy prey. Jirku, *ThLZ* 75, col. 118, attempts to explain the

issued to the Assyrian conqueror the lot which accords his right to take possession of and to plunder Israel and Damascus. The background of this symbolic action is probably formed by the ancient custom of dividing up the common land by lot at certain intervals.[a] So that no one can later accuse Isaiah of falsifying it after the event, he registers it in the presence of two respectable and reliable witnesses. One of them, Uriah, was the high priest of the Jerusalem sanctuary, according to II Kings 16.10–16. Here, as in 7.3ff. we can see that Isaiah had unrestricted access to the ruling class of his country, which may have been granted to him because of his ancestry, of which we have no knowledge, or else because of his standing as a prophet.

It is obvious that the process of registering the deed and the naming of the child occurred about the same time. If it were not until this moment that Isaiah lay with the prophetess, then there would be far too long an interval before the second symbolic action (v. 3).[b] Either the 'prophetess' had already borne a son, which in view of the male name is probably the simplest explanation, or else her confinement was due to take place only a short time hence. The title given to Isaiah's wife has frequently given rise to lively debate. Whereas many see in it only a reference to the prophetic significance of her children and the position of her husband (cf. 'mayoress'), others are probably right in supposing that she was a prophetess in her own right.[c] This in its turn suggests that Isaiah himself did not make any distinction in principle between himself and his professional colleagues.[d] In any case, their child is meant to become a living sign of the truth of his father's prophecies. Isaiah is so certain of what he has to say that he does not have to fear that he is saddling his son with a name which will later bring him mockery and scorn, with every child calling after him: 'Look, there comes the son of the false prophet.' Before the child is old enough to utter the first coherent sounds, the words 'father', and 'mother', the

---

name on the basis of the vocabulary of Ugaritic, in which *mhr* signifies 'servant, soldier', which would give the name the meaning 'Warrior of prey, hastening to rob'.

[a] Cf. above on 5.8.

[b] Cf. also Lindblom, StKHVL, 1957–1958, 4, p. 29.

[c] Cf. Hylander, *Monde Oriental* 25, 1931, pp. 53ff.; C. R. Reynolds, *JTS* 36, 1935, pp. 182ff.; Gunneweg, FRLANT 73, 1959, p. 102; cf. Ex. 15.20; Judg. 4.4; II Kings 22.14; I Chron. 34.22; Neh. 6.14; now cf. also Jepsen, *ZAW* 72, 1960, p. 268.

[d] Cf. Duhm and Procksch, *ad loc.*

danger which threatens the Davidic kingdom will be removed. This
means that the prophet is setting a limit of about nine months. Within
this period, the states allied against Judah will have become the spoils
of the Assyrian King Tiglath-pileser.

CHAPTER 8.5–8

Siloah and the Euphrates

5 And Yahweh spoke again to me and said:
6 'Because this people have despised
　the waters of Shiloah that flow gently,
　⟨they shall fade away⟩ᵃ before Rezin and the son of Remaliah
7 ⟨　　　　　⟩ᵇ Therefore, behold the Lord is bringing up
　against them
　the waters of the Euphrates, mighty and many,
　the king of Assyria and all his glory.
　And it will rise over all its channels
　and go over all its banks
8 and sweep on towards Judah, ⟨flooding⟩ and ⟨overflowing⟩,ᶜ
　reaching even to the neck.
　And the span of its wings
　will fill the breadth of your land, Immanuel.'

[5–8] Verse 5 makes a loose association between the prophecy of
warning which it introduces and which concludes with v. 8 and what
is recounted in 8.1–4, by dating the revelation recorded here after
that which precedes it. The key to the understanding of this passage
lies in the expression 'this people' in v. 6, where it means, as in v. 11,
the population of the southern kingdom (cf. v. 8a). The people of
Judah are reproached that they have despised the 'waters of Shiloah

　ᵃ Read *ūmāśōś* and cf. Lindblom, StKHVL, 1957–1958, 4, pp. 44f. The extant
text would have to be translated 'and rejoice in' Rezin and the son of Remaliah,
against which there are strong grounds of syntax and content. There is no other
mention of the existence of a party in Judah which sympathized with the enemy.
In view of 7.2 it would be remarkable for the whole people to be threatened in this
way as the result of the attitude of one group.
　ᵇ Cf. *BH.*
　ᶜ Read with Lindblom, StHKVL, 1957–1958, 4, p. 45, *šāṭōp weʿābōr.*

that flow gently', melting in fear before the king of Damascus, Rezin, and the Israelite king, Pekah (cf. 7.3, 9; II Kings 15.27). The 'waters of Shiloah'[a] do not refer to the tunnel of Shiloah first built by Heze-kiah,[b] but a channel with a very slight fall which led the water from the spring of Gihon along the edge of the eastern hill of the city.[c] These waters of the Shiloah channel are contrasted with the 'mighty and many waters of the river', which according to biblical usage (cf. Josh. 24.15) refers to the Euphrates. One must take care not to inter-pret this contrast on the basis of 7.3, which records that the decisive encounter between the prophet and king Ahaz concerning the threat-ened siege of the city took place at the end of the conduit of the upper pool on the road to the Fuller's Field; for the latter merely gives the place at which the incident occurs, but is not concerned with the question whether in Isaiah's view the king was justified in examining the water supply of the capital or not. Similarly, the present passage is not concerned whether the king has any occasion to provide a new reservoir, but, as is implied by the contrast between native and foreign waters, with the foolish decision taken in the matter of whether to trust the nation's own God or the Assyrian king (cf. 7.4 above). Consequently, the waters of the channel of Shiloah which are rejected are a symbol of what has been despised at home, Yahweh himself as a helper in every time of trouble.[d] Isaiah prophesies that the very pro-tection sought from the Assyrians will bring about the ruin of the country, and that, in metaphorical terms, the mighty and many waters of the Euphrates will overflow the country. Because the people will not take refuge in God's protection, it will feel God's punishment.

The meaning of v.8b is disputed. Apparently the image of the river is now abandoned and replaced by that of a bird. But whether this bird has come to rob (cf. Hos. 8.1; Ezek. 17.1ff.), or has settled over the country with outspread wings to protect it, cannot be decided with certainty. If the half-verse comes from Isaiah himself,

---

[a] The name *šilōaḥ* is, as is shown by the article, intended to be a proper noun. From its derivation from *šālaḥ* II, 'to stretch out, to send', it can be translated with Procksch as 'the sender'. This does not mean that its name conceals a special meaning capable of a theological interpretation.

[b] Cf. II Kings 20.20; II Chron. 32.30.

[c] Cf. J. Simons, *Jerusalem in the Old Testament*, Leiden, 1952, pp. 175ff.; L. H. Vincent and M. Steve, *Jérusalem de l'Ancien Testament* I, Paris, 1954, pp. 289ff.; Lindblom, StKHVL, 1957–1958, 4, p. 43.

[d] Following Elliger, *ZAW* 53, 1955, p. 18, against Gressmann, *Messias*, pp. 239ff. and Kaiser, ATD 17, 1960, pp. 82f.

then the bird is to be understood as the Assyrian army, from whose attack no escape is possible in the whole country. The purpose of the concluding cry 'O Immanuel' would then be to remind anyone reading the 'testimony'[a] of what was said in 7.10–17: Yahweh's warning for the Davidic kingdom remains in force beyond the period of peace which begins with the defeat of the Aramaeans and Israelites. In the other case, the bird would have to be taken as Yahweh himself (cf. Pss. 17.8; 36.7), who settles over his country to protect it, and here v. 8b would have to be regarded as an addition written in a period which saw 7.14–16 as a prophecy of salvation. If the two possible interpretations are weighed against one another, it seems more likely that Isaiah is the author, since a redactor would perhaps have given clearer expression to a hope which contradicted his text (cf. 29.5f.), and this means that the wings can be thought of as different sections of the army.

Whether this prophecy of warning was ever uttered by Isaiah, or was first made public when the prophecies gathered together in his 'testimony' were written down, can no longer be decided with certainty. However, it is notable that it lacks any direct address, so that the form in which we find it at present must derive from the time when it was written down ('this people' in v. 6).

In applying this prophecy to his own situation, the Christian must remember that a simple application of Old Testament texts, ignoring the cross and resurrection of Jesus Christ, is forbidden to the church of the New Testament. According to Protestant thought, it is neither the task of the church as the church, nor of the Christian as a Christian, to give specific and binding political instructions, but to convince, educate and comfort the conscience by the preaching of the law and the gospel revealed in Jesus Christ.[b]

[a] Cf. the comment on 6.1.

[b] Cf. the detailed discussion by K. E. Løgstrup, *Die Ethische Forderung*, Tübingen, 1959, pp. 122ff.

CHAPTER 8.9–10

God is with us

9 ⟨Know it⟩,[a] you people, and be dismayed.
   Give ear, all far places of the earth.
   Gird yourselves and be dismayed.
10 Take counsel thoroughly, that it may fail.
   Speak of the matter; it will not stand.
   For God is with us.

[9–10] Repeated attempts have been made to isolate this short hymn of triumph from its present situation, and to interpret it on the basis of situations other than that assumed by its immediate context,[b] without coming to any definite result. As far as its content is concerned, it can easily be associated either with the prophecy of warning against Judah which precedes in vv. 5–8, or with the confession of the prophet which follows in vv. 11–15. If the hymn is read in association with the prophecy of warning, it gives him assurance that the Assyrian attack which is to come will no more attain the aim it sets itself, of destroying Judah, than her present enemies Aram and Israel. Since v. 8a prophesies extreme danger, but not real annihilation, there is no direct contradiction between the two passages. As 10.5ff. shows, Isaiah saw Assyria as Yahweh's rod of correction, but not as the instrument of Judah's destruction. If the hymn is read in association with the verses that follow, it provides the basis for the warning in vv. 11ff.: because God is with his people, those who fear him have no reason to be terrified at the intrigues of the enemies of their country. But since by including such a hymn of triumph Isaiah would have removed the ultimate seriousness of his previous prophecy of judgment against Judah, it is improbable that he himself included it when he wrote the testimony[c] in which he gathered together his prophecies from the period of the war with Syria and Ephraim.

ᵃ Cf. *BH*.

ᵇ Cf. Lindblom, StKHVL, 1957–1958, 4, p. 32. Fichtner, *ZAW* 63, 1951, p. 22, also sees this passage as belonging to the period of the war with Syria and Ephraim, but at the same time deletes the phrase 'For God is with us' and regards it as an oracle of Yahweh, while Eichrodt regards it as an oracle of consolation for the disciples in the face of the preparations for war on the part of the coalition against Assyria and against Judah.

ᶜ Cf. above on 6.1.

Consequently, it should be regarded as a later interpolation adapted to the needs of worship.

The background to the hymn, which could in fact have been a fragment of a psalm which was generally known at the time, but has not come down to us, is probably formed by faith in the ultimate inviolability of the city of God, such as is expressed in Pss. 46, 48 and 76.[a] Although enemies conspire against Jerusalem, they will not be able to conquer the city of God, because Yahweh will annihilate them. In Ps. 46 we also encounter the phrase 'Immanuel', 'God with us', in a comparable context. The enemies of the people of God and of the city of God will not attain the goal that they have set themselves, because God's goal is different. Only that part of human plans and devices which is in accord with his plan and purpose will attain its aim (cf. Pss. 33.10f.; 81.12; Prov. 21.30). If the significance of the similarities to the passage described above are taken seriously, it is clear that the phrase 'God is with us' was not regarded by the redactor as a guarantee of salvation, effective as by magic, but that he was aware of the presence of the God whose ultimate aim is of course a fellowship of salvation with his people, but who brings about his salvation not by overlooking sin, but by judging it.

The church of the new covenant will be reminded here of the promises given in Matt. 28.20; 16.18 and John 5.21–24.

CHAPTER 8.11–15

Right Standards

11   For Yahweh spoke thus to me, when his hand seized me, and
        he warned me
        not to walk in the way of this people, saying,
12   'Do not call difficulty,[b]
        all that this people call difficulty,
        and what it fears, do not fear
        and do not dread.

---

[a] Cf. Weiser, *The Psalms*, and Kraus, BK XV, on the psalms referred to.
[b] On the literal meaning of *qešer* cf. Driver, *JTS*, N.S. 6, 1955, pp. 82ff.

13   Yahweh Sebaoth, him you shall regard as ⟨difficult⟩ᵃ
      and he shall be your fear and your dread.
14   And he will become the ⟨reason for difficulty⟩ᵇ and stone of
      offence,
      and a rock of stumbling
      to both houses of Israel,
      and a trap and a snare
      to the inhabitants of Jerusalem.
15   And many among themᶜ shall stumble
      and shall fall and be broken
      and shall be snared and taken.'

[11–15] The introduction in v. 11 gives the whole passage the character of a confession on the part of the prophet. In content, it consists of a prophecy of warning and a threat. Isaiah explains here how he attained an unshakable peace, while the court and the people were seized by profound emotion because of the news of an alliance against the Davidic dynasty between the Aramaean state of Damascus and Israel (cf. 7.2). His own attitude is not in some way the consequence of a better political insight or a more robust nature, but of divine inspiration. In a state in which he felt himself seized by God,ᵈ a state probably anticipated by bodily and mental tension, he heard the warning voice of Yahweh, which sets to right all distorted earthly standards. The plural form of address in v. 12 clearly identifies Isaiah with a group which is not described more closely, and opposes him to 'this people', the people of the southern kingdom in general. One can hardly be wrong in supposing that in the short period which had passed since his call in 735, a body of followers (cf. the comment on v. 16) had gathered about him, to whom he at once imparted this warning, and to strengthen whose faith he may have composed the testimonyᵉ of which the present passage also forms a part.

ᵃ Cf. *BH*.
ᵇ Read, with Driver, *lᵉmaqšir*.
ᶜ Cf. Gk and Vg.
ᵈ For the expression 'to be seized by the hand of Yahweh' cf. I Kings 18.46; II Kings 3.15; Ezek. 1.3; 3.22; 33.22, and the remarks of F. Haeussermann, *Wortempfang und Symbol in der alttestamentlichen Prophetie*, BZAW 58, Giessen, 1932, pp. 22ff., and Seierstad, *Die Offenbarungserlebnisse der Propheten Amos, Jesaja und Jeremia*, SNVAO, 1946, II, 2, Oslo 1946, pp. 176ff., who points out that the phrase does not have any particular empirical state of affairs in mind, but merely attributes an extraordinary happening to the work of Yahweh.
ᵉ Cf. the comment on 6.1.

The people's self-assessment at the present moment is based entirely upon the difficult situation which they face in the aims adopted by the enemy alliance.[a] They regard themselves as in apparently insurmountable danger, which appears to drive them into the arms of the Assyrian king, as the only escape (cf. 7.2). The community of those who have recognized God in his deity, and who believe that he meant seriously the promises he gave when he set up the royal dynasty and the people, must not follow the rest of the people in this course. They must never lose sight of the fact that Yahweh Sebaoth is Lord over all possibilities (v. 13, cf. the comment on 6.3) and is therefore the true ruler of history, who really casts into hopeless difficulty those who do not fear him but fear men. Whoever fears God thinks of him as the living God, who watches over the maintenance of his will. Consequently, the real danger for the southern kingdom does not lie in the intentions of the allies, or in groups which sympathize with them, but in the failure to be aware of the constant presence of God who judges it (cf. 18b). For those who believe he is a firm rock, to which they can flee in every danger (v. 14a, cf. 17.10; Deut. 32.4; Pss. 18.2; 31.2f.; 42.9; 62.7; 71.3), but for those who rebel a stone of offence and of ruin (vv. 14b–15, cf. Luke 2.34; Rom. 9.33; I Peter 2.8). Just as someone wandering in the night suddenly stumbles over a stone and falls to the ground, or on a mountain steps upon a loose fragment of rock and falls, the people of the covenant, in all three states, both in the northern kingdom and the double kingdom of Jerusalem and Judah, will be smitten unexpectedly by the judgment of God. And just as wild animals fall into the nets and snares of the trapper as they flee from the hunter, they will fall into the hands of God as they flee from human power. When these images are applied to political reality they mean that in their faithless efforts to avert the danger the whole people of the covenant will themselves fall into difficulties which will bring them great numbers[b] of dead and prisoners. By imparting this revelation to his disciples and writing it down for the future, Isaiah was preparing the holy remnant which

[a] That *qešer* alludes to a party within Judah which sympathized with the enemy, as suggested recently by Lindblom, StKHVL, 1957–1958, 4, p. 30, and Fohrer, cannot be confirmed, but is likely in view of 7.6, since the son of Tabe-el must have had some adherents.

[b] By contrast with its equivalents in English and German, the Hebrew *rabbīm* must be understood not in a partitive but in a generalizing sense; cf. my essay *Der Königliche Knecht*, FRLANT 70, Göttingen 1959, p. 90; J. Jeremias, *The Eucharistic Words of Jesus*, rev. ed., tr. N. Perrin, 1966, pp. 227ff.

was to endure in the catastrophe (cf. 6.13), and would recognize the hand of God in the blows that fell.

CHAPTER 8.16–18

I Hope in Him

16 Let me bind up the testimony,
⟨seal⟩ᵃ the teaching through my disciples,
17 and I will wait for Yahweh,
who is hiding his face
from the house of Jacob,
and I will hope in him.
18 Behold, here am I, and the children
whom Yahweh gave to me
they are from Yahweh Sebaoth,
who dwells on Mount Zion.

[16–18] Whereas the previous passage only retains the character of a confession by the prophet because of the introduction in v. 11, the present passage belongs to the same category by its whole content. In the moment of his call, Isaiah experienced the presence of God, who is holy and brings judgment. Thereafter he heard his voice time and again, and delivered the message given to him. But what was foretold to him at the beginning of his career (cf. 6.9f.) was constantly confirmed: the people did not hear his voice. His struggle for the faith of the king and the people at the beginning of the war with Syria and Ephraim had remained without success. Thereupon Yahweh had commissioned him to prophesy to him at the same time a coming judgment (cf. 7.10–17; 8.5–8, 12–15) and so to take up again the theme of his prophecies before the outbreak of hostilities (cf. 2.6–22; 3.1–15; 3.16–4.1; 5.1–7, 8–24; 10.1–4; 9.8–20; 5.25, 26–30). This meant that in the first instance his activity was concluded. It now became his task to await in silence the confirmation of his word. The present passage is the conclusion of his prophecies from the year 733, albeit enlarged along the same lines by vv. 19–22; Isaiah himself

ᵃ Cf. *BH*.

seems to have written them down upon a roll as a witness for the future, and they form the substance of the so-called 'testimony'[a] of 6.1–9.7.

Just as Isaiah displayed the sheet 8.1–4 in the presence of Uriah and Zechariah, the son of Jeberechiah, he now proposes to bind up and seal what he has written down in the presence of his disciples (v. 16). The way in which this careful preservation was carried out was that the written roll was first wrapped in linen and then sealed. Then it was placed in an earthenware jar which was likewise closed with a clay seal (cf. Jer. 32.14; Isa. 29.11). The discoveries at Qumran have provided ample evidence of this practice. The word *tōrāh*, instruction (cf. the comment on 2.3), signifies, like *teʿūdā*, a solemnly proclaimed exhortation and testimony, the prophet's preaching as legitimized by God. Whom the word *limmudīm*, disciples, actually refers to is no longer known, since further evidence is lacking. They are probably to be sought among the temple personnel, to whom perhaps prophets in training also belong.[b] But the meaning of the action is unequivocal: they will subsequently be able to testify that Isaiah did not compose or edit his prophecies later on the basis of what had happened, but that he wrote them down and sealed them in this form and no other.[c] We must not overlook the note of lamentation in his confession (v. 17). Like one whose prayer is a lamentation (cf.

[a] Cf. the comment on 6.1.

[b] Cf. A. R. Johnston, *The Cultic Prophet in Ancient Israel*, Cardiff, [2]1962, p. 62; also Jer. 35.4 and G. Widengren, *Literary and Psychological Aspects of the Hebrew Prophets*, UUÅ 1948, 10, p. 115; but cf. *ibid.* p. 69 n. 4.

[c] With regard to its syntactical structure and to its meaning v. 16 is disputed. In accordance with the rule followed here, the punctuation of the second infinitive is altered to make both absolutes, understood in a cohortative sense. Because of the continuation in v. 17 there are difficulties in interpreting it as an infinitive. Depending upon whether one takes the statement in v. 16 in a literal or a metaphorical sense, it will be translated either 'through my disciples' or else 'with' or 'in' my disciples. If it is taken metaphorically, Isaiah is comforting himself with the thought that his work has not been entirely without success, but that he has found a group of adherents, in whose hearts it is preserved like a well wrapped and sealed roll of writing. One must admit that this interpretation is possible. But the literal interpretation of a passage must be preferred as long as it can be maintained meaningfully and without artificiality. – Fohrer, who prefers the metaphorical interpretation, deletes 'through my disciples' as a later addition. – Reference to Jer. 7.9f. (Duhm) and Isa. 5.5f. (Lindblom) shows that the alteration of *ḥatōm* into *ḥātōm* is to be preferred to the Massoretic text and the view now taken by Rignell, *StTh* 10, 1957, p. 47, as does the consideration of the context. Rignell regards v. 16 as a reference back to the procedure described in 8.1–4.

Ps.25.3, 5; 71.14; [Isa.40.31]; Lam.3.25) he is affirming that he
looks forward to the intervention of his God which will confirm his
words, God who has turned his face away from his people and thereby
delivered them up for judgment (cf. Num.6.25f.; Pss.80.3; 51.11).
The Hebrew words for both 'wait' and 'hope' really signify a condition of acute tension.[a] Hope is the tense expectation of some future
possibility of life, towards which man strains inwardly.[b] Isaiah, however, is not looking forward simply to his own future, but in the first
place to the fulfilment of the divine proclamation of judgment and in
the second place to the future of his people.[c] For within his expectation of the fulfilment of his prophecy of judgment there is contained
the tacit hope that those who escape in the catastrophe will be convinced of the rightness of his prophecy and so return to God (v.18).
Like a witness in a public hearing, he defends the truth of his words
with his whole being and with his children. These words form a
conscious parallel to the first 'Here am I! Send me' (6.8). Isaiah
knows that God's words are true. Just as on that occasion he had
placed himself at God's disposal as a messenger, he now stands with
his children as a living word in the midst of his people. Their names,
with the meaning they carry (cf. the comment on 7.3 and 8.3), are
known to everyone. They point to the imminent fall of Israel and
Damascus, to the coming judgment upon Judah, to the remnant, and
to the opportunity of repentance which has been missed, and yet
which still remains. The God who gave him these children, and
appointed those names for them, will not abandon him (cf.50.7ff).
He solemnly refers to him who has taken responsibility for the
prophet's own words and actions, Yahweh Sebaoth, who appears as
judge in his sanctuary upon Zion (cf.Ps.50).

[a] The verb *qwh* is related to the Accadian word *qū*, 'a measuring line', the
cuneiform sign for which originally represented a weight which drew out the
thread as it was spun.

[b] Cf. Emil Brunner, *Das Ewige als Zukunft und Gegenwart*, Zürich, 1955, p.7:
'What oxygen is to the lungs, hope is to human existence.'

[c] Lindblom, StKHVL, 1957–1958, 4, p.49, rightly.

CHAPTER 8.19–22

A Warning against Superstition

19 And when they say to you,
'Ask those who return^a and the knowing ones,
who chirp and mutter.
Should not every people consult its gods,
the dead on behalf of the living?'
20 To the teaching and to the testimony!
If they do not speak in this way,
there is no dawn for them.^b
21 They will pass away in accordance with them,^c
oppressed and hungry.
And when they hunger, they will be enraged
and will curse their king and their God,
and will look upwards ²²and glance down at the earth.
But there is distress and darkness,
gloom and anguish,
the thick darkness of those who are driven out.

[19–22] Isaiah speaks once again, to fortify his disciples against superstitious voices which may attempt to shake them in their faith in the word of God which he has proclaimed (v. 19). In times of distress, superstition is always rife where true faith is lacking, and the followers of many magical practices now come into the light of day because of the threat from the coalition with Syria and Ephraim, and attempt to persuade the people to seek an interpretation of the future by means of mysterious conjurations. Just as in the night before the decisive battle on Mount Gilboa Saul went away in disguise to consult the witch of Endor (cf. I Sam. 28), the people are now being asked to consult the spirits of the dead, who are known as 'those who return', and because of their mysterious knowledge, 'the knowing ones'. It was generally recognized that all practices of this sort in Israel carried a sentence of death (cf. Lev. 19.31; 20.6; Deut. 18.10f.; Lev. 20.27),^d but the attempt would have been made to persuade the

---

^a According to Eichrodt, *Theology of the Old Testament* II, p. 215, the Hebrew '*ōb* is perhaps related to the Arabic root '*wb*, 'to come back', and would then originally refer to the dead person as one who returns, a *revenant*. Cf. also Baumgärtel, *TDNT* VI, pp. 364f.

^b Hebrew 'it', i.e. the people, the population of Jerusalem and Judah.

^c *bāh* refers, according to Rignell, *StTh* 10, p. 49, to *tōrāh* and *te'ūdā* in v. 20.

^d Cf. the comment on 2.6.

people that this was nothing but unjustified prejudice: for people everywhere consulted their dead, because they were regarded as sharing in the gods' knowledge. Isaiah is firmly convinced that there is no way which can lead to a happier future for his people if it ignores the teaching and exhortation given in his prophecies. Only when the people recognize that their continuance depends entirely upon their genuine trust in God (cf. the comment on 7.9) and consequently accord real belief to his words, can they escape from their distress. At the moment people are afraid of the approaching enemy and are seeking counsel among the dead, instead of listening to his words. This means that their distress will become greater and greater, in accordance with his prophecies. Plagued by hunger (cf. 7.15, 21, 23a, 24) they will curse their king and their God, because they see no possible escape, and will finally stagger into slavery in a foreign country (vv. 21–22).

CHAPTER 9.1–7[a]

The Great Feast of Liberation and Peace

1   *But there will be no gloom*
    for (the land) which is being oppressed.[b]
    As in the past
    ⟨Yahweh⟩[c] dealt contemptuously
    ⟨with the plain of Sharon and the mountain of Gilead⟩,[d]
    and land of Zebulun
    and the land of Naphtali,[e]
    so later he will make glorious
    the way of the sea,
    the land beyond the Jordan,
    the circle of the nations.

ᵃ 8.23–9.6 in Hebrew and German.

ᵇ Verse 1a is a redactor's gloss.

ᶜ With Alt, 'Jesaja 8.12–96, Befreiungsnacht und Krönungstag', *Kleine Schriften* II, p. 209, add 'Yahweh'.

ᵈ Cf. *ibid.*, pp. 209ff.

ᵉ *'arṣā* is an Aramaism, or else an old accusative; cf. Rignell, *StTh* 10, and Gesenius-Kautsch, 28th ed., §§90f.

2   The people who walk in darkness
     see a great light.
     On the inhabitants of the land of deep darkness[a]
     a light shines.

3   Thou makest ⟨the rejoicing⟩[b] great,
     thou increasest the joy,
     they rejoice before thee,
     like the rejoicing at the harvest,
     as they rejoice
     at the dividing of the spoil.

4   For the yoke of his burden,
     and the bar[c] of his shoulder,
     and the stick[d] of his oppressor
     thou breakest as on the day of Midian.

5   For every boot
     treading in tumult,
     and ⟨every⟩[e] garment
     rolled in blood,
     will become burnt,
     food for the fire:

6   'For to us a child is born,
     a son is given to us.
     And the government will be
     upon his shoulders.
     He called his name:
     He who plans wonders[f]
     Mighty God,
     Everlasting Father,
     Prince of Peace
     . . . .'[g]

Throne names given to a new King on his accession. Salvation hopes of Isaiah are tied to the Davidic line of Kings

7   ⟨   ⟩[g] Great is the rule
     and no end to the peace
     upon the throne of David,
     and in his kingdom,

[a] The Massoretic punctuation, which gives 'shadow of death', derives from a popular etymology. For the real derivation of the word cf. the Accadian ṣalāmu, 'to be black'.

[b] Cf. *BH*.

[c] Actually 'the rod'.

[d] The mention of *šēbet* together with the yoke implies, as stated by Dalman, *Arbeit und Sitte* II, p. 120, that it was a substitute for the ox-goad.

[e] With Alt, *Kl. Schriften* II, p. 214, add *kōl*.

[f] Cf. Wildberger, *ThZ* 16.4 (*Eichrodt-Festschrift*), 1960, p. 316.

[g] Only the end of the fifth throne name is preserved.

because he sets it up
and upholds it
with justice and with righteousness
from now unto eternity.
The zeal of Yahweh Sebaoth
will do this.

[1–7] Albrecht Alt is responsible for having demonstrated the correctness of the chapter division of the Latin Bible,[a] and the fact, assumed by Matt. 4.15f., that 9.1–7 forms a unity.[b] In the two campaigns of Tiglath-pileser in 734 and 732 there took place the separation of the western, eastern and northern provinces of Israel, assumed by v. 1, and their transformation into Assyrian provinces.[c] The faith of the Israelites was thereby faced with the question whether God had abandoned his people and his land for ever to the enemies of Israel, or whether he intended to reunite them and awaken them to new life under a glorious ruler, corresponding to the ideal picture described in the royal psalms. Here, as in 10.33–11.8, Isaiah is making a confession of faith in the future of his people, which is based upon God's purpose of salvation. For the sake of his glorification in the sight of the nations he will fulfil the promises he has given, and bring to reality an empire in which all Israel is united and at peace, under a second David. This oracle of salvation falls quite naturally into five stanzas. First, v. 1 promises a reversal, brought about by God, of the fate of the separated districts. The second, vv. 2f., takes on the tone of a hymn, and describes the rejoicing of the redeemed before their God. The third, vv. 4f., gives the reason for this, with its reference to the liberation and to the final victory of Yahweh over his enemies. In the fourth, v. 6, the people themselves join in the hymn and proclaim the enthronement of the redeemer. In the fifth and last stanza, corresponding to the *Abgesang* or *envoi* of the mastersingers, the prophet emphasizes that the change will be an enduring one, and that he has confidence in the fulfilment of his words. If one wishes to describe the literary category into which this unique poem falls, one might call it a prophetic hymn of thanksgiving transformed into a prophecy of salva-

[a] See above, p. 123 note a.
[b] For an opposite view cf. Lindblom, StKHVL 1957–1958, 4, pp. 39f., Fohrer and Eichrodt, *ad loc.*, as well as H. P. Müller, *EvTh* 21, 1961, pp. 408f. and H. W. Wolff, *Friede ohne Ende*, BSt 35, Neukirchen, 1962, pp. 60f.
[c] Cf. Alt, *Kleine Schriften* II, pp. 206ff. The present interpretation follows Alt directly only in the understanding of 9.1.

tion.[a] The prophetic character as a whole is explicitly emphasized by the conclusion. Consequently, it is pointless to relate this prophecy to the birth of a prince or the enthronement of a Davidic king during Isaiah's lifetime.[b] For Isaiah, at his encounter with Ahaz, the ruling line of the royal house of Judah lay under judgment (cf. 7.15; 11.1).

[1] *The change of fortune.* The prophet, who had foretold the total collapse of the northern kingdom itself (cf. chs. 7 and 8), added to his 'testimony' a prophecy of salvation for the Israelite districts annexed by Assyria in connection with the war with Syria and Ephraim. The anger of God is not the end of all he has to do, but a transition to a new act of grace. For the sake of his glorification in the sight of the nations (cf. v. 7)[c] he will not abandon his people of the twelve tribes in the future. He himself will bring a new prosperity and freedom to the land which is oppressed at his command.[d] In 734, Tiglath-pileser III separated the coastal districts belonging to the kingdom of Israel and transformed them into a province called Du'ru after its capital Dor.[e] In 732 the same fate befell the north and the east. The plain of Jezreel and Galilee became the province Magidū with Megiddo as its capital, and the land across the Jordan, the province Gal'azu.[f] These areas, the 'way of the sea' presumably being the coastal district,[g] the 'circle of the nations', Galilee, and the 'land beyond the Jordan', which as seen from Jerusalem was of course Transjordan,[h] are once again to be restored to glory by Yahweh; and that

[a] Cf. von Rad, *The Problem of the Hexateuch and other Essays*, pp. 230f.; Lindblom, StKHVL 1957–1958, 4, p. 34.

[b] M. B. Crook, *JBL* 68, 1949, pp. 213ff., interprets the passage of Joash, and it is not necessary to oppose his view explicitly. But the suggestion of Rignell, *LuQ* 7, 1955, p. 34, that the child is Israel, is too bold.

[c] Cf. Ezek. 36.36; 37.28; Isa. 44.23.

[d] This, however, does not mean that he does not make use of any human assistance in the process, as the poem is understood by Gressmann and Alt. They also make the enthronement follow immediately upon the act of liberation, without there being any recognizable outward connection between the two, far less any congruence in time.

[e] Cf. Alt, *Kleine Schriften*, II, p. 157.

[f] *Ibid.*, pp. 210f.

[g] Procksch thought this referred to the road from the country east of the Jordan to Galilee, while Rignell took it for the road along the west side of the Sea of Galilee.

[h] Rignell's suggestion that the expression alludes to names in use before the settlement, so that it represents the ancient promises given before the entry, in which case the land beyond the Jordan would be west of the Jordan (*StTh* 10, 1957, p. 52) is not convincing.

means being taken into the federation of his new and strengthened people.[a]

[2–3] *The rejoicing of the redeemed.* Just as a wanderer after a long and fearful night joyfully greets the rising sun, the liberated people will receive the salvation given to them by God. The light that will appear to them is the presence of God which annihilates his enemies (cf. 10.17; Pss. 50.2; 27.1; 104.2).[b] It is not the hand of man (cf. 31.8) but the direct intervention of God which will drive out the enemy. The prophet's account turns at once into a hymn, which anticipates the celebration of the great acts of God. Consequently, in v. 3 he addresses himself directly to God. The redeemed will rejoice before the face of Yahweh as at the harvest or the sharing out of spoil. For the people of that time, the harvest possessed a much more pointed significance than at the present day, where the food supply, at least in time of peace and in Europe, has become almost independent of the seasons. Then, as for many people today in other parts of the world, it signifies the end of a long period of hunger.[c]

[4–5] *The inauguration of the kingdom of peace.* In accordance with the practice in hymns, there now follows the reason for the rejoicing. What the prophet has referred to in the second stanza is now described in detail and confirmed. Those who are enslaved under the burden of tribute and forced labour are again compared to draught animals who are urged to their work by their driver with a stick. Here the image and the reality coincide (cf. Ex. 5.6ff.; Job. 39.7). But the burdensome yoke of foreign rule will be taken from them, and will be broken by Yahweh as previously on the day of Midian. Then Gideon, the saviour inspired by God, struck the Midianites who were camping in the plain of Jezreel (cf. Judg. 6.33ff.). Just as Yahweh freed the north at that time (cf. Judg. 7.9ff.), he will free it again now. The help given at that time was transitory, and wars and the tumult of war once again prevailed among the nations. This day of Midian will not merely hold back the nation's enemies for a certain period. It will

[a] Ginsberg, *Eretz Israel* 5, 1958, pp. 61ff., does not convince me by his suggestion that v. 1 contains a contrast between the time of Pekah and that of Hoshea.

[b] Cf. also 30.27ff.

[c] Cf. H. Guthe, *Palästina*, Bielefeld and Leipzig, ²1927, p. 41: 'The days spent on the threshing floor are the most joyful in the whole year for the farmer and his family, and indeed for the whole village.' It is natural that the joy of harvest should be recalled to describe the utmost degree of joy: 'The main occupation of those who live in the country is agriculture, and what does the farmer enjoy more than the harvest?'

make all wars whatsoever impossible in the future. What the congregation anticipated in the songs of Zion in the sacred feast (Pss. 49.9f.; 76.4) will now finally be fulfilled: in one last great battle the enemies of the people and of God will finally be conquered, and warrior's boots and bloodstained military cloaks will be done away with for ever as useless (cf. 2.4).

[6] *The enthronement of the saviour king.* The fourth stanza has an even loftier theme: the night of liberation is followed by the day of coronation. The herald[a] comes to those who have been set free with the news that a descendant of David has ascended the throne,[b] his rule once again including the whole people of the twelve tribes. 'To us a child is *born.*' But as Ps. 2.7 clearly shows, this is no more than an expression for the adoption of the king by God in the moment in which he ascends the throne.[c] In the case of this king all the enthronement ceremonies are more than an ideal meant to be achieved later, but never in fact attained.[d] They are simply a further testimony of what God has already brought to reality through him: the government has been given to him. As a sign of this the sceptre lies upon his shoulder (cf. Ps. 110.2). And the titles he bears, which set out the programme for his reign and promise him good fortune,[e] are given to him by his father when he is raised to the status of a son: He who plans wonders; Mighty God; Everlasting Father; Prince of

[a] Cf. Alt, *Kleine Schriften* II, pp. 220ff.

[b] Von Rad, *Old Testament Theology* II, pp. 171ff., and W. Harrelson, *Muilenberg-Festschrift*, 1962, p. 151, regard the avoidance of the royal title for the bringer of salvation as a polemic against the kings of Jerusalem who no longer had any loyalty to Yahweh, or else as an emphasis on Yahweh as the only king, cf. Isa. 6.5.

[c] Mowinckel, *He That Cometh*, Oxford, 1956, pp. 102–110, sees v. 6 as the proclamation of the birth of a prince. He regards the whole passage, vv. 2–7, as post-Isaianic or pre-exilic. Lindblom, StKHVL, 1957–1958, 4, pp. 36ff., also regards v. 6 as the proclamation of the physical birth of a royal child, who is in fact Immanuel, whom he identifies with Hezekiah. He cautiously rejects the objection to this view which is based on II Kings 16.2 and 18.2: 'Unfortunately enough the chronological notices in II Kings referring to Ahaz and his son Hezekiah are, as we know, very uncertain and inconsistent. But much can be said in favour of the opinion of those in older and more recent time who hold that Immanuel is Hezekiah' (*ibid.*, p. 41). He regards vv. 2–7 as composed by Isaiah and v. 1 as secondary.

[d] Cf. von Rad, *Old Testament Theology* I, pp. 320f. On the royal ritual of Judah cf. his *The Problem of the Hexateuch and Other Essays*, pp. 222ff.

[e] Cf. W. Vischer, ThSt(B) 45, 1955, pp. 40ff.; H. Wildberger, ThZ 16.4, pp. 314–32.

Peace. The fifth and last seems to be lost.[a] The first name signifies that this king will need no outside advice and that his own plans, which extend to the whole world, will attain their goal, because God guides his thoughts (cf. 25.1; Ps. 20.4).[b] The second[c] emphasizes the fulness of his power and is reminiscent of the 'spirit of heroic virtue' (11.1; cf. also Pss. 20.6; 21.1, 13). Only here and in Ps. 45.6 is the king referred to as 'god' in the Old Testament. The concept of the king as the son of God in physical terms, which is found particularly in Egypt, was transformed in Jerusalem, according to Pss. 2.7; 89.26f.; and II Sam. 7.14, into a relationship of father and child that derived from an act of adoption. The meaning of this name is unequivocal: it describes the king as the legitimate representative of God upon earth. The next title has in mind his enduring (cf. II Sam. 7.16), fatherly, beneficent, and righteous rule.[d] The last extant name, 'Prince of Peace', is reminiscent of the divine name from Judg. 6.24, 'Yahweh is peace', and also of Isaiah 11.6–9 (cf. also Ps. 72.3, 7).[e] For the Israelites, peace was more than the absence of war or the continuation of war by other means; peace is a term for the condition in which all

[a] It is necessary especially because of the fivefold Egyptian throne name; cf. H. Frankfort, *Kingship and the Gods*, Chicago, 1948, pp. 46f.; A. H. Gardiner, *Egyptian Grammar*, Oxford, ²1950, pp. 71ff. H. Ranke, *ZÄSA* 79, 1954, pp. 72f., pp. 73f., gives an Egyptian example of an imaginary fivefold royal title: 'The leader–free from greed; the Great One–free from meanness; destroying lies, creating truth, coming at the voice of him who calls.'

[b] 'Counsel', *y's*, includes in Hebrew both the decision and its carrying out. Cf. J. Pedersen, *Israel, its Life and Culture*, I–II, London and Copenhagen, 1926 (1954), pp. 128ff.; S. Mowinckel, *ZAW* 73, 1961, pp. 297f.: ' "Counsel" therefore forms part of the psychical armament of the ruler; he has "counsel" in himself, puts it into operation and affirms it, and ensures that it continues in being.'

[c] For the translation 'Mighty God' cf. Deut. 10.17; Jer. 32.18; Ps. 45.5, 9; Gressmann, *Messias*, p. 245; McClellan, *CBQ* 6, 1941, pp. 276ff.; Wildberger, *ThZ* 16.4 pp. 316f.

[d] Gressmann, *Messias*, p. 245, refers to the attribute applied to the Egyptian king: 'who ever and eternally gives life like his father Re every day'. Widengren, *Sakrales Königtum*, Stuttgart, 1955, p. 106 n. 70, refers to such Mesopotamian divine epithets as 'Father of the Land'. For the Israelite conception cf. Lam. 4.20 and also – with some caution – the Hymn of the Courtiers to Rameses II in Kees, *Religiongeschichtliches Lesebuch*, ed. Bertholet, 10, Tübingen, ²1928, p. 41; and especially with W. Vischer, ThSt(B) 45, p. 44, Pss. 132.12–14; 89.26ff.; 21.4–6 and I Kings 2.45.

[e] W. Harrelson, *Muilenberg-Festschrift*, p. 153, suggests that this is an allusion to Judg. 6.24, but in spite of v. 4 this seems far-fetched. Similarly he believes that the other throne names contain allusions to charismatic judges.

things, human beings, animals and plants, follow their destiny undisturbed. Thus it only exists when all creatures recognize God in his
deity and live and act accordingly.[a] In the background of the throne
names is the royal ideology of Jerusalem, which in its turn is influenced by that of Egypt. David himself, when he ascended the
throne of the ancient Jebusite capital, took on a similar throne name
in four parts, or, if one includes his father's name, in five parts: 'David,
the son of Jesse; . . . the man whom Elyon has set up; the anointed
of the God of Jacob; the favourite of the warriors of Israel.'[b] With
the coming of this king, the history of the human race, characterized
by unrest, strife and devastation, approaches its conclusion. He will
bring to the world an all-embracing and never-ending salvation,
because he and his descendants will exercise their office on this earth
as the true representatives of God. The third title does not have in
mind the immortality of this king.

[7] *The envoi.* In the last verse it seems that the prophet himself is
again the speaker. Once more he gives a free summary of what has
been said in the previous stanza, and at the same time carries it a step
further. Only now does he introduce the name of David. Only now
does it become clear what is the source of the prophecy. The new king
will exercise his rule in full power. Peace will never end in his kingdom, as the kingdom itself will not end, because his throne is sus-
tained by justice and righteousness.[c] With the conclusion Isaiah
avoids the objection that he is only uttering human desires and
dreams: for the zeal of Yahweh Sebaoth will carry out everything
which is prophesied here. God is a personal force, not a neutral being
underlying the world. He plays a living part in everything he has
created. He will not share his honour either with men or with gods.
Just as he demands of his adherents that they serve him only (cf.
Ex. 20.5; 34.14; Deut. 4.24), he does not abandon them again for the
sake of his glory in the sight of the nations (cf. Isa. 37.22; 42.13;
63.15). Since he has begun his work with Israel, he will finally bring
it to its consummation in this way, for this is in accordance with his
holiness and his glory, and with his uniqueness.[d]

[a] For the concept 'peace' cf. von Rad, *TDNT* II, pp. 402ff.
[b] Cf. II Sam. 23.1 and H. Cazelles, *Mélanges Bibliques A. Robert*, TICP 4, pp. 122ff.
[c] For justice and righteousness as the supports of the throne cf. H. Brunner,
VT 8, 1958, pp. 426ff. For the Israelite picture of the righteous king cf. below on
11.1–5.
[d] Cf. the definition of the zeal of Yahweh in Dilmann-Kittel, *ad loc.*, '. . . the

CHAPTERS 9.8–21ᵃ AND 5.25–30

'For all this his anger was not turned away'

8 The Lord sent a word against Jacob
and it fell upon Israel.

9 And all the people became aware of it,ᵇ
Ephraim and the inhabitants of Samaria;
⟨[Yet] they spoke⟩ᶜ in pride and arrogance of heart:

10 'If bricks fall, we will build with dressed stones;
if sycamores are cut down, we will put cedars
in their place.'

11 So Yahweh raised up their ⟨adversaries⟩ᵈ
and stirred up their enemies:

12 Aram before and the Philistines behind,
that they might eat Israel with open mouth.
For all this his anger was not turned away,
and his hand was stretched out still.

13 But the people did not turn to him who smote them,
and they did not seek Yahweh Sebaoth.

14 Then *Yahweh* cut off *from* Israelᵉ head and tail,
palm branch and reed in one day.

15 *The elder and courtier were the head,*
and the prophet who preaches lies was the tail,

16 And the leaders of this people led them astray,
and those who were led by them were ruined.

Despite Divine warning the people still spurned God.

---

energy of his holiness, by means of which he gives his glory to no other, lovingly
protects and cherishes everything undertaken for the purposes of his holiness, and
consumes like fire everything that resists his will.' Cf. also Vriezen, *An Outline of Old
Testament Theology*, pp. 149f. For the meaning of the Isaianic expectation of the
coming saviour-king for Christian faith cf. the end of the comment on 10.33–11.9.

ᵃ 9.7–20 in Hebrew and German.

ᵇ Perhaps, as Buhl suggests in Bentzen, we should read *wayyedᵉᶜū*, cf. *BH*.
Winton Thomas, *JTS* 41, 1940, p. 44, and Ap-Thomas, *JTS* 41, 1940, p. 162, see
here the root *ydᶜ*, 'to be humbled', and translate: '. . . and the whole people shall
be subjugated.'

ᶜ Cf. *BH*.

ᵈ Read *ṣōrᵉrāw* with Budde.

ᵉ 'Yahweh' and 'from Israel' are later interpolations. Similarly 'Yahweh' may
originally have stood in place of 'Lord' in vv. 8 and 17.

17 Therefore *the Lord* did not spare[a] their young men
and had no compassion on their fatherless and widows;
for they are all godless and wicked,
and every mouth speaks folly.
For all this his anger was not turned away,
and his hand was stretched out still.

18 For the guilt burned like a fire,
that consumes briars and thorns;
that kindles the thickets of the forest,
and they roll up high in smoke.

19 Beneath the wrath of Yahweh Sebaoth the earth bent down, [b]
and the people became like ⟨consuming fire⟩,[c]
and no man had mercy on his brother.

20b Each devoured ⟨his neighbour's⟩[d] flesh.

20a They snatched on the right and remained hungry,
they ate on the left and were not satisfied.

21 Manasseh Ephraim, and Ephraim Manasseh,
[and] both togther, they [campaigned] against Judah.
For all this his anger was not turned away,
and his hand was stretched out still.

....
....

5 25 Therefore the anger of Yahweh was kindled against his people
and he stretched out his hand against them and smote them.
And the mountains quaked and their corpses remained
as refuse in the midst of the streets.
For all this his anger was not turned away,
and his hand was stretched out still.[e]

26 But he is raising a banner for ⟨a people⟩[f] from afar
and is whistling for them from the ends of the earth,
and see, swiftly, speedily, they will come!

[a] Cf. *BH.*

[b] With W. L. Moran, *CBQ* 12, 1950, pp. 153f., this form is to be regarded as the 3rd sing. fem. perf. of *nwʿ* with an enclitic *mem.*

[c] Cf. *BH.*

[d] Cf. *BH* and place v. 20b in front of v. 20a following Steinmann and Fohrer.

[e] Many scholars regard the whole poem as a proclamation of future punishment and in vv. 11a, 12a and 14a alter the consecutive imperfects into simple imperfects. It is impossible to be certain about the right rendering of the tenses. With Guthe, König, Procksch, Fischer, Kissane, Steinmann, Ziegler and Fohrer, among recent commentators, the Massoretic text has been followed as far as possible. On the relative simultaneity of the imperfect cf. Grether, *Hebräische Grammatik*, §80e.

[f] Cf. *BH.* The *mem* is once again enclitic.

27 None is weary and none stumbles among them.
They will not slumber and will not rest.[a]
They do not loosen their waist-cloth,
and none of their sandal-thongs is broken.

28 Their arrows are sharp,
and all their bows strung.[b]
Their horses hoofs are like flint,
and their chariot wheels like the whirlwind.

29 Their roaring is like a lion.
When ⟨they roar⟩[c] like young lions
and growl and seize their prey
and carry it off, there is none to rescue.

30 *And it thunders over it on that day like the roaring of the sea.*
And if one looks at the land, behold, darkness,
⟨*brightness*⟩[d] *and light darkened in rain squalls.*

9.8–21 and 5.25–30. This poem concerning the anger of God
against the northern kingdom[e] is interrupted by the interpolation of
the so-called 'testimony of Isaiah' (6.1–9.7), from the period of
the war with Syria and Ephraim, into the collection of prophecies
beginning with 2.1. Only the last stanza was allowed to remain in its
former place, albeit in fragmentary form. Its beginning and the bulk
of its content were later linked by means of 10.4b with the woe,
10.1–4a, which probably originally belonged to 5.8–24. Commentators
have generally regarded 5.26–30 as the true conclusion of the poem.
This view is firmly supported by the metre (3+3), by the consistent
use of a stanza of seven lines (apart from the interruptions in 5.14 and
5.25), and by the fact that 5.25b appears to require a prophecy of
judgment following it. 9.8–21 and 5.25 are shown to be a unity by
the refrain which recurs in 9.12, 17, 21 and 5.25. 5.25 is clearly
meant to be preceded by the reason for what it describes, but this has
been lost in the course of the transpositions, either intentionally or by
an oversight. It looks back over God's punishments and judgments in

[a] A gloss, Cf. Ps. 121 4a.
[b] Literally, 'trodden'. The bow was strung immediately before use by standing
on the lower end and forcing the upper end down with the arms.
[c] Cf. *BH*.
[d] Read with Zolli, *ThZ* 6, 1950, p.232, ṣaḥ.
[e] L. Rost, *Israel bei den Propheten*, BWANT IV, 19, 1937, pp.44f., has clearly
shown that in vv.8, 12, 15 and 21 Israel means the northern kingdom. The
decisive verse is v.21; it speaks of 'the battle between the two tribes Ephraim and
Manasseh, which is only interrupted in order to attack Judah'.

the past, its purpose within the whole poem being to provide an accusation on which the judgment which follows is based. Its closest parallel is Amos 4.6–12. It has frequently been supposed that the tenses found in the Massoretic text should be altered so that the whole forms a single prophecy of the future. But such retrospective surveys of the history of man's unfaithfulness and God's punishments seem to have been firmly rooted in the Israelite festival worship from the earliest times. The oldest complete cultic hymn in the Old Testament, the Song of Deborah (Judg. 5), already provides evidence of such a usage. There, vv. 6–8 look back to the period of Israel's unfaithfulness, in the manner of a confession of guilt, and this is followed in v. 11 by a reference to a remembrance of Yahweh's previous acts of salvation in the form of a hymn sung by two alternating groups of singers.[a] Both elements are present in Ps. 78[b] and also in the covenant liturgy of the later Dead Sea community (cf. the Damascus Document, column I). They also form the theological framework of the Book of Judges, as of the whole Deuteronomic history. Apparently Isaiah also shared a similar tradition. But he reapplied it, like Amos, in accordance with his prophetic mission, which was determined by the unfaithfulness of Israel, and concentrated upon the aspect of wickedness showing how it moves relentlessly towards its consummation and conclusion. In spite of the continued division of the nation into northern and southern kingdoms, Isaiah feels himself responsible for the whole of Israel. It is possible that even in his time pilgrims came from the north to the great feast of Yahweh at Jerusalem, and his words here may be specially addressed to them (cf. Jer. 41.5). But since according to the belief of the Old Testament the prophet's word is more than merely the foretelling of a future event, since it actually brings about the future,[c] he did not in fact need direct witnesses of his preaching from the north. The very general terms in which the mention of the word of God in v. 8 and the judgment which follows are expressed make it impossible to fit each statement to the history as we know it. Verse 21 can scarcely assume the events of the war with Syria and Ephraim, but is a general reference to the internal division of the people of God in the period following David, if it is correct to

[a] Cf. Weiser, *ZAW* 71, 1959, pp. 67ff.; *The Psalms*, pp. 30ff., 42ff.; Noth, *EvTh* 12, 1952/53, pp. 6ff.

[b] Cf. Eissfeldt, BAL 104.8, 1958.

[c] Cf. Grether, *Name und Wort Gottes im Alten Testament*, BZAW 64, 1934, pp. 103ff.; Johnson, *The Cultic Prophet in Ancient Israel*, Cardiff, ²1962, pp. 37ff.

relate 5.25 to the earthquake mentioned in Amos 1.1 and 2.13ff.
Since in the concluding prophecy of judgment 5.26–29 the Assyrians
are not mentioned by name, the prophecy must come from the period
before the war with Syria and Ephraim.[a] In spite of uncertainty
about details and obvious gaps, the message of the whole poem is
clear: Yahweh's word of judgment will bring his work to its irrevo-
cable conclusion, because the people have not turned to their God.

[8–12] *The first stanza: God's judgment upon those who despise his word.*
God has uttered a word against the northern kingdom, in order to
warn it and call it back to the right path, which it had abandoned in
the years of economic prosperity during the first six decades of the
eight century. It does not matter to Isaiah which prophet proclaims
this word. A prophet always points beyond himself to him from whom
his calling comes. This word of warning and judgment, once it has
been proclaimed with authority, is effected in history. It has descended, full of power, upon the people of the covenant, by whom, as
is shown by vv.8 and 9, the inhabitants of Samaria and Ephraim are
meant. But those who have heard it have failed to recognize that
when God speaks, he is also acting (cf. 55.10f.; I Sam. 3.11; Hos. 6.5;
Ps. 107.20; Heb. 4.12). Instead of repenting and changing God's mind
by walking in obedience to his will, the people of the central province
and the capital of northern Israel, who are representatives of the
opinion of the whole country, consciously and deliberately rejected a
warning. Whatever blows were to fall upon them in any future war,
they felt themselves able to deal with them by their own power. If the
ancient brick buildings and sycamore trees were to fall at the hands of
hostile invaders (cf. II Kings 3.25; Mal. 1.4), they would rebuild
what had been destroyed and make it even finer. The prophet's word
brought about the precise opposite of what might have been expected
from it by him who uttered it. It provoked the people into an even
more wicked rebellion against God (cf. 6.9ff.; Jer. 1.10). God followed
his words by acts: he roused the enemies of Israel, the Aramaeans of
Damascus and the Philistines, and gave them the power to make a
pincer movement against Israel and inflict heavy defeats, associated
with the annexation of territory.[b] (The power of the Philistines,
which, from the very earliest times, had caused severe difficulties to

---

[a] Here I explicitly withdraw the literary-critical view of the passage advanced
in the first German edition.

[b] For 'devour' in the sense of victorious military undertakings cf. Jer. 2.3;
30.16; 51.34; Ps. 79.7.

Israel, had not been finally crushed, even by David. Together with the Aramaeans, they continued to be greatly feared throughout the period when the nation was divided, until the intervention of the Assyrians crippled them or made them Israel's natural allies.)ᵃ But this was to be only the beginning of the great divine judgment which was to come. The hand of God's judgment still remained stretched out over his people (cf. Ex. 6.6; Deut. 4.34; Ps. 136.12; Isa. 30.30).

[**13–17**] *The second stanza: the blow strikes both high and low in the nation.* Verse 13 gives the reason for the continuing anger of Yahweh: even a severe punishment had been unable to turn the people from their perverse ways. If the people had returned to their God, by subjecting themselves to his will in an act of true repentance (cf. 30.15; 7.3),ᵇ they would have sought him with their whole heart (cf. Amos 5.4, 6; Ex. 18.15; I Sam. 9.9; II Kings 22.18; Jer. 37.7) and he would have inaugurated a new period of salvation. Instead, he sent out his new judgment of punishment over the whole people, whose religious and moral foundations were weakened by the guilt of their political and spiritual leaders, and who were rebelling against their God in their deeds and words. Though there are different degrees of responsibility, the ultimate guilt is the same. Consequently, God's judgment falls not only upon the leaders, but upon the whole people. High and low, head and tail, the noble and magnificent palm branch and the plain reed, the ordinary man, are all destroyed (cf. 19.15; Deut. 28.13, 44).ᶜ Here Isaiah is probably thinking of the events associated with the revolution of Jehu (cf. II Kings 9–10).ᵈ But the new dynasty turned out to be no better (v. 16), so that God had to inflict fresh blows upon his misguided people in the form of terrible wars with the Aramaeans. Neither those in the flower of their youth, nor the widows and orphans who were specially committed to Yahweh's protection (cf. 1.17; 10.2), were spared, for what was not merely godless behaviour, but also godless language (cf. 3.9), had become widespread. But even this did not bring the divine judgment to an end.

[**18–21**] *The third stanza: civil war and fraternal strife.* By failing to

ᵃ Cf. Eissfeldt, *ZDPV* 66, 1943, pp. 115ff.; Noth, *The History of Israel*, 2nd ed., pp. 238ff.

ᵇ For the prophetic use of *šūb*, cf. H. W. Wolff, *ZThK* 48, 1951, pp. 129ff.; W. L. Holladay, *The Root* šūbh *in the Old Testament*, Leiden, 1958, pp. 116ff.

ᶜ Verse 15 is a later, factually correct, but also superfluous explanation of the simile by a later hand.

ᵈ Cf. Fohrer and Eichrodt, *ad loc.*

acknowledge the power of Yahweh at work in all the disasters they have suffered, the people became deeper and deeper entangled with their guilt, so bringing down upon themselves an ever more inexorable divine judgment. Just as a fire lit at the edge of a wood and not properly watched takes hold in the bushes and tufts of grass and weeds, and finally consumes the whole forest in smoke and flames, un-expiated guilt[a] spread throughout Israel in fearful acts of self-inflicted damage. Internecine hatred, nourished by an insatiable lust for power, divided the people, so that brother attacked brother in civil war. Whether Isaiah is thinking here of the struggles for the throne which followed the death of Jeroboam, which were perhaps followed also by tension between Ephraim (cf. II Kings 15.14) and Manasseh (II Kings 15.25), is uncertain, and unlikely if we assume that some sort of chronological sequence has been maintained, since the earthquake referred to in 5.25 is probably that which took place during the reign of Jeroboam (cf. Amos 1.1; 2.13ff.). Perhaps Isaiah is alluding here in general terms to the inner tension within the northern kingdom (cf. Gen. 48.14ff.; Judg. 6.35; 8.1), unless he has in mind other concrete events in the ninth century, of which the tradition is no longer extant. On the same assumption, the attacks upon the southern kingdom which are also mentioned should be seen as referring not to the war with Syria and Ephraim, but to that between Jehoash of Israel and Amaziah of Jerusalem and Judah (cf. II Kings 14.8ff.). However, the conflagration was not limited to the northern kingdom. It also extended to the south. All Isaiah's prophecies of warning against his own homeland are evidence that he did not see this invasion simply as that of a wicked wolf seizing an innocent lamb. All the guilt of the holy people of the covenant, whose holiness was tarnished, received in it a just punishment. And yet he is clearly dominated by the feeling that this civil war is unnatural, for it holds out no future for the attacker. Ultimately, it remained for Isaiah 'a sign of the progressive disintegration of the Israelite state',[b] and therefore of the hand of God, visiting and punishing Israel, and still not ready to forgive. But even this inner self-destruction did not bring the people to their senses.

[5.25] *The fourth stanza: the earthquake.* The lines which describe the next stage in the intensification of the people's sin have not been preserved. The extant material opens with a description of God's

[a] For the meaning of *riš'ā* cf. Deut. 25.2; Ezek. 18.20.
[b] Rost, *Israel bei den Propheten*, p. 45.

action as a consequence of the people's blindness: once again, God
sent his stern punishment. Though one might suppose that it consisted of a fresh war, described in terms of a theophany of judgment
(cf. Judg. 5.4; Ps. 18.8 = II Sam. 22.8; Joel 2.10, etc.), the reference
to bodies lying untended and in heaps in the streets points to a real
earthquake.[a] It is a terrible thing to fall into the hand of the living
God (Heb. 10.31), but it is fatal for the individual, as it is for the
people, not to recognize the fact. Because the people of the covenant
ultimately regarded all these blows merely as 'natural' events, God's
hand remains stretched out over them, ready for new acts of judgment.

[26–30] *The fifth stanza: God's patience is now finally exhausted.* He will
call up a terrible and irresistible enemy from a distant and unknown
country. The prophet lets his audience hear everything from the
gathering of the enemy army to the tumult of destruction as it
advances. In the far distance (cf. 49.1) Yahweh sets up a standard as a
sign to the people whom he has chosen as the instrument of his anger,
for them to gather together (cf. 13.2).[b] Just as the bee-keeper attracts
his numerous and teeming swarm of bees with an irresistible whistling
(cf. 7.18),[c] Yahweh calls up the enemy from the ends of the earth.
For Isaiah, as for his fellow believers, the central point of the world
was naturally seen as being in Jerusalem, the city in whose sanctuary
the true God appears and brings about the proclamation of his word
(cf. 2.2f.; Ps. 72.8; Zech. 9.10; Ecclus. 44.23). The end of the earth is
the circular edge of the disc of the earth, washed by the primeval sea.
It is certain that by this people Isaiah means the Assyrians, whose
king Tiglath-pileser III first attacked the states of northern Syria in
740, and in 738 received tribute from Damascus and Israel. For the
people of Judah, the nations of Mesopotamia inhabited a far country
(cf. 39.3). With a few telling strokes Isaiah pictures the attackers:
nothing stops them (v. 27). They march rapidly and without rest,
well armed and constantly ready for battle. The leather girdles round
the waists of the warriors and the thongs of their sandals are rigid and
taut, and spur the army on to take no rest. The archers are always
ready to shoot (v. 28). The chariots and cavalry also need no pause to
relax; for the unshod feet of the horses are as hard as flint, so that

[a] With Fohrer, this can be taken to refer to the earthquake mentioned in
Amos 1.1.
[b] Military banners consisted of a staff carrying the image of a god or an animal;
cf. Galling, *BRL*, cols. 160ff.
[c] Cf. the comment on 7.18.

even upon rocky ground they are not damaged (cf. Amos 6.12). Like a destructive whirlwind they drive over the whole country. At the end of his poem, emphasizing the hopelessness of the situation, the prophet involuntarily passes to the *qīnā* metre: there is no escape from this enemy. His battle cry will chill the blood and stun all the senses (v. 29). As a traveller at night, or a shepherd, starts at the roaring of a lion (cf. Amos 3.8)[a] seizing his prey with deadly certainty and carrying it off, the people of the covenant will succumb to the attackers, without hope of escape. Wherever God's church allows itself to be led into a careless sense of security, relying upon its election, instead of answering the call to obedience in faith (cf. John 5.24), then like the rest of the world it comes under God's temporal and eternal judgment. Only undivided faith, regarding God's promise and his command with equal seriousness, has any right to be consoled by the saying that the gates of hell will not prevail against the church (cf. Matt. 16.18; II Cor. 5.10; Rev. 2.5; 16.23; 3.3, 16ff.).

It is difficult to say how v. 30 is to be understood in this context. At first sight, and in itself, it gives the impression of being incomplete. Looking at the land ought to be paralleled by looking to the sky. Similarly, the words 'on that day' arouse the suspicion that v. 30 contains traces at least of a later redaction.[b] The real problem is what is referred to by the phrase 'over it'. In accordance with the gender of the Hebrew word for 'prey' it may relate to this, which would provide a firm connection with what precedes, but the older versions suggest another interpretation. The idea of judgment is there transferred to the attackers, with Yahweh himself as the subject of v. 30a. This would mean that the whole verse was an addition, to answer the questions posed by the later, probably post-exilic, community. How far it is an alteration of an authentic saying of Isaiah can no longer be decided. When the community of the second temple considered the sayings of the great prophet, they were concerned with the question why Israel suffered the punishment of God, while the unbelieving Gentile world was apparently allowed undisputed domination over Israel. The Assyrian empire had long ago disappeared, but only to be replaced by other nations. The redactor is assuring the community of his own time that these nations also must come under judgment. Just as Assyria collapsed under God's blows, the powers which rule Israel

---

[a] According to Guthe, *Palästina*, [2]1927, pp. 73f., the lion only withdrew beyond the Euphrates in the twelfth century of our era.

[b] Cf. 3.18; 4.2; 7.18, 20,23; 10.20; 11.10, 11; 12.1; 17.4; 19.16, etc.

in its place will also disappear. The thundering breakers fall over a
ship to smash it against the rocks,[a] and the end of all the enemies of
God will be similar. They will be like a traveller over whom a sudden
and impenetrable darkness falls, so that he wanders from his way and
dies in a stony wilderness or in a ravine.

CHAPTER 10.5–15

Woe to the Self-Confidence of Assyria

5 Woe to Assyria, the rod of my anger,
  and the staff ⟨in the hand⟩[b] of my fury.
6 Against an impious nation I send him,
  and against the people of my wrath I command him,
  to take spoil and to seize plunder,
  and to tread them down like the refuse of the street.
7 But he does not so imagine it,
  and his heart does not so think;
  for his heart [intends] to destroy
  and to cut off nations not a few.
8 For he says:
  'Are not my princes all kings?
9 Was not Calno like Carchemish?
  Was not Hamath like Arpad?
  Was not Samaria like Damascus?
10 *As my hand found the kingdoms of the idols,*
   whose graven images were greater than those of Jerusalem and Samaria, –
11 Shall I not do what I have done
   to Samaria and her idols,
   to Jerusalem also and her images?
12 *But it shall come to pass, when the Lord has finished all his[c] work on*

[a] The comparison of Yahweh with the roaring of the sea may have been
inspired by the similarity in sound between the breakers and the roaring of a lion,
which according to Delitzsch gave rise to the name Sierra Leone, when those who
first landed there confused the thundering of the breakers with the roaring of a
lion.

[b] Read with Ginsberg, *JBL* 69, 1950, p. 54, *bᵉyad-mā* with enclitic *mem*.

[c] The form *yᵉbaṣṣaʿ* seems to have been derived by the interpolator from an
inverted reading of the last word of the preceding verse, *ᵃṣabbēhā*, P. W. Skehan,
CBQ 14, 1952, p. 236.

Mount Zion and on Jerusalem, ⟨he⟩ᵃ will punish the arrogant boasting of the king of Assyria and the pride of his eyes. ¹³For he says:

13 By the strength of my hand I have done it,
and by my wisdom, for I have understanding.
I ⟨have⟩ᵇ removed the boundaries of peoples,
and have plundered their treasures,
and like a hero ⟨I have brought down⟩ᶜ those who sat on thrones.

14 My hand has found like a nest
the wealth of the peoples;
and as one gathers eggs that have been forsaken
I have gathered the whole earth.
And there was none that moved a wing
or opened the beak and chirped.'

15 Shall the axe vaunt itself over him who hews with it,
or the saw magnify itself against him who wields it?
As if a rod should wield him who lifts it,
or as if a staff should lift him who is not wood!

This woe against Assyria cannot be dated with certainty. Many exegetes consider that it belongs to the year 701, in which Sennacherib attacked the rebellious states of Syria and Palestineᵈ with 'the fearfulness of weapons',ᵉ but none of the events mentioned in v. 9 occurred later than the year 717, in which Sargon II conquered Carchemish. We know of two occasions in the last two decades of the eighth century BC in which the Davidic kingdom took part in alliances against Assyria. The first occurred in the year 713, and the second in the year 705–701. If one can suppose that the background to v. 11 is the fact that the king, on some occasion no longer known to us, gave expression to his arrogant contempt for his vassal in Jerusalem and for his God, it is probable that it refers to Hezekiah's part in the revolt of the year 713–11, which was led by Ashdod.ᶠ In later adaptions of the book of Isaiah as it was handed down, the text has been corrupted by transpositions, interpolations and false links. By opposing Jerusalem and Samaria to the other kingdoms, and thereby contradicting the contrast between Jerusalem and Samaria in the

ᵃ Cf. *BH.*
ᵇ Cf. *BH.*
ᶜ Cf. *BH.*
ᵈ Cf. Duhm, Marti, Schmidt, Steinmann, Balla, Pfeiffer, *RSO* 32, 1957, pp. 130f., Fohrer and Eichrodt.
ᵉ Cf. *AOT*, 2nd ed., p. 352.
ᶠ Cf. Procksch, Fischer and Zeigler.

following verse, v. 10 betrays the fact that it is a later interpolation. Verse 12, which interrupts the self-glorification of the Assyrian king, and is written in inelegant prose, does not belong to its present context. In vv. 16–19, a later writer added a conclusion to comfort his contemporaries.[a] We can only guess at the concrete *Sitz im Leben* of this prophecy. One can think of it as uttered either at the royal court, or at a service of petition in the temple. In the woe, Isaiah holds firmly to the view he had expressed earlier, that Assyria was called up by Yahweh to be a rod of punishment for his unfaithful people. Because Assyria itself was presumptuous and despised its true Lord, it was doomed to destruction.

[5–7] *God's woe upon Assyria.* Yahweh himself speaks in this announcement of his resolve to judge Assyria. He chose it as the instrument of the punishment exercised by his righteousness (cf. 5.26–29; 7.18–25; 8.5–8; 10.27b–32) and gave it a free hand to rob and destroy. But Assyria showed by its attitude towards the cities and kingdoms which it had conquered, that it sought to be more than the instrument of divine providence. It was concerned with nothing more than the unlimited increase of its own power.[b] The question whether there was ever any possibility of the Assyrians knowing that they were sent by Yahweh is not posed by Isaiah. For him there is only one God at work in the history of the world, calling the nations or commanding them to withdraw. By his ability to exercise moderation after the victory, which he assumes was possible in the case of Assyria (cf. Rom. 2.14f.), the king should have been able to show that he did not go beyond the commission given him. Anyone who is sent by God and acknowledges that he has been sent, does works of righteousness. Anyone who is intoxicated with power, tramples on human rights and behaves presumptuously and arrogantly, loses his historical commission, and comes under the judgment of the ultimate guardian of what is right.

[8–14] *The self-glorification of the Assyrian king.* As a reason for the divine woe which he has pronounced Isaiah presents the king of Assyria, whom we suppose to be Sargon II, as the speaker. He knows only his own power in the world, his own will. It is incomprehensible to him that the weak king of Judah can dare to show the slightest degree of self-assertion towards him. By comparison with Hezekiah,

---

a Cf. below.

b To the Hebrew the heart was the seat of the mental and spiritual powers and faculties, cf. Baumgärtel, *TDNT* III, pp. 606f.

all his commanders and govenors are mighty kings. In order to emphasize the fullness of his power and his certainty of victory, he lists the easy successes of the years immediately previous. The conquered cities are named in a geographical succession from north and south, so that the listener is made aware of the threat to Judah implied by their progress. Carchemish, the last refuge of Hittite coloniala civilization, paid for its attempt at rebellion in 717 with the loss of its freedom. Its population was deported. Calno (cf. also Amos 6.2), the Kullani of the cuneiform text,b which lay east of Antioch, and which had already been conquered in 738 by Tiglath-pileser III, together with Arpad, which lay north of Aleppo, and which competed with Calno during the eighth century for the hegemony of northern Syria, may have taken part in 720 in the movement of revoltc led by Yaubidi of Hamath, which ended in failure. Damascus, which was conquered and destroyed in 732 in association with the war with Syria and Ephraim, took part, like Samaria, which was annexed in 722/21 by Sargon, in the unsuccessful revolt of 720. What difference, the king asks, is there between Samaria and Jerusalem? Both cities believe in the same God. Thus they are equally at his mercy. In 722/21 it seemed to him to have been made clear that the God of Israel possessed no real power. For him, Yahweh was no different from the idols of the states in the rest of the Syro-Palestinian world. That the worship of Jerusalem made no use of images was either unknown to him or of no importance. The prophetic legend found in II Kings 19.10–13 = Isa.37.10–13 seems to have drawn its material from these two verses. Verse 12 refers back to v.7 and emphasizes the arrogant attitude of the king. At the same time, it also reflects the expectation of the consummation of history upon Zion, which is found in Pss.46, 48 and 76, and occurs repeatedly in the prophet's preaching (cf.17.12–14; 29.1–8; 30.27–33; 31.4f., 8f.; Ezek.38f.; Joel 3.14–17; Zech.9.14–16; 12.1–9; 14.2ff.; Dan.11.45). Since for the reasons given above the verse must be regarded as an interpolation, it is best understood as coming from the time of the Diadochi, in which case Assyria would be a cryptic reference to the Seleucid rule (cf.19.23f.).

a Cf. Moortgat, 'Geschichte Vorderasiens bis zum Hellenismus', in Scharff und Moortgat, Ägypten und Vorderasien im Altertum, Munich, 1950, p.413.

b Cf. B. Meissner, Könige Babyloniens und Assyriens, Leipzig, 1926, p.162; Elliger, Eissfeldt-Festschrift, Halle, 1947, p.97.

c Cf. A. Jepsen, AfO 14, 1941/44, p.170.

The king explicitly stresses that he owes all his success to his own power and ability (v. 13). He regards himself as the only wise statesman of his time, and so fails to recognize that man owes all his achievements and successes to the gift and command of his creator. Isaiah is not interested here, any more than in vv. 6f., in the way the Assyrian king actually thought of himself. He is only concerned with his attitude in practice judged against the faith in his own heart. From a human point of view Sargon had every right to be proud of his achievements. Like his predecessors, he had altered and laid down the boundaries of the nations. As a much feared general, he had deprived the rebellious kings of their throne, as it were by a stroke of his hand. Like a boy who collects eggs from an abandoned nest, he has seized the kingdoms of the earth without any significant resistance (v. 14). But God would have conceded all this to him as part of his commission to chastise the people who formed the central figure of history, if he had given God the honour due to him. But as it is, the wisdom he claims is foolishness (v. 15). For a tool can no more boast against the hand which uses it, as though it moved itself, than man can boast in the sight of God, the Lord of all that happens (cf. Rom. 3.27; I Cor. 1.29; 3.21; 4.7; 1.31; Rom. 15.17). The only attitude which man can properly adopt with regard to his own works is, in the words of the Old Testament, 'I am not worthy of the least of all the steadfast love and all the faithfulness which thou hast shown to thy servant' (Gen. 32.11), and in the words of the New Testament, 'What have you that you did not receive?' (I Cor. 4.7). In the sight of God, man exists only as a creature, whose domination has been given to him by God (Gen. 1.28), and who looks for his future from God (Gen. 12.1ff.; Phil. 3.13f.). Otherwise he is subject to judgment. – Isaiah takes up the image of v. 5: Assyria is nothing more than God's tool, a rod in his hand. Fohrer[a] recalls 31.3 and says: 'It is flesh and not spirit.'

CHAPTER 10.16–19

Yahweh's Chastising Fire

16 Therefore the Lord Yahweh Sebaoth will send
    wasting sickness against his stout ones,

[a] *Ad loc.*

    and beneath his glory a burning will be kindled,
    as a fire breaks out.

17   And the light of Israel will become a fire
    and his Holy One a flame,
    which will burn and devour his thistles,
    and his briars in one day.

18   The glory of his forest and of his orchard
    ⟨will disappear⟩,ᵃ from the soul to the flesh;
    like a sick man it will waste away.

19   And the remnant of the trees of his ⟨forest⟩ᵇ will be so few
    that a child can write them down.

[16–19] There can be no doubt that in its present context the passage is meant to be understood as a description of the divine judgment upon Assyria prophesied in 10.1–15. Procksch tried to resolve the strange tension between the descriptions of a peaceful landscape and of the mobility of the Assyrian army by supposing that a prophecy of warning originally addressed to Israel was separated from its true context when the book was being edited, and was then falsely applied.ᶜ As v. 17 clearly shows, this poem is not a prophecy of a genuine conflagration or a parching drought, but is a vision influenced by the tradition of the theophany of judgment. There are nevertheless strong objections to the authenticity of these verses. On the one hand there is a tension between v. 16 and v. 17, since a wasting disease means the beginning of a long process of decay, whereas the fire carries out its work of destruction in a single day; in the second place, there is a contradiction between v. 17 and v. 18, for in the first it is the weeds, and in the second the glory of the trees of the forest and the orchard which is destroyed. In addition, it can be shown that the author of this passage has borrowed numerous expressions and images from other prophecies of Isaiah. The images for punishment are taken from 17.4 and 9.18f. The conception of Yahweh as light is reminiscent of 9.2, and that of Yahweh's chastising fire of 30.30. The thistle and briar go back to 5.6; 7.25 and 9.18, but reverse the order in which they typically occur in Isaiah. The destruction in a single day is derived from 9.14; the image of the orchard contains echoes of 29.17 and 32.15, but here applies to the enemy in a negative sense.

ᵃ With Bruno read *yikleh*.

ᵇ Cf. *BH*.

ᶜ Procksch, *ad loc.*; Budde, *ZAW* 41, 1923, p. 194 (and also Koppe, as early as 1780); Eissfeldt, *Introduction*, p. 312.

Even the concept of the small boy who can count those trees which remain seems to have been suggested by another saying of Isaiah, 11.6.[a] Thus the whole passage is recognizable as the scholarly work of a man who felt the lack of a prophecy of punishment and needed one which referred to the contemporary oppressors of his people, to be read in the course of worship. Although we do not know with certainty when this addition was made, it is possible, as in the case of 10.12, that it was during the time of Seleucids, in which prophecy was replaced by a scholarly apocalyptic. While Israel, the congregation of the second temple, is trembling before its oppressors, the preacher points to God's help; Isaiah wrote merely not for his contemporaries, but his vision looked forward to the last days. God has overthrown Assyria and Babylon, and brought about the fall of the Persian empire. He will also avert the danger from the Greeks. The armies which appear unconquerable will be desolated by wasting disease and destroyed by Yahweh's *kābōd*, his fullness of power and glory, which from the earliest times had been thought of as a fiery splendour (cf. Pss. 97.1f.; 50.2.f; Ex. 24.15ff.; Ezek. 1.1ff.; I Kings 19.12). The light of Israel (cf. Pss. 27.1; 36.9) will become a fire to the Gentiles. Just as the farmer burns the weeds at the edge of the field during the harvest, Yahweh will exterminate the wilful enemies of his people with all their glory. What today is bursting with health is dead and gone on the morrow. What people tremble at today not even a child will fear tomorrow. God's judgment will strike the enemy with such force that only a handful will escape. Here we have expectations such as are expressed at greater length in the apocalypse of Isaiah (chs. 24–27) and in the Book of Daniel.

CHAPTER 10.20–23

A Remnant will Return

20   In that day it will come to pass:
     the remnant of Israel will no longer lean,
     nor the survivors of the house of Jacob,
     upon him that smote them,   — *is the enemy of the people – Meaning*
                                   change again indicates the late date
                                   of this oracle.

[a] Cf. Duhm, Marti and Fohrer, *ad loc.*

      but will lean upon Yahweh,
      the Holy One of Israel, in faithfulness.

21   A remnant will return,
      a remnant of Jacob,
      to the Mighty God.

[Handwritten margin note: Return is to YAHWEH - NOT NECESSARILY TO THE PROMISED LAND. Cf. with 9.6. The Monarchy is a thing of the past - Indicates a post exilic setting for this oracle. (Carroll). See Below.]

22   For though your people,
      O Israel,
      were as the sand of the sea,
      [only] a remnant of them will return.
      Destruction is decreed,
      overflowing righteousness.

23   For the Lord Yahweh Sebaoth
      will carry out the decreed destruction,
      in the midst of the whole earth.

[20–23] The present prophecy assumes the oracle of judgment in vv. 16–19, and is therefore at least a secondary interpolation. Duhm has accurately expressed the difficulty of the passage from the point of view of literary criticism when he says: 'According to II Kings 16 Ahaz relied upon Assyria, but was not struck down, whereas Hezekiah was struck down, but did not rely upon Assyria'. The attempt to place the oracle in the year 738, in which Menahem of Israel paid a tribute to Tiglath-pileser,[a] fails in the first place because no fighting took place between the northern kingdom and Assyria at that time, and secondly because the prophecy can only be understood in association with a preceding prophecy of doom. In addition, it must be observed that v. 21 gives the impression of being a quotation drawn from 7.3 and 9.6, while v. 22 derives from Hos. 1.10; Gen. 22.17; 32.12 and Isa. 28.2ff.;[b] and v. 23 has a parallel in 28.22.[c] While there are difficulties in ascribing the passage to Isaiah himself, for there are no prophecies attributable to him which look beyond the year 701, it seems likely that it was composed by the same or a similar hand as was at work in vv. 16–19. An unknown writer, steeped in the thought of the great prophet, and living in a period in which the actuality of Isaiah's message apparently belonged to the past, emphatically stresses that God's anger still extends over his people. Anyone in Israel who relies upon its oppressors and consequently transgresses the commandment

   [a] So Steinmann.
   [b] Cf. Duhm, Marti, Fohrer and Eichrodt, *ad loc.*
   [c] Fichtner, *ZAW* 63, 1951, p. 26, regards 10.23 instead as a displaced saying of Isaiah himself, which I do not consider likely.

to worship Yahweh alone (Ex. 20.3) will be judged by God (cf. Dan. 11.32ff.). But in these days the hope which lies behind Isaiah's prophecy of judgment will ultimately be fulfilled, that the purified and holy remnant (cf. 7.3; 1.26; [6.13]) will be saved from the catastrophe. The divine title 'Mighty God', 'Hero God' which is very rare in the Old Testament, and occurs in 9.7 as the title of the saviour-king, emphasizes the unique and decisive power of Yahweh to direct the wars and the kingdoms of this world according to his plan. The emphatic reference to the remnant is an exhortation to unconditional loyalty in the time of temptation. As long as men do not place their trust wholly and exclusively in God, they are subject to the decree of judgment of him who is Lord of all lords.[a] His righteousness will pour out like a stream over the earth, destroying every sinner. This judgment will not be limited to Israel, but in accordance with the real belief of Israel will come upon all nations, and will then bring the longed-for time of salvation.[b]

CHAPTER 10.24–27a

'My People, be not Afraid of Assyria'

24 Therefore thus says the Lord, Yahweh Sebaoth:
    'Be not afraid, my people
    who dwell in Zion, of Assyria,
    who smites you with a rod
    and lifts up its staff against you as Egypt did.
25 For in a little, a short while,
    ⟨my⟩[c] wrath will be exhausted
    and my anger ⟨wholly concluded⟩.'[d]
26 Then Yahweh Sebaoth will swing the scourge against them,
    as he struck Midian at the Rock of the Raven,
    and will lift his rod over the sea,
    as he did against Egypt.

[a] On the divine name Yahweh Sebaoth cf. the comment on 6.3.

[b] On the ambiguous concept of judgment cf. the comment on 10.17 and Weiser, *The Psalms*, pp. 47ff.

[c] Cf. *BH*.

[d] With Driver, *JTS* 38, 1937, p. 39, read *we'appī 'al tēkel yittōm*, with *tēkel* being understood as a substantive derived from *kll* with the meaning 'completion'.

27a And it will come to pass in that day:
His burden will depart from your shoulder
and his yoke will ⟨disappear⟩ᵃ from your neck.

[24–27a] This oracle of salvation, like the preceding one about the remnant which shall return, breathes the atmosphere of a zealous study of the scripture. Verse 24, with the phrase 'my people who dwell in Zion', is reminiscent of 30.19; the image of the rod recalls 10.5 and 30.31. The beginning of v.25 is found almost word for word in 29.17 and 26.20. The allusion to the day of Midian has a parallel in 9.4, but is introduced here on the basis of Judg.7.25. Assuming what has been said in vv.20–23, the passage is addressed to the congregation, to prepare in it the remnant which will be able to endure in the ultimate judgment of Yahweh's wrath. Thus it is equally possible that it comes from the days of the threat from the Greeks, to which Assyria had become a cryptic name for the Seleucid domination. The act of salvation which God was to carry out for Israel would be a repetition of that at the beginning of its history. 'From his own time, the writer looks back to the time of distress in the pre-eschatological period, which corresponds to the oppression in Egypt.'ᵇ Just as Israel found a helper in God, first in Egypt and then in the danger from the Midianites, so now God will not ultimately abandon them. The congregation who believe in the God who has proclaimed his nature and his purpose of fellowship in history can constantly return to the testimony of the fathers in their own day, in order to understand their own position in the light of the revelation that has already been given.ᶜ In the fundamental note of this oracle of salvation, that it will be fulfilled 'soon', we can see that all true faith is at the same time an imminent expectation (cf. Rev.22.20). For anyone who does not acknowledge that God can show himself gracious here and now is ultimately excluding God entirely from his life. These concrete expectations are no more to be fulfilled directly at the present time than in the past. In the midst of danger and persecution, God will constantly bear witness to himself before his worshippers in such a way that they obtain power and courage for the next step (cf. II Cor.4.8ff.). The consummation of history itself is in God's power (cf. Mark 13.32; Acts 1.7f.). It is the part of the church to bear witness to this hour and to await it (cf. Matt.25.1–13).

ᵃ Cf. *BH*.
ᵇ Fohrer, *ad loc.*
ᶜ Cf. Noth, *EvTh* 12, 1952/53, pp.6ff.

CHAPTER 10.27b–32

The Enemy from the North

27b ⟨He goes up from Samaria⟩ᵃ
28   and falls upon Aiath.
     He passes through Migron,
     he directs his baggage train towards Michmash.
29   They have crossed over the ravine,
     in Geba they make their quarters for the night. ᵇ
     Ramah trembles,
     Gibeah of Saul has fled.
30   Cry aloud, O daughter of Gallim!
     Hearken, O Laishah!
     ⟨Answer⟩,ᶜ O Anathoth!
31   Madmenah is in flight,
     the inhabitants of Gebim flee for safety.
32   This very day he stands in Nob,
     he shakes his fist against the mount of the daughter of Zion,
     against the hill of Jerusalem.

[27b–32] This passage is one of the most obscure of all the prophecies of Isaiah, the moment one fails to recognize its unique and
direct actuality. To some extent it offers a parallel to the prophecy of
judgment from the early period in 5.26–29, the subject of which is
likewise the irresistible and victorious progress of an enemy army.
The phrase 'this very day' in v. 32 suggests that it belongs to the days
before the beginning of the siege of Jerusalem in the year 701,ᵈ that is
in the period in which Isaiah uttered 14.24–27 and 31.4–9, and
looked forward to the destruction of the Assyrians by Yahweh, while
the people looked for help to Egypt (cf. 30.1–5, 6–7; 31.1–3). The
prophet had repeatedly impressed upon the people that they could
look for help from Yahweh alone (cf. 28.16; 30.15), though for a long
time without success (cf. 30.9, 15f.). Thus the announcement of the
approach of the enemy army may be thought of as an appeal to make
a decision to rely on Yahweh as sole helper.

ᵃ Cf. *BH* and Procksch, *ad loc.*

ᵇ Others translate: 'Geba shall be our quarters for the night'; cf. Duhm,
Bentzen, etc.

ᶜ Cf. *BH.*

ᵈ Schmidt thinks this refers to the war with Syria and Ephraim; Procksch to
715; and Steinmann, Pfeiffer, *RSO* 32, 1957, pp. 150ff. and Fohrer to 701.

In the course of the redaction of the book, the text has not remained unscathed. Its opening verse has been so corrupted that the original reading cannot be restored with certainty. The extant Hebrew text would have to be translated '. . . and the yoke of fatness will be destroyed'. The period of salvation proclaimed in 10.24–27a will bring such an increase of power and of population that Israel will be able to shake off the yoke of foreign rule. This image seems so ill chosen that one can regard it as a later corruption, caused by a wrong division of the sentence and vocalization. Whereas some scholars read 'Rimmon' on the basis of the consonantal form of the Hebrew word 'fat', *š-m-n*, for practical reasons we ought rather to read Samaria, *š-m-r-n*.[a] The concluding verses 33 and 34 were wrongly associated with this prophecy, at a time when the poem was no longer understood as a prophecy of warning against Jerusalem, because of its present context. Herder already recognized that they formed the introduction to 11.1ff.[b] Isaiah's hearers become the witnesses of a rapid succession of announcements which make known to Jerusalem the advance of an enemy army (vv. 27b–28). It is probable that he had the Assyrians in mind. Since the enemy did not choose the broad military road, which led from Bethel to Jerusalem in three or four hours, but deviated first towards Ai, which lay south-east of Bethel, and which appears under the name Aiath,[c] they seemed to have in mind a punitive expedition against the border towns of the northern kingdom. It is no longer certain whether Migron is the name of a town or a district. In any case, the army advances to Michmash, which seems to have surrendered without resistance. Since the baggage train follows to this point, there seems to be no direct danger to Jerusalem. It looks as though the enemy intends to set up his quarters for the night in Michmash. It is clearly already evening. But then comes a new and terrifying message: under cover of darkness, the combat troops are crossing the deep *Wādi eṣ-ṣuweniṭ*[d] (v. 29). To do so, it was necessary to descend about three hundred feet from Michmash into the bottom of the valley and then to climb over five hundred feet to Geba, the present day *jeba'*. This journey of three miles would have taken two

[a] On Rimmon cf. Duhm; for an opposing view cf. Dalman, *PJB* 12, 1916, pp. 43f.; for Samaria cf. Procksch, *ad loc.*

[b] *Vom Geist der Ebräischen Poesie* II. 2, *Sämtliche Werke*, ed. B. Suphan, 12, Berlin, 1880, p. 289 (433); cf. more recently Bruno, *ad loc.*

[c] On the places and roads cf. Dalman, 'Palästinische Wege und die Bedrohung Jerusalems nach Jesaja 10', *PJB* 12, 1916, pp. 37ff.; Ai is *et-tell* near *dēr dubwān*.

[d] It is described by Dalman, *ZDPV* 25, 1905, pp. 163ff.

hours at the most. It meant that the enemy had entered the territory of Judah. The intention was obvious: if he moved his quarters for the night here, then by early morning he would appear before the walls of Jerusalem. There is no longer any restraint in the villages in the plain before the city: Ramah, today *er-rām*, is seized by feverish excitement. Inhabitants of the ancient royal city of Saul, Gibeah (cf. 1 Sam. 10.26; 11.4), take to flight (v. 29b). The message of doom spreads like wildfire during the night and in the first light of morning. Gallim, perhaps identical with *ḥirbet ka'kūl*, cries out in fear. In Laishah, nowadays *el-'esāwīye*, the cries of terror are heard from the neighbouring villages and are taken up: 'The enemy comes, the enemy comes!' Already Anathoth where Jeremiah was later to be born (Jer. 1.1), and which is now *'anāta*, joins in the clamour (v. 30). Madmenah, perhaps *ḥirbet ṣōma*, takes to flight. The people of Gebim try to seek refuge behind the walls of Jerusalem (v. 31). The terrible message is on their lips: the enemy will soon be in Nob (v. 32). Nob, the ancient city of priests (cf. I Sam. 21.1ff.) is today called *rās el-mešārif* 'the look-out point'. This is the point from which the traveller first sees the walls and towers of the holy city. It is four miles from Geba to Nob, and one and a half from Nob to Jerusalem: before the sun is high in the heavens, the enemy will appear before the walls of the city, and besiege the fortress and the residential parts of the city. The battle of nations before the gates of Jerusalem is beginning. Nothing further is said about the siege or its conclusion. Whether the enemy attains his goal of conquering the capital, or whether he meets his end here, depends upon whether the people of Jerusalem at last honestly repent (cf. 31.6) and recognize that their help is from God and not from the cavalry of Egypt (cf. 30.16; 31.1–3). Thus this passage bears witness to a faith in God, who can instantly provide help.

Points of Literary Criticism on 10.33–11.16

In recent exegesis, the whole of ch. 11 has provoked dispute, with regard both to its outward limits and internal sub-divisions, and also to its origin and the date of its composition. 10.33f. are regarded as the conclusion of 10.27b–32, either authentic or composed by a redactor. As in the case of 9.1–7 [which the German versions, following the Hebrew, divide as 8.23 and 9.1–6], this view is based upon the traditional chapter divisions, and of course this corresponds to the view

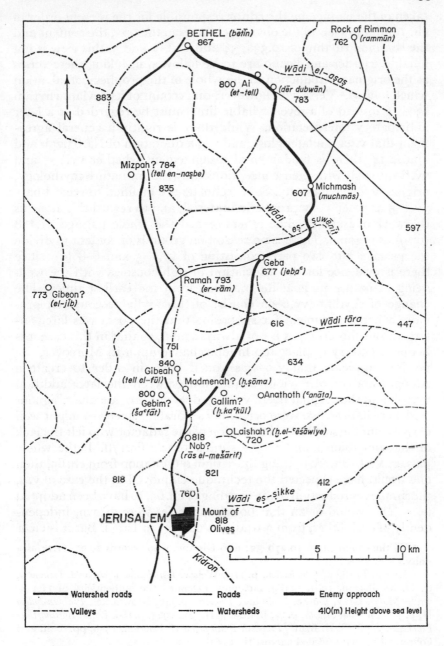

Watershed roads · · · · · Roads ▬▬▬ Enemy approach

- - - - Valleys ········· Watersheds 410(m) Height above sea level

taken of the passage by the editor responsible for the present order of ch. 10. But in view of the obvious changes in the text, the content and the common rhythm of 10.33a, 34 and 11.1–2 and 5, this view is not tenable. Herder and Bruno are to be followed in taking these verses as the original introduction to the whole of the prophecy of salvation which follows.[a] Verse 33b, however, on account of its deviant rhythm (3 + 2 instead of a seven-syllable line) must be regarded as a later anticipatory interpretation. While there is rightly a general agreement that v. 3a is a later gloss, and v. 9 a quotation of Isa. 65.25b and Hab. 2.14, there is fundamental disagreement whether vv. 1–5 and vv. 6–8 (or 9), with their conceptions drawn from nature mythology, originally formed a unity. Some scholars are inclined to regard only vv. 1–5 as specifically prophetic material, and to regard this alone as the work of Isaiah,[b] while others regard the whole passage 11.1–8 (or 9) as original. There is no reason on grounds of content to divide the passage into two parts consisting of vv. 1–5 and 6–8 (9), since there is evidence for the association of righteousness with the well-being of nature in Israelite tradition from the earliest times. The change of rhythm (vv. 6–9a consist of three-syllable couplets) provides a better argument for supposing that the poem was later enlarged. But this criterion is not always sound, so that in this case it is better not to try to place too much reliance upon it. Moreover, the possible suspicion that v. 9 was added later, in order to create a stronger and more obvious connection between the later addition vv. 6–8 and the original poem vv. 1–5, does not provide unambiguous evidence that the two were originally separated, since v. 9 might well derive from the scholarly observation of the redactor who felt the lack of the conclusion found in the similar oracle 65.17ff. If the whole passage vv. 6–8 were nothing more than a quotation from ch. 65, then one would have expected the technique employed in the case of v. 9, the simple reproduction of the wording of ch. 65, to have been adopted here. This would mean that both prophecies were drawn, independently of each other, from a tradition current in Israel. But it is clear

[a] Cf. the comment on 10.27b–32; also Kissane, who regards 10.27–11.14 as a unity.

[b] Duhm, Eissfeldt, *Introduction*, p. 319; Weiser, *Introduction to the Old Testament*, tr. D. M. Barton, 1961, p. 189, etc. have defended the authenticity of 11.1–5, while Marti, Gray, Guthe, Hölscher, *Profeten*, p. 348, Mowinckel, *Psalmenstudien* II, p. 308, *He That Cometh*, p. 17, Budde, *ZAW* 41, 1923, p. 189, Balla, *Botschaft der Propheten*, p. 475, S. H. Blank, *Prophetic Faith in Israel*, London, 1958, pp. 16off. and Fohrer, *ad loc.* have argued against that of the whole passage.

that vv. 11–16 were not joined to 11.1–9 (or 10.33–11.9) till later. Whereas vv. 1–9 deal with the rule of the saviour-king and its consequences, vv. 11–16 describe Yahweh's acts for the redemption of Israel. Considerable suspicion is cast on v. 10 by the fact that its opening words are exactly the same as those of v. 11. It serves as a link between vv. 1–9 and 11–16. The latter passage clearly assumes the existence of a world-wide diaspora, and therefore comes from the period of the exile, or, more probably, from the post-exilic period. Thus the task remains of fitting 10.33–11.9 into the career of Isaiah. The impression produced by 11.1–9 when considered in isolation, that the prophecy assumes that the Davidic monarchy has already been brought to an end,[a] is removed once the link between 10.33a, 34 and 11.1–9 is recognized. Here we are dealing with a true prophecy. The Davidic monarchy has not yet disappeared from the stage of history. Moreover, the complete annihilation of the Davidic dynasty, assumed by v. 1, did not in fact take place.[b] If the text itself suggests that it derives from Israel's monarchical period, there is no fundamental objection to the view that Isaiah is the author. Since we know nothing of the prophet's activity under Manasseh from the book of Isaiah itself, the passage can be understood either, following Buber, as Isaiah's answer to the disappointment over Hezekiah,[c] or, following Procksch, as composed during the war with Syria and Ephraim, since in 7.17 the prophet explicitly foretold a gloomy future for the royal house during this period. This also raises the possibility that it was actually uttered in the worship of the Jerusalem temple, for at the great harvest festival the election of the Davidic dynasty was explicitly recalled.[d] Thus it is possible that Isaiah opposed a false trust in God's promises, as an unconditional pledge of the people's self-confidence, with this prophecy of salvation, which by comparison with current expectations (cf. II Sam. 7.12ff.; Lam. 4.20) was quite inadequate. Otherwise, one must consider the possibility that it was uttered among his disciples (8.16).

[a] Cf. Mowinckel, *Psalmenstudien* II, p. 308; *He That Cometh*, p. 17.
[b] Cf. Duhm, *ad loc.*
[c] *The Prophetic Faith*, p. 148.
[d] Cf. Weiser, *The Psalms*, pp. 44, 62f.; H. J. Kraus, BHTh 13, 1951; BK XV on Ps. 132; *Worship in Israel*, pp. 183ff.

The Empire of Peace of the King from the Stem of Jesse

33   Behold the Lord Yahweh Sebaoth
      lops the boughs with terrifying power,
      the great in height are felled,
      and the lofty sink low.

34   The thicket of the wood is cut down with iron
      and the ⟨poplar⟩ᵃ falls ⟨in its majesty⟩. ᵇ

11 1   But a shoot will come forth from the stump of Jesse,
      and a sprout ⟨spring out⟩ᶜ of his roots.

   2   And the spirit of Yahweh shall rest upon it,
      the spirit of wisdom and understanding,
      the spirit of counsel and might,
      the spirit of knowledge and the fear of Yahweh.

   3   ⟨   ⟩ᵈ
      He shall not judge by what his eyes see
      or decide by what his ears hear;

   4   but with righteousness shall he judge the poor
      and decide with equity for the meek of the earth.
      ⟨But the villain⟩ᵉ he shall smite with the rod of his mouth,
      and the wicked he shall slay with the breath of his lips.

   5   And ⟨   ⟩ᶠ righteousness shall be the girdle of his
      waist,
      and faithfulness the ⟨band⟩ᵍ about his loins.

   6   Then the wolf shall dwell with the lamb,
      and the leopard shall lie down with the kid;
      and calf and the lion cub ⟨shall feed⟩ʰ together,
      and a little child shall lead them.

   7   Then the cow and the bear ⟨shall be friends⟩;ⁱ
      their young shall lie down together.
      Then the lion shall eat straw like the ox.

ᵃ With Bruno read *wᵉhallibnē.*

ᵇ With Bruno read *bᵉ'edrō.*

ᶜ Cf. *BH.*

ᵈ 'And his delight shall be in the fear of the Lord' is a gloss. Driver, *Textus* 1, 1961, p. 129, argues in favour of the suggestion of Perles that the clause is an abbreviation of 11.2ab.

ᵉ Cf. *BH.*

ᶠ With König and Driver, *JTS* 38, 1937, p. 39, read the article, lost through a haplography.

ᵍ Read with Driver, *JTS* 38, p. 40, *'esūr.*

ʰ Cf. *BH.*   ⁱ Cf. *BH.*

8   The sucking child shall play at the hole of the adder,
    and the weaned child shall put his hand on the viper's den.
9   *They are not evil and do not destroy*
    in all my holy mountain;
    for the land is full of the knowledge of Yahweh
    as water covers the sea.

[**10.33–34**] *Yahweh's judgment upon the king and the people.* The almighty Lord Sebaoth[a] will fall like a gardener with his shears, or like a woodman with his axe, upon the trees, the Davidic kingdom. The common people, who are compared with the thickets of the wood, and the royal house, the proud poplar, are equally condemned to ruin.[b] These will be the days of distress prophesied to Ahaz at the encounter by the Fuller's Field, which were to be harder for the royal house than the defection of the northern kingdom in the days of Rehoboam (cf. 7.17). The king and the people, who do not believe, will not endure (7.9).

[**11.1–5**] *The righteous ruler of the future.* But the judgment is not God's last word. Behind it lies his purpose of salvation, his resolve to consummate the work he has begun. Of course the royal house itself is condemned to ruin. But just as David was once chosen in a truly miraculous way from the insignificant family of Jesse (cf. I Sam. 16.1–13; II Sam. 7.18) to receive the highest honour, once again a new shoot[c] will spring up from the root stump[d] of the family, a second David[e] (v. 1). Just as the spirit of Yahweh once rested upon David (cf. I Sam. 16.13; II Sam. 23.2f.),[f] the second David will also be equipped for his office by the spirit,[g] which will bring about agreement between the will of God and that of the king[h] (v. 2). What this

a Cf. the comment on 6.3.

b Cf. Isa. 2.13; Amos 2.9; Ezek. 31.2ff.; 17.9ff.

c Cf. *ṣemaḥ* in Jer. 23.5; Zech. 3.8; 6.12. Cf. Eichrodt, BFChTh 25.3, 1920, p. 42 n. 1.

d Cf. Isa. 40.24; Job. 14.8.

e With Mowinckel, *He That Cometh*, pp. 161f., to speak of a *David redivivus* should be regarded as inappropriate.

f For the date of the 'last words of David' cf. Johnson, *Sacral Kingship in Ancient Israel*, Cardiff, 1955, pp. 14f.; on the wording and translation cf. de Boer, *SVT* 4, 1957, pp. 47ff.

g On the concept of the spirit in the Old Testament, cf. Johnson, *The Vitality of the Individual in the Thought of Ancient Israel*, Cardiff, 1949, pp. 35ff.

h Cf. Baumgärtel, *TDNT* VI, pp. 365f. On the endowment of the king with the spirit cf. I Sam. 10.6, 9f.; 16.13; II Sam. 23.2f.

means is set out in the three pairs of concepts which follow. It is a spirit of wisdom and understanding. Wisdom is the ability to act in accordance with the existing circumstances. Understanding is the clear appreciation of the situation. In this case both gifts have in mind the judicial capacity of the king,[a] which determines his activity in internal and foreign policy. The wisdom of Solomon in judicial matters was particularly famous (cf. I Kings 3.16–28). (In very similar terms, Jeremiah [23.5f.] was later to prophesy a righteous branch who would act as king with understanding, and exercise justice and righteousness in the land.[b]) In the power of the spirit, the future king will have no need of human advisers, with their selfish attempts to influence him. His judicial wisdom and ability to distinguish between appearances and reality will enable him to plan aright, and he will also possess the power to translate his decisions into action: for upon him rests the spirit of counsel and heroic might (cf. 9.6). He will exercise his office in the knowledge of God and the fear of Yahweh. For the Israelites, knowledge is not merely or even in the first place an intellectual faculty (cf. Gen. 4.1). Because the whole of reality is constantly determined anew by God, all dealings with it are simultaneously an encounter with God. Consequently, there is no knowledge of God without action. 'The knowledge of God means to "cease" from idolatry and sin, to "turn" to Yahweh and to "seek" him, to "adhere" to him, and "fear" him; it means to exercise love, justice and righteousness.'[c] In the Old Testament, the fear of Yahweh is as it were a summary of everything that can be said about the right attitude of man to God.[d] When Yahweh reveals his power and deity in violent natural phenomena or in historical upheavals, it is man's part to bow before him in awe.[e] The king of the time of salvation will not presume upon his power, but will know in his every act that he must give an account to God for every step he takes. He will be a wholly devout and righteous king, because God himself has given him his spirit.

Consequently he will also prove this in the exercise of his office.

[a] Cf. Lindblom, *SVT* 3, 1955, pp. 198; Noth, *SVT* 3, 1955, p. 234; and Porteous, *SVT* 3, 1955, p. 254.

[b] The independence of Jer. 23.5 from Isa. 11.1 is discussed by Weiser, ATD 20, *ad loc.*; Porteous *op. cit.*, p. 254, is uncertain, cf. Rudolph, HAT 12, 2nd ed., p. 136.

[c] Cf. Botterweck, *Gott Erkennen*, BBB 2, 1951, p. 97; also Bultmann, *TDNT* I, 696ff.; Mowinckel, *Die Erkenntnis Gottes bei den alttestamentlichen Profeten*, Oslo, 1941, pp. 5ff.

[d] Cf. Eichrodt, *Theology of the Old Testament* II, pp. 268ff.

[e] Cf. the references in Kaiser, *Der Königliche Knecht*, FRLANT 70, 1959, p. 78.

Whereas men have to rely in their judicial decisions upon what they see and what is testified to them by the disputants, the king who is to come from the family of Jesse will share in God's ability (cf. I Sam. 16.7; I Peter 1.17) to see and decide on things as they really are (v. 3). All other human judgment is a premature leap in the dark, constantly threatened by emotions and by ignorance of the true situation (cf. I Cor. 4.3–5). Consequently, when it is carried out, the ultimate decision is always reserved to the verdict of God. The incorruptibility of the king and judge is exemplified by his attitude towards those who are without possessions and in need (v. 4). Every state is known to exercise the rule of law only in so far as it honours the rights of its weakest members. In this expectation, Isaiah shares the royal ideology of Israel, and indeed of the whole of the ancient East.[a] The king will judge his people in righteousness (cf. Ps. 72.2), which he loves (Ps. 45.7). This is the proper virtue of a ruler (II Sam. 23.3; Isa. 9.6f.). He manifests it by helping the poor and needy, the widows and orphans (Pss. 45.4; 72.4, 12f.; Isa. 10.2; 32.1; Ex. 22.22), and is thereby doing the work of God himself (Pss. 9.9; 68.5; Job 5.15f.). In the proverbial wisdom, the incorruptibility and correctness of a king's judgment is praised in similar terms:

A king who sits on the throne of judgment
winnows all evil with his eyes (Prov. 20.8).

And again:

Oracles are on the lips of a king;
in pronouncing judgment his mouth will not transgress (Prov. 16.10)[b].

Whoever has been recognized by the coming saviour-king as a transgressor of the covenant ordinance will be condemned to death. The evil-doer is the man who has been found guilty in the course of the trial (cf. I Kings 8.32; Ex. 9.27; 23.1, 7; Isa. 50.9). It is the king's duty to punish him (cf. Ps. 101; Prov. 20.26). Whether this is a reference to the idea that the very word and breath of the king is sufficient

---

[a] Cf. the references *ibid.*, pp. 25f.; also the inscription of Darius I on his rock grave, which is strikingly reminiscent of expressions in Ps. 101 and which reads in part. 'What is right I love, wrong I hate. It is not my pleasure that the exalted harm the lowly through wrong.' E. Hertzfeld, *Altpersische Inschriften* I, Supplement to *Archäologischen Mitteilungen aus dem Iran*, Berlin, 1938, pp. 4ff., quoted in F. König, *Die Religion Zarathustras*, CRE II, Freiburg, 1951, p. 624.

[b] Translation following that of Steuernagel, HSAT, 4th ed. Cf. also the Ugaritic texts, Gordon 127. 45ff.; 2 *Aqht* V. 4ff.; and E. Hammershaimb, *SVT* 7, 1960, pp. 89ff.

to bring death to the wrong-doer and criminal (cf. Job 15.30), or whether the rod of his mouth and the breath of his lips are metaphors for his judicial sentence, which is upheld by his power to carry it out,[a] is uncertain. If the first were true, the king would share in the holiness of God. But here again, this holiness would not be his own natural power, but the effect of the spirit of God. What was glorified in the royal psalms in the Old Testament, as the pattern intended by God for the anointed king and his kingdom,[b] God ultimately intends to bring into being by sending the king from the family of Jesse. Isaiah has clearly recognized that the ruling house of David in no sense fitted this picture. Consequently, God would once again make a complete new beginning. As he is, man is and remains a sinner, who cannot change by his own power (cf. Jer. 13.23). Only the grace of God, which follows his judgment, can create man anew, so that he does the will of God. Just as the belt holds together the clothes and gives freedom of movement and dignity to him who wears it, so the second David, inspired by the spirit of God, owes his dignity to his righteousness, and his ability to rule, and therefore the endurance of his reign (cf. 9.7) to his trustworthiness and loyalty (v. 5).[c] He will rule in a way pleasing to God and man.

[6–9] *The restoration of peace between man and animals.* At the present time, the whole creation is profoundly disturbed by human sin. According to priestly belief, peace had prevailed in the beginning between men and animals. The end of this peace was not affirmed by God until after the flood (Gen. 9.2f.). The people, exposed from their earliest days to danger in the house, on the farm, and in the open country, longed for the restoration of the lost peace. At present they had to fear for their cattle. Numerous enemies threatened them, from the wolf to the lion. They had to fear for their little children, who thoughtlessly played with the bright and colourful poisonous snakes and received fatal bites.[d] Like his contemporary Hosea, Isaiah also expects that in the time of salvation which is to come, peace will be restored between men and animals (vv. 6–8; cf. Hos. 2.18). He has in

[a] Cf. the 'spirit of (heroic) might' in v. 2.

[b] Von Rad, *Old Testament Theology* I, pp. 319ff.

[c] For this concept cf. Quell, *TDNT* I, pp. 232ff.

[d] Guthe, *Palästina*, [2]1927, p. 76, mentions as particularly feared snakes which were still to be found in the first third of the present century the cobra (*Naja naje*), the small horned snake (*Cerastes*) and the great yellow snake (*Daboia xanthina*). G. L. Harding, *The Antiquities of Jordan*, 1959, pp. 19f., says that the cross-marked adder and the horned viper are still to be found.

mind not so much the existence animals lead with one another, as the removal of the damage and danger to which they give rise for man.[a] This expectation is not without an inward connection with the promise of the saviour king which precedes it. He is to bring right-eousness into the world. Where righteousness truly prevails, the whole world is brought into the condition intended for it by God.[b] Thus the latter addition in v. 9 is not a mere blind interpolation. It does of course restrict the prophecy to the holy mountain, the city of God, in a way which does not follow from the authentic words of Isaiah.[c] But it expressly emphasizes that this change will take place only because, and not until, the land is full of the knowledge of God, and when all exercise righteousness under the guidance of the one who alone is righteous.

For the present-day reader, these words raise two related ques-tions. He is unable to look forward, like the Old Testament, to a time in which lions eat grass, because of his knowledge of natural history. He believes that there was conflict in the animal world at the very beginning, before there were men. The question how this came to be, and why it is so, remains ultimately unanswerable.[d] But this un-answerable question directs him towards the creative foundation of all life, God the creator. It is not sufficient to turn the entire final stanza into a metaphor for peace among the nations. But it can serve as a metaphor for the statement that in the future which God is pre-paring for his creation, everything will be transformed, and that there will no longer be distress and weeping in it, according to the vision of the apocalyptic writers (cf. Rev. 21.1ff.). Again we are aware that the great outward transformation in the history of Israel did not take place in the way in which Isaiah expected, and in the time to which he looked forward. Judaism holds firmly to the expectation of the coming saviour-king, the Messiah, and daily prays to God for him to

---

[a] Cf. perhaps Amos 5.19.

[b] Cf. also Isa. 35.9; 65.25; Ezek. 34.25; Lev. 26.3ff.; *ANE1*, 2nd ed., p. 38, lines 13ff. For the Israelite conception of the status and responsbility of the king by contrast to the conceptions of the Ancient East as a whole cf. S. Mowinckel, *SN* IV, 1959, pp. 283–93.

[c] 'Hill' here can, however, also be taken in the sense of 'hill-country'.

[d] This is regarded by modern man as what Goethe described as an *Urphänomen*, a basic element of experience. Cf. his *Maximen und Aphorismen*, Aphorisms 433 and 1207. – But cf. the conclusion of Goethe's 'Novelle', *Gedenkausgabe*, ed. Ernst Beutler, vol. 9, pp. 477ff.

appear.[a] When faith is faced with and tried by the question why the promise has still not been fulfilled, despite all the suffering of the Jews, the answer given is that of the Hassidic Rabbi Schmelke of Nikolsburg: 'Today, just as yesterday, all their prayers are for nothing but bread, for nothing but the satisfaction of bodily needs.'[b] And with regard to the condition of the world, which is obvious to everyone, there is truth in this. Christian faith has always asserted that the prophetic oracles concerning the future king from the time of David were fulfilled in Jesus of Nazareth.[c] When he appeared, these expectations were not simply fulfilled in the literal sense, but were reinterpreted. Since then, the kingdom of God is realized for the believer in the church. There the time of salvation is present in the kingly rule of Christ who is preached (cf. II Cor.6.2). The righteous judgment, which takes no account of persons, takes place since the coming of Jesus in the presence of the Lord who is proclaimed (cf. John 3.16ff.; 5.24f.).[d] But with the prophets of the old covenant, the church waits for God's power and glory to be revealed once and for all, in his Son, before all flesh. Every testimony to this future possesses only a provisional validity (cf. I Cor.13.12); for it speaks of a reality of which no one can anticipate the way in which it will come into being. Consequently, all Christian future hope is of its nature pure hope, *purissima spes*,[e] which leaves to God everything of which he is capable. It is based solely upon the promise that Christ is the first fruits of those who sleep (I Cor.15.20), and upon the testimony of the Spirit, the transformation of those who have received the preaching of the crucified and risen Christ (cf. II Cor.1.22). And yet this hope is never valid merely for the soul of the individual, or for the renewal of the individual in another form, but is always true of the world as well. Because it is God's creation, it will not relapse into nothingness; it will itself be transformed and consummated (cf. Rom.8.19–22; Rev.21.1).

   [a] Cf. Danby, *Mishnah*, Berakoth.

   [b] Cf. Buber, *Tales of the Hasidim: the Early Masters*, p.185.

   [c] On the question of Jesus as the son of David cf. W. Michaelis in *Der Historische Jesus und der kerygmatische Christus*, Berlin, 1960, pp.317ff.

   [d] Cf. Bultmann, *Essays Philosophical and Theological*, tr. J. C. G. Greig, London, 1955, p.200.

   [e] Cf. Gogarten, *DUZ* IX, 24, 1954, pp.3ff.; Luther, WA 29, 327ff.; 43, 204f.; Conf. Aug. XX 17.

CHAPTER 11.10–16

The Liberation and World Domination of the People of God

10 *And it will come to pass in that day:*
the root of Jesse, which stands as a banner to the people,
for him shall the nations seek,
and his dwelling shall be glorious.

11 In that day it shall come to pass:
again the Lord will ⟨lift up⟩ᵃ his hand,
to redeem the remnant of his people,
which is left from Assyria and Egypt,
from Pathros and from Cush and from Elam,
from Shinar and from Hamath and from the islands of the sea.

12 And he will raise a banner for the nations,
and will assemble the outcasts of Israel
and gather the dispersed of Judah
from the four ends of the earth.

13 Then the jealousy of Ephraim shall depart,
and the oppressors of Judah shall be exterminated.
Ephraim shall not be jealous of Judah,
and Judah shall not oppress Ephraim.

14 Then they shall fly towards the sea to the ⟨foot hills⟩ᵇ
of the Philistines,
and together they shall plunder the sons of the East.
Edom and Moab ⟨shall be⟩ the possession of their hands,
and the sons of Ammon shall obey them.

15 Then Yahweh will ⟨dry up⟩ᶜ the tongue of the sea of Egypt,
and will wave his hand over the Euphrates with the ⟨scorch-
ing⟩ᵈ of his breath
and will smite it into seven channels,
that men may cross it in sandals.

16 And there will be a highway for the remnant of his people
which is left from Assyria,
as there was for Israel
when they came up from the land of Egypt.

This prophecy of salvation is only loosely joined to what precedes it
by v. 10, the ideas of which are drawn from 11.1; 5.26; 11.12 and

ᵃ Cf. *BH.*
ᵇ Cf. *BH.*
ᶜ Cf. *BH.*
ᵈ With Dahood, quoted by H. D. Hummel, *JBL* 76, 1957, pp. 94f., read *bāʿō-ma*,
an infinitive absolute of *bʿh* with an enclitic *mem.*

2.3. 11.1–16 is strikingly reminiscent in its conceptions of 10.24–27 and probably originated in the post-exilic period, when there was a widespread Jewish diaspora. Verse 13 assumes the existence of the Samaritan schism. Accordingly, the oppressors of Judah must be identified with the Ptolemies and, as can be seen from v.16 with its emphasis on Assyria-Syria, with the Seleucids. We must bear in mind the possibility that this prophecy of salvation assumes the political situation at the end of the third century BC, if not the beginning of the second century.[a] The passage can be divided into vv.11–12, the liberation of the diaspora, vv.13–14, the new unity and growing power of the people of the covenant, and vv.15–16, the highway for those who are returning home. Once again, God's gracious hand is seen hidden behind the terrible divine judgment that has taken place since 722/21. Just as in the beginning he set his people free from servitude to Egypt, and made them a great power, he will once again redeem them and bring them to a new prosperity. **[10]** The editor of the book sought to link his own prophecy of salvation with that which came from Isaiah. What God has now promised to do will in fact be fulfilled in the time of the saviour-king prophesied by Isaiah. The second David will become the centre about which all the nations will gather,[b] turning to him in their troubles with a petition for counsel and judgment. What Ps.2.8ff. promises to the king will at last be fulfilled.

[11–12] *The liberation of the diaspora.* The whole oracle of salvation extending to v.16 could have been uttered on a single occasion as God's answer, through the lips of an unknown prophet, to the lamentation of the congregation at the dispersal of the people of God (51.9ff.). But it is more likely that it owes its origin to the desire of a scribe to complete the prophecy handed down to him with new features which accorded with the situation of the community of his own time. In any case, it assumes the wretched fate of servitude in foreign countries, and foreign rule at home. In this situation, the people and their spokesman look back to the beginnings of the nation's history: God helped them then; he will do so again. From Assyria, where the ruling class of the northern kingdom had disappeared in 721, from Egypt, where many had fled after the downfall of Judah (cf. Jer.43.7), from Upper Egypt[c] and Nubia,[d] from Elam,

---

[a] Cf. also Procksch, *ad loc.*
[b] Cf. Ps. Sol. 17.31f. and P. Volz, *Eschatologie*, Tübingen, 1934, pp.177f.
[c] =Pathros.   [d] =Cush.

the country east of Mesopotamia, from Mesopotamia itself,[a] where the exiles wept by the waters of Babylon (cf. Ps. 137), from Syria,[b] and even from the distant Greek islands, where according to Joel 3.6 Phoenicians and Philistines had sold people from Jerusalem and Judah as slaves, Yahweh will call back the remnants of his people to their homeland. The remnant here, as in v. 16, refers not merely to that part of the people which remained after the judgment in their own country (cf. 7.3; 10.20–22; 6.13), but also that part of diaspora Judaism which had remained conscious of its distinctiveness. This change of usage shows clearly that the passage does not go back to Isaiah himself. Moreover, a diaspora as widespread as this was far outside his experience, but is entirely in accord with the reality during the rule of the Diadochi. The scribe found that the prophecy of Deutero-Isaiah (49.22f.; cf. 43.5–7) foretold that the captives would be brought home by those who had formerly oppressed them, and repeated this message, in the expectation that its fulfilment was imminent: just as Yahweh gave the enemy the sign to attack and destroy (cf. 5.26), he will also give them his sign to bring his worshippers home.

[13–14] *The new unity and growing power of the people of the covenant.* From the time of the division of the kingdom, the people of God had repeatedly inflicted grave wounds upon themselves in internecine wars, and had thereby weakened their power to resist outside enemies. At the beginning of the third century the Samaritan schism had also broken the last links between north and south. But the scribe trusts that in the time of salvation, as previously in the days of David's empire, all feuds between the tribes will be buried (cf. also Jer. 3.18; Ezek. 34.23; 37.15–28).[c] Their forces united, they will restore the boundaries of David in the west and the east, and defeat their ancient hereditary enemies, the Philistines in the west, and the Edomites, Moabites and Ammonites in the east, who had stabbed them in the back in the days of Nebuchadnezzar (cf. II Kings 24.2; Lam. 4.21).

[15–16] *The highway for those who return.* In order to emphasize these prophecies, and once again drawing his material from the conceptions of Deutero-Isaiah, the scribe finally paints a picture of the highway which Yahweh will set up for his people to return home by (cf. 40.3; 41.17ff.; 42.15ff.; 43.1ff.). The special emphasis on Egypt (v.

[a] =Shinar.

[b] Hamath represents Syria.

[c] Cf. 27.6 and O. Ploeger, *Theocracy and Eschatology*, tr. S. Rudman, Oxford, 1968, p. 78.

15), and particularly on Assyria (vv. 15 and 16), points once again to the concrete situation which the congregation had to endure, the domination and the wars of the Diadochi, which had meant imprisonment and slavery for many Jews.[a] But Yahweh will not remain idle. As at the Exodus of the children of Israel under Moses, he will dry up the tongue of the sea of Egypt, that is, the Red Sea (cf. Ex. 14.f; Zech. 10.11; Isa. 51.10) and make the Euphrates evaporate, so that only pitiful trickles remain, which will offer no hindrance to the returning exiles. The highway is laid down as at the beginning of history: the liberated people are travelling home. The stylization of the future hope in accordance with the saving acts of the past on which Israel's faith was based does not imply a mechanical repetition of these events; its intention is rather to remind the congregation, through the example of these events, of the power of their God, and so to provide a foundation for the present message of hope.[b] The remnant of the people, in v. 16 as in v. 11, is formed by the inhabitants of the homeland and the diaspora of Syria (which the unknown author, following a late usage, calls Assyria), who had remained conscious of their distinctive nationality and religion.

CHAPTER 12.1–6

The Hymn of Thanksgiving of the Redeemed

1   And you will say in that day:
    'I will give thanks to thee, Yahweh, for after thou wast angry with me,
    thy anger turned away and thou didst comfort me.
2   Behold, ⟨in⟩[c] God is my salvation,
    I trust and am not afraid.
    For my strength and ⟨my song⟩[d] is ⟨Yahweh⟩[e]
    and he has become my salvation.'

[a] Cf. the Letter of Aristeas 12; I Macc. 1.10, 34.
[b] Cf. also Fischer, ad loc.
[c] With 1Q Isa read 'el, lost through haplography.
[d] Cf. BH.
[e] The tetragram is presumably to be regarded, with S. Talmon, VT 4, 1954, p. 207, as an explanatory marginal gloss, which came into the text later.

3 You shall draw water with joy
from the wells of salvation,
4 and will say in that day:
'Give thanks to Yahweh, call upon his name,
make known his deeds among the nations.
Proclaim that his name is exalted.
5 Sing to Yahweh, for he has done gloriously;
⟨let this be known⟩[a] in all the world.
6 Shout and sing for joy, O inhabitants of Zion;
for great in your midst is the Holy One of Israel.'

The unknown editor to whom we owe the preservation of the words of the prophet Isaiah seeks to assure the congregation of the second temple, sorely tried by the troubles of their own time, that the prophecies of the coming empire of the king of peace, of which they have just heard (cf. 11.1–6), will certainly be fulfilled. In that day, the coming of which God alone knows, they will experience the grace of God in such overwhelming fullness, that as in the Exodus from Egypt (cf. Ex. 15) they will sing their hymn of thanksgiving (vv. 1aβ–2) from a full heart, and in a song of praise (vv. 4–6) glorify the name of their God before the whole world. Through the power of hope, the congregation are to endure their present trials, and even now praise their redeemer in anticipation of the consummation. The background of this thanksgiving is provided by an ancient practice in the sacred law, according to which the condemned man had to pronounce a confession of his guilt and a hymn in praise of the might of the righteousness of God which was revealed in the trial (cf. Josh. 7.19).[b] So here the congregation acknowledge both the righteousness of the divine judgment, which still weighs heavily upon them, and also their faith that the purpose of salvation which will ultimately be revealed lies behind this judgment. The fact that this prophetic thanksgiving which concluded the prophecies of judgment and salvation concerning Jerusalem and Judah, and is intended to edify, is steeped in the language of the psalms, is not sufficient to show that it does not come from Isaiah himself. The clearest argument in favour of this view is the assumption and purpose of the hymn, for which no appropriate setting in the prophet's own preaching can be found.

[a] With the *Qere* and 1Q Isa (facs.), read *mŭda'at*.
[b] Cf. F. Horst, *ZAW* 47, 1929, pp. 50ff. = *Gottes Recht*, ThB, Munich, 1961, pp. 162ff.

[1-2] *The hymn of thanksgiving of the redeemed.* On that day,[a] in which Yahweh will send his saviour-king from the stump of Jesse and lead his scattered people back to their homeland in a second Exodus, the thankful congregation will sing their hymn. Throughout the centuries they have learned that the hand of God is stretched over them in wrathful judgment (cf. 9.12, 17, 21; 5.25; [10.4].) His anger is now averted. In a Jerusalem purified from all sin (cf. 4.3f.; 11.9) the congregation of the redeemed, the holy remnant (cf. 10.20; 7.3; 6.13) gathers together for a joyful thanksgiving (cf. Pss. 30.11f.; 52.9; 71.21f.; 86.12f.; 118.21). Yahweh has heard the lamentation and prayer of his congregation, 'When wilt thou comfort me?' (cf. Ps. 119.82). In the transformation, in accordance with the word of the prophet, of the time of judgment into the coming of salvation they have recognized the power of their God. Thus they know that in God alone, and in trust in him, can they find the possibility of life, ample land, and salvation (cf. Isa. 26.1ff.). In the words of the song of praise of the people of the first Exodus, the redeemed of the second and last Exodus will give thanks to their God (cf. Ex. 15.2 with 12.2b). This short hymn contains both the characteristic elements of a thanksgiving: the introduction, which expresses the resolve to give thanks, acknowledgement or praise, and always contains Yahweh's name, and the actual account which provides the basis of the thanksgiving and is introduced with 'for'.[b]

[3-6] *The song of praise of the redeemed.* Verse 3 looks first towards the expected and longed-for time of salvation. Then the redeemed will draw water with joy from the wells of salvation. Though it is not impossible that this verse refers to the rite in the Jewish feast of Tabernacles, which consisted of drawing water from the spring of Gihon, following which it was solemnly poured out before the altar, bringing to the minds of the congregation the well-being and fruitfulness of the coming year,[c] yet it is possible that we have here a metaphor with a

---

[a] 'In that day' is the favourite stylistic device of the redactor for adding further sayings to the material already present, cf. 3.18; 4.2; 5.30; (7.18, 20, 23); 10.20; 11.10, 11; 17.4; 19.16, 18, 19, 23, 24; 23.15, etc.

[b] Cf. Gunkel-Begrich, *Einleitung in den Psalmen* 7.3 and 4; Weiser, *The Psalms*, pp. 56ff. 35ff. – The suggestion of C. Westermann, *The Praise of God in the Psalms*, pp. 15ff., that the usual designation of the literary category, 'song of thanksgiving', should be replaced by 'declarative praise' is worthy of considerable attention for the reasons he adduces.

[c] Cf. Mowinckel, *Psalmenstudien* II, pp. 100f. At a later period Isa. 12.3 was

double meaning, already separated from the concrete cultic action: the people expect to receive all their strength, in joyful trusting faith, from their God, the source of life (cf. Ps. 36.9; Jer. 2.13; 7.17),[a] while they are constantly strengthened in this trusting faith by returning time and again to the book of the prophet whose name, 'Yahweh is salvation', Isaiah, is alluded to three times altogether in vv. 2 and 3.[b] Overwhelmed by the fullness of blessing the members of the congregation exhort one another to glorify and give thanks to their God. The purpose of this is the glorification of Yahweh before the nations. They are to learn of his acts of revelation and will ultimately come to give him the honour which is his due.[c] Special emphasis is twice laid here upon the name Yahweh. It is to be proclaimed in all its greatness. This demand is not associated with earlier magical conceptions of the spell cast by a name. The name of God is a gift, and the essence of his historical act of revelation in Israel (cf. Ex. 23.21). It is a guarantee of Yahweh's presence in the world.[d] Consequently, the glorification of his name and the proclamation of his mighty acts in history are identical. Verse 4 borrows words from Pss. 105.1 and 148.13, the first of which looks back to the history of salvation and the second of which contains an exhortation to every creature to praise God; thus it serves to remind those who are aware of this of the whole range of thought of those psalms, which expounds in detail what is only hinted at here. Verse 5 echoes Ex. 15.1. As in the very earliest days, during the Exodus from Egypt, God will act gloriously on behalf of his people in the time of the consummation of history, and will liberate them. Because all manifestations of salvation are concentrated upon Zion, the site of Yahweh's revelation, the people of Jerusalem in particular will have cause to break out into joy and singing at the presence of their God, the holy one of Israel (cf. 1.4), which no longer brings ruin upon them. Thus the aim of history, which through every judgment is moving towards its consummation, is the presence of God in his church (cf. I Cor. 15.24; Rev. 21.3ff.). The church of the old covenant

---

recited during this rite. H. J. Kraus, *Worship in Israel*, p. 226, thinks the *Sitz im Leben* of the passage is a feast of thanksgiving of the nation.

[a] The background to this metaphor is the summer drought, as result of which water comes to be regarded as a divine gift.

[b] Procksch.

[c] Cf. Ps. 22.22–31; 9.11ff.; 57.9ff.; etc.; and also Gen. 12.3; Ezek. 36.23, 36; 37.28; Isa. 43.8–13; 44.6–8; 45.18–25.

[d] Cf. Bietenhard, *TDNT* V, pp. 255ff.

looked forward to this consummation in the continuance of the world of space and time and of its own institutions, even though this was to lie beyond the great judgment. The church of the new covenant knows that it has no enduring city here, but seeks that which is to come (Heb. 13.14). It looks forward to a new heaven and a new earth according to the promise it has received (II Peter 3.13), without being able to anticipate in conceptual terms God's new creation; for 'it does not yet appear what we shall be, but we know that when he appears we shall be like him, for we shall see him as he is' (I John 3.2). Just as Israel, in the trials of its faith, was strengthened by the author of this hymn and by his vision of the consummation, the pledge of which it possessed in the prophet's words of judgment, which had come true, so the church of Jesus Christ can rejoice at the day in which it will be united with its risen Lord in an eternal fellowship (cf. I Thess. 4.17b).